BLOOD ON THE NASH AMBASSADOR

HUTCHINSON RADIUS

BLOOD ON THE NASH AMBASSADOR

INVESTIGATIONS IN AMERICAN CULTURE

Eric Mottram

HUTCHINSON RADIUS

Hutchinson Radius

An imprint of Century Hutchinson Ltd
62–65 Chandos Place, London WC2N 4NW

Century Hutchinson Australia Pty Ltd
89–91 Albion Street, Surry Hills,
New South Wales 2010, Australia

Century Hutchinson New Zealand Ltd
PO Box 40–086, Glenfield, Auckland 10, New Zealand

Century Hutchinson South Africa (Pty) Ltd
PO Box 337, Bergvlei, 2012 South Africa

British Library Cataloguing in Publication Data
Mottram, Eric
Blood on the Nash Ambassador: investigation in American culture.
1. American culture, to 1983
I. Title
306′.0973

ISBN 0–09–182364–1 (cased)
ISBN 0–09–182354–4 (paper)

Printed and bound in Great Britain by
Anchor Press Ltd, Tiptree, Essex

Contents

Preface

The related essays that constitute this book are the result of investigations into American culture carried out since the 1960s. From research for university and conference lectures, papers and discussions, information and ideas were relocated for publication in a wide range of journals and books, some scholarly and some for a general readership, but always with the purpose of stimulating further cultural study of the USA. consideration of this particular field of cultural studies.

Thanks are therefore due to the editors of the publications where the essays first appeared, and to the staff and students of all the places where their materials were initially offered and discussed:

King's College and the Institute of United States Studies, University of London. The American Studies Resources Centre of the Polytechnic of Central London. Kent State University, Ohio; Eötvös University, Budapest; New York University and the American Council for Learned Societies; universities in Tunis, Valencia and Vienna; University of Wales conferences at Gregynog; the University of Hyderabad; Bulmershe College of Further Education, Reading; the Universities of Warwick, Nottingham, and Durham; and the many annual conferences of the British Association for American Studies.

Dr. Clive Bush actively promoted the publication of these essays in book form, as well as being a student, colleague, and good friend and supporter since the 1960s. The author offers his deep gratitude to Dr. Dale Carter for instigating and editing this book for the press. Without his exacting standards and his persistent enthusiasm it is doubtful if it would have reached anything like the levels required by Neil Belton, the editor at Radius – to whom also my lasting thanks.

E.M.

1

'The Persuasive Lips':
Men and Guns in America,
the West

I

In June 1974, Tim Findlay reported the shoot-out between Los Angeles police and the Symbionese Liberation Army for *Rolling Stone*. Fully covered by TV, police fanaticism and the fantasies of Cinque entered every home:

> People sat in their living rooms, watching an epic battle of American insanity, commenting to each other about the cases of ammunition being unloaded from the FBI car, about the small grin on the cop's face as he threw the bolt home on his rifle before firing another round into the blazing little bungalow in south Los Angeles. His base-ball cap and clumsy flak jacket along with his bolt-action rifle made him appear as a boy playing at a game in which all the battles are heroic spectacles – where just the imaginary bad guys fall dead.

> The camera pans closer . . . cinque, the soul of the SLA . . . Was like the rest, an ultimate victim, whether of his own fantasies or of police fanaticism or of both.[1]

George Longo volunteered for the Viet Nam war as a manhood test: 'I was trained to kill. I wanted to go and get that bronze star. It was a way to become a man, handling all those rifles and things.' He survived the test as a psychologically sick man, one of many reported in Caryl Rivers' 'The Vertigo of Homecoming.'[2] It begins in childhood.

As a child, Nicholas Payne ambushed a neighbour's piano with a small calibre rifle fired from a tree. Years later, the hero of Thomas McGuane's novel, *The Bushwhacked Piano*, recalls his ecstasy:

1

One thing Payne thought of continually was the time he blasted the piano with his .22, the beautiful splintering of excessively finished wood, the broken strings curling away from liberated beams of spicy piano light, the warm walnut stock of his .22, the other spice of spent shells, the word hollowpoint, the anger of the enemy, the silver discs the bullet made on the window, the simple precision of a peep sight, the blue of barrel steel, the name Winchester when you were in America, the world of BB caps, Shorts, Longs, and Long Rifles, the incessant urge to louse up monuments, even the private piano monuments he perforated from a beautiful tree with an almost blinding urgent vision of the miserable things ending in an uproar of shattered mahogany, ivory, ebony and wire. No more Bach chords to fill the trees with their stern negation. There's no room here for a piano, he remembered righteously. No pianos here please.[3]

The depth of the morality in this luxurious 'righteousness' of individual anarchistic power is encapsulated in one sentence from E.L. Doctorow's novel *The Book of Daniel*, published the year before McGuane's, in 1971. In this work on the lives of children whose parents were electrocuted in 1953 on a charge of giving America's atomic secrets to 'the Enemy,' the son, Daniel Isaacson, asks himself: 'Why is shooting straight a metaphor for honesty?'[4]

The gun politics of American business neurosis are exemplified in Louise Thorensen's account of her husband, William Erness Thorensen III, son of the president of the Great Western Steel Corporation, thief, and assault-and-battery artist, who hired an assassin to kill his brother in 1965 and owned a seventy-ton private weapons arsenal. As the U.S. attorney said at the time of his arrest in 1967: 'The guy has so many munitions, I don't know whether the government should prosecute him or negotiate with him.' His wife was aquitted of shooting him in self-defence.[5] Thorensen's mansion arsenal is not uncommon. The Minutemen of America, led by 'maximum leader' Robert Bolivar DePugh, is a national paramilitary organization of Right wing extremists who oppose any kind of liberalism, including the United Nations. It has affiliations with Lincoln Rockwell's American Nazi Party and the Reverent Kenneth Goff's militants in the Soldiers of the Cross organization. A round-up of the New England Minutemen in 1966 revealed one million rounds of rifle and small arms ammunition, 125 single shot and automatic rifles, ten dynamite bombs, chemicals for bomb-making, considerable radio equipment, five mortars, twelve .30 calibre machine guns, twenty-five pistols, 240 hunting, throwing, and machete knives and cleavers, one bazooka, six hand grenades, three grenade launchers, fifty 80-millimetre mortar shells, and a cross-bow with curare-tipped bolts.[6] The co-ordinator was Milton Kellogg, a wealthy businessman with a huge private armoury. In 1967, Rich Lauchli, a founding member of the Minutemen, was arrested in Southern Illinois with a cache of over 1000 Thomson sub-machine guns. DePugh himself was discharged from the US Army Signal Corps, diagnosed as suffering from 'psychoneurosis, mixed type, severe, manifested by anxiety and depressive factors and schizoid personality.' He founded the Minutemen to counter 'the International Communist conspiracy.' His library includes Guevara, Giap, Mao, Grivas, H.C. Lea's three-volume classic, *Materials Towards a History of Witchcraft*, the four-volume Department of State publication *Documents on German Foreign Policy, 1918–1945*, Major-General J.C. Fry's *Assault Battle Drill*, and assorted works by Von Clausewitz, Nietzsche, and others. He claims he can quote *Mein Kampf* from memory, and the connection with the Nazi regime is, of course, standard in such cases.

The monthly journal, *Guns*, carries advertisements for models of many weapons, ranging from the Waffen-SS PPK, 'favorite of all German officers in World War II,' to the Israeli UZI submachine gun: 'the most successful submachine gun on the market today.' *Guns* also advertises firing version of historic American weapons, Nazi-Wehrmacht eagle pins, 'detective holsters' for off-duty policemen, SS-Panzer black field caps, and 'authentic German issue' Stahlheiem helmets complete with insignia including that of the Death's Head SS. The April 1974 issue carried a full-colour centre-fold pin-up of John Wayne in *McQ*, on the back of which was a full-colour photograph of a woman's left leg in black fish-net stockings. Her hand is just withdrawing a '.22 short calibre Cold Lady Deringer' from her pink satin and lace garter. (A note adds: 'only one "r" in

Deringer on the modern Colts'). Derringer was a Philadelphia gunmaker who popularized this weapon with thieves, gamblers, and whores in the pre-Civil War years. Some of the guns were only 3½ inches long. Deringer did not take out a patent, so the type flourished. *Guns* not only roots heavily for the National Rifle Association and the Shooters Club of America, but also helps circulate Gestapo identity discs, 'German lockblade survival knives,' and every kind of weapon and war souvenir. It represents the main myth of masculinity in a society that insists on individual survival in a competitive free-for-all, and in which the main lethal combination is alcohol, a car, and a gun, in various arrangements.[7] The FBI reports that of the 18,520 murders committed in the United States in 1972, 54 per cent were done with hand guns, 12 per cent with long guns, and 34 per cent by all other means. 31 per cent of the murders occured within families or between estranged lovers, and 41 per cent resulted from disputes and quarrels, mostly between people who knew each other. Criminals were responsible for about 28 per cent. In the same year, there were 2,900 accidental deaths from gunshot, 10,000 gun suicides, and 200,000 accidental gun injuries. A Gallup poll of 1972 showed two out of every five Americans in favour of a bill suggested by Congressman Michael Harrington and Senator Philip Hart: to bar hand guns except for the police, the military, licensed gun clubs, licensed security guards, and antique gun colletors. It has little chance of becoming law, for reasons that are part of the American social and individual imagination.

That the National Rifle Association can at any time instigate 500,000 or so letters opposing gun control has enabled Congress to permit city slaughter to continue. In 1974 murder rates rose to somewhere in the region of 1 in 10,000, two thirds with firearms and more than half with handguns. The *Los Angeles Times* reported a Chicago man who killed his brother recently because 'he didn't say happy birthday to me.' To counter such permissive habits, the National Council to Control Handguns has been formed. The *Christian Science Monitor* estimates that a crime with a gun is committed every two minutes in America. But regulation of guns cannot be put through unless there is a radical change of attitude towards male machismo in the States. In 1974, Baltimore initiated a gun bounty of fifty dollars, with no questions asked. The weapons, mostly family-owned, poured into police headquarters: people needed a little quick money. Their state of mind remains unchanged. Guns are historically part of human rights in America.[8]

American gun culture originated in agrarian frontier society, but survives when only 5 per cent of the population lives from farming, which is itself now a highly industrialized business. America alone among modern industrial societies clings to the 'unrestricted availability of guns' as acceptable and safe.[9] The Second Amendment to the Constitution says that 'the right of the people to keep and bear Arms shall not be infringed,' but, contrary to widespread belief in the United States, this relates to the need for 'a well-regulated militia' and not an armed civilian population. In Richard Hofstadter's words: 'the state of the law still abets assassins, maniacs, impulsive murderers, and potential terrorists at the expense of the general population and civic order.' In the 1974 article, 'The Politics of Gun Control,' Congressman Michael Harrington provides a succinct summary of the position today: G. Gordon Liddy's advocacy of an 'open, clear dialogue' between the White House and the firearms lobby via 'mutually helpful conferences at the White House with representatives of firearms organizations, manufacturers, and gun publications'; the squalid victories of the National Rifle Association (assets worth nineteen million dollars, and an annual budget of nearly eight million) and its allies; the large number of hunting and sporting publications (twenty one million Americans hunt, spending twenty seven million dollars on hunting licences and another twenty seven million on taxes for guns and ammunition); an estimate of sixty million households with guns; the social and political pressures the gun lobby is able to bring to bear over a wide range of issues; and the fact that, even though in eight Gallup polls carried out between 1959 and 1972, the proportion in favour of a police permit to buy guns never dropped below 68 per cent, no such legislation has ever been enacted.[10] A South Dakota politician is reported as holding that '[o]ur constituency is very emotional about guns. Guns are a way of life and their attitude is: if you take away my guns, you'll take away my wife next.' A *Wall Street Journal* editorial sees gun ownership as a major cultural division: 'The real pressure for gun control comes from cosmopolitan America, which sees it as the plainest common sense. The real resistance comes from the redoubts of bedrock America, which sees gun control as another symptom of encroachment by a new culture.' The strategy of the gun lobby is therefore to play on nostalgia for the frontier, self-reliance, individual strength and 'rugged' masculinity (the key advertizing adjective in *Guns*), and on the fact that, as Richard Hofstadter puts it, millions of American boys learn that their graduation 'from toy guns [to] the first real rifle of their own' is a 'veritable rite of passage that certifie[s] arrival at manhood.' Gun-owners belong to a radical tradition of self-defended individualism in a mass society where they live under total surveillance and increasingly know it. As Chicago's Deputy Police Superintendent observed in 1974: 'What's the use of city law when you can walk twenty feet across the city limits and buy an arsenal?'

How men are permitted to act within the state depends on the myth-model of self in society. In the historical development of the United States, based as it has been on a combination of Calvinist élitism and Darwinian natural selection which determines that the strongest are the fittest to survive, the competitive nature of both frontier and capitalist *laissez-faire* thrusts towards identity and conquest. Gunmen generate Americanism since they use technology to survive, either in a lawless culture or in a culture where the laws which are traditionally supposed to foster community are eroded by laws which command self-reliance. The hero becomes the lawless star permitted in an uncertain community, a figure not only permitted but needed to justify the system, to exemplify heroic reward for energy placed at the disposal of manhood and survival. Perry Miller's *The Life of the Mind in America* shows how codified law was resisted during the nineteenth century. When it met on 12 October 1776, Jefferson's committee decided against 'a code, the text of which should become the law of the land' because it would keep 'the rights of property . . . in the air' at the expense of criticism and litigation. Lawyers began to rule America from that date onwards, and, alongside them, gun-law and law-enforcement through weapons. It was argued almost from the outset that the chaos of common law was an analogue of the chaos of nature and that it neither should nor could be systematized. Arguments from nature inferred that it was unnatural to be restricted by recognizable and inherited legal system.[11] James Fenimore Cooper's Natty Bumppo became the arch-resistance myth of the anti-coders. The good gunman and the bad begin to blur. The gunman repeatedly becomes sheriff or marshal and a good man becomes a gunman. In the urban western genre, private eye and cop, killer and law-enforcement agent are identified in the ambiguous roles of Bogart and Cagney, and today in the figure of Shaft, the Black inheritor of the uncodified West.

II

The technological morality of gangster and police movies provides a full iconography from the Thirties onwards. The obvious symbolism of black and white shirts is there in cowboy films, of course, together with other ancient characterizations: blonde and brunette, fair and darker skins. But clothing and other 'extensions of man' furnish gangster films with their own mythical technology. Large hats and heavy coats signify police in Thirties gangsterdom. The Cadillac 1926 touring model in *Little Caesar* (Edward G. Robinson), the 1930 Nash Ambassador in *Each Dawn I Die* (Cagney), and the 1928 La Salle and 1927 Lincoln in *The St Valentine's Day Massacre* show how the automobile can be used for intimidation as well as mobility. Cigars become a form of communications technology. The gangleader who continually orders his up-and-coming henchmen to change his suits emulates and parodies class shifts in society at large. Scenes in tailors' shops and clothing stores therefore become crucial moments, since fashion and status are emblematic of money and power, and since, in the iconography of the capitalist city, money is the most visible form of energy control. The standard weapons in the city's civil war armoury are the .38, the sawn-off shotgun, and the submachine-gun, all of which are manufactured by an arms industry that claims moral neutrality. As in the Western, hands placed above the shoulders remains the key icon of vulnerability. The victim cannot reach his gun, nor can he protect his face, his stomach, or his groin.

The plots intersect clothing and cars, guns and money. The characters they draw together include the cop, dick, private eye and priest, the lawyer, mother, girlfriend or moll, the boyfriend (a few homosexual variants around) and the gunman. The dangers lie, not so much in the cops and detectives (who act as predictable agencies of law), as in the irrational, whether in sex or in the passionate involvements of killing, which themselves often reach orgasmic abandon. Danger arises either when sexuality undermines mobility or when the erotic starts to govern the use of gun, knife, and sword, of bullet and cigar, and, to some extent, of car and bike. Behind both the gangster movie and the Western lies the legislative permissiveness of the prime agencies of gun-manliness: the gun lobby and the armaments manufacturers and importers. During the 1970s, TV took over the gun scene. The police-hero saga in particular played a major part in fuelling the cult of 'masculine mystique' rife in TV and cinema movies of the period. In 1955, the plot of Nicholas Ray's *Rebel Without a Cause* turns, rather as it does in John Frankenheimer's *All Fall Down* (1961), on the use of telephone, alcohol, car and gun as familiar instruments in middle-class life. Both Jim Stark's cry to his impotent father – 'We're all involved!' – and his quiet retort to Buzz's taunts concerning his masculinity – 'You've seen too many movies' – express their very ubiquity. The middle-class kids use cars as instruments in a twentieth-century medieval tournament. The justification for Plato's use of the gun, however, is pure twentieth-century America – 'I need it' – whilst his cry to the Black servant encapsulates the film's indictment of the entire middle-class assumption of security and superiority. Once the fearful Plato takes the gun from under his pillow, the plot moves towards senseless killing. First he protects himself from middle-class teenage thugs in black leather. Then the police move in, their target high-school kids on the run from parents rather than Cagney on the run from a System which in *Public Enemy* (1931) had insisted on World War I and prohibition.

Within this pattern gun technology, like any other technology, modified morality and attitudes to law. The arts moved in. The

Depression of the 1930s was accompanied by a rediscovery of national cultural roots, and the tale of Billy the Kid became a ballet. To the generation of the 1960s, the police were legalized gunmen, since they were never off duty as far as their weapons were concerned. Some Americans still felt protected, others felt entirely vulnerable. But the issue had been stated at least as far back as 1835 when De Toqueville suggested that being American technically meant unlimited individual power. There then follows the concomitant challenge: how come I am not as powerful as God's programme of self-reliance claims for me? Just who is permitted to be an élite in what is assumed to be an egalitarian structure? Wild Bill Hickok was a small-time thug, gambler, and drunkard who used a rifle to shoot the McCanles gang (three unarmed men) at a safe distance.[12] But his dime novel myth was sealed when he was played in a 1937 De Mille movie by Gary Cooper, star of endless good dumb men roles and one of Hollywood's major investments. In 1946, Henry Fonda portrayed Wyatt Earp as a charming, shy and good marshal in Ford's *My Darling Clementine*. Andy Adams' *Log of a Cowboy* (1903) recalls one side of the Mastersons, Wyatt Earps, 'Doc' Hollidays, and other such 'peace officials' from 'the trail days': 'The puppets of no romance ever written can compare with these officers in fearlessness. And let it be understood, there were plenty to protest against their rule; almost daily during the range season some equally fearless individuals defied them.'

In fact, when Earp was on the Dodge City payroll, he and Bat Masterson augmented their income through gambling and prostitution. The cowboys nicknamed them 'The Fighting Pimps.' As lawman and gambler, Earp and Doc Holliday robbed a stagecoach of $80,000 and murdered the driver and one passenger.[13] The gunfight at the O.K. Corral on 26 October 1881 saw the slaughter of those who could have made a case against them. One version says Wyatt's brother Virgil, town marshal at Tombstone, Arizona, acted as peace-officer (his brothers as deputies) and only shot when shot at. Another version holds that the Earps wished to kill Ike Clanton because he had seen them try to rob a stage-coach. A third says the two clans were feuding over women, and a fourth that the Clantons headed a cowboy gang out to kill the Earps. Wyatt's account in the Tombstone *Epitaph* claims the Clantons were threatening the Earps. In all these ambiguities, what is certain is that the Earps were acquitted and Wyatt Earp died peacefully at the age of 81 in 1929. It is also certain that the Earps used six-shooters.[14] In February 1974 a Tombstone, Arizona, business man auctioned Earp's .22, a seven-shot revolver made by the American Standard Co. of Newark, New Jersey, and given to him by Doc Holliday in 1884. In *My Darling Clementine*, self-reliant survival in a hostile environment is an essential myth: Fonda's Earp dances at a church celebration as avenger and free man. Alan Ladd's *Shane* (1953) is rather more honest, since it portrays a gunfighter who fails to settle into a community when his abilities are no longer needed. He leaves because he lives on the edge of hysteria and might draw at any time. Law finally means settlement and family. Director George Stevens' last shots show Shane riding off into the geology of America. A roller-skating rink has now been laid out over the O.K. Corral.[15]

As weapons technology has developed, so the boundaries between hero, villain and fool have become increasingly blurred. As Marx puts it in the *Grundrisse* (1857–8): 'Is Achilles possible side by side with powder and lead?'[16] The crucial fusion in America, as elsewhere, brings together invention, the factory, and mass-production techniques under state or private capitalism:[17] 'The triumph of violence depends upon the production of armaments, and this in turn depends on production in general, and thus . . . on economic strength, on the economy of the State, and in the last resort on the material means which that violence commands.'[18]

Although the idea of a projectile spinning in a barrel was expounded to the Royal Society in 1747, the objective was to make it spin tightly. The smooth-bore wheel-lock musket had appeared in Germany in about 1500, and rifles were well-known by 1525, but until the Thirty Years War they were still primarily used as sporting instruments. Accurate weapons were too expensive for common warfare, and rifles were difficult to load in field conditions and on horseback. Franklin is said to have advised American generals to use bows and arrows rather than guns at the beginning of the Revolution.[19] Experience made the soldiers listen respectfully. Experiments in 1838 with the service musket led the Royal Engineers to advise soldiers to aim 130 feet into the air above a man at 600 yards in order to hit him.[20] During the Franco-Italian Wars of 1494–1559, the invention of the horse-pistol enabled a key-wound spring lock to make a rough-edged wheel spark from a piece of pyrites. This weapon could be fired twice in succession, which meant that a cavalry-man could fire once, charge, and fire again without reloading.[21] By 1630, French perfection of the flint-lock enabled a strong spring to drive a flint against a roughened metal plate fixed over a firing pan into which sparks fell. In the 1660s, Louis XIV equipped his army with it; and during the 1688 English Revolution the flint lock was again in evidence. Though it remained a luxury, this weapon was not seriously challenged until 1807, when the crucial invention of percussion-powder led a Scottish Presbyterian clergyman named Alexander Forsyth to seek a patent.[22] In 1816 an English painter, Joshua Shaw, invented a percussion cap using fulminate of Mercury as a detonator. Subsequently, the so-called American System introduced the mass production of fully interchangeable parts and thereby changed the economy of weapons manufacture and distribution. Army rifles produced in this fashion were exhibited at the 1851 Great Exhibition, although the method had been witnessed by an excited Thomas Jefferson in Paris as early as 1782. Jefferson wrote back to the States: 'I put several [locks] together myself, taking pieces at hazard as they came to hand, and they fitted in the most perfect manner. The advantages of this when arms need repair are evident'.[23]

Eli Whitney began manufacturing muskets comprised of interchangeable parts for the American government after 1794; Simeon North did the same for pistols; and in 1819 the two main Army arsenals adopted the method. After the American victory in the war with Mexico had demonstrated the value of the Colt revolver, invented a decade earlier, the manufacture of small arms increased rapidly. By 1853 Colt had developed an armoury employing 1,400 machine tools.

How quickly the Colt entered the dreams of the righteous is confirmed by John Greenleaf Whittier's 'Letter – From a Missionary in the Methodist Episcopal Church South, in

Kansas, To a Distinguished Politician. *Douglas Mission*, August, 1854.' The poem speaks in the voice of a Christian slave-addict, panicked by the Yankee abolitionist onslaught against the divinely-ordained institution of slavery, and about to abandon the South in favour of Cuba:

> . . .Methinks I hear a voice come up the river
> From those far bayous, where the alligators
> Mount guard around the camping filibusters:
> 'Shake off the dust of Kansas. Turn to Cuba –
> (That golden orange just about to fall
> O'er ripe, into the Democratic lap;)
> Keep pace with Providence, or, as we say,
> Manifest Destiny. Go forth and follow
> The message of *our* gospel, thither borne
> Upon the point of Quitman's bowie-knife
> And the persuasive lips of Colt's revolvers.
> There may'st thou, underneath thy vine and fig-tree,
> Watch thy increase of sugar cane and negroes,
> Calm as a patriarch in his eastern tent!'
> Amen: So mote it be. So prays your friend.

Locksmiths, explosives, men, and the American System came together to produce the gunman's means. During the Middle Ages, Armytage writes, gunpowder not only 'helped to render both the catapult and the medieval castle obsolescent, so further weakening the feudal system,' but also 'stimulated other sciences [such as] chemistry, metallurgy, mechanical engineering, [and] surveying.'[24] The beginnings of the machine gun were already evident in the fourteenth century ribaudequin, 'a multi-barrelled mobile weapon and a small barrel mounted on wood,' whose development prompted alterations in 'the fortifications and designs of towns . . . defense in depth supplanting the simple keep or castle tower.' The rifle was first effectively used in the War of Independence by America's 'Minute Men.' After Forsyth's early nineteenth century patenting of percussion-powder, the improvements next called for and perfected were a weatherproof action and better bullet design. Joseph Whitworth, who set up in Manchester in 1833, constructed many pioneering tools, standardized the thread of screws, and by 1855 had become the world's most distinguished tool-maker. The British government called on him to improve the design of barrels and projectiles, develop an accurate rifle, and then experiment with the production of heavy guns using a casting technique which involved submitting molten metal to hydraulic pressure before it cooled. The issue was the Crimean War. The orders that Whitworth supplied for the Confederate Army during the American Civil War enabled him to experiment further with large steel castings using a hydraulic press rather than a steam hammer. While the results did not appear until 1870, Whitworth's company was big enough by 1874 to come under the Limited Liability Act. In 1883, the American Gun Foundry Board visited his works at Openshaw, near Manchester, and reported that the production process 'amounted to a revelation.' In the United States, the main issue for Samuel Colt was the Mexican War, which promoted small arms manufacture from 1846 onwards. In 1854, Colt's factory impressed John Anderson, a British inspector of machines reporting to a Parliamentary Committee on Small Arms. His assembly line techniques were also admired by the British pioneer of such systems, James Nasmyth, who witnessed 'perfection and economy such as I have never seen before. . . . You do not depend on dexterity – all you need is intellect.'[25] The Lee-Enfield was produced according to American principles at Enfield, near London, from 1851. Within three years, Anderson's factory was turning out 2,000 guns a week. These labour, technology, and mass-production intersections show at least something of the international connections between weapons and politics. The Lee-Enfield ultimately secured British rule in India and other colonies.

Samuel Colt perfected his first six-shooter in 1832. The gun, which was company manufactured from 1836 onwards, could be fired with one hand and was therefore essential to cavalry. It was first put to political use by the Texas Rangers against Comanche Indians in June 1844, and was used widely during the Civil War. Colt's factory was designed by the brilliant mechanic and organizer Elisha K. Root. The machine-gun, like the torpedo and the electrically-fired mine, was also developed during the Civil War. Originating as a ten-barrel revolving rifle rotated by hand-crank, invented by R.J. Gatling in 1861 as, in his own words, 'a labour-saving device for warfare,' it eventually fired 200 rounds a minute, and was widely adopted where a small number of men fought a large number of 'natives.' These later developments were made in France during the Franco-Prussian War in 1870.[27] The machine-gun went on to be used by Mark Twain in the slaughter at the end of *A Connecticut Yankee at King Arthur's Court* in 1889, and by Theodore Roosevelt's 'rough riders' in Cuba in 1898.[28] In 1854, Horace Smith and Daniel B. Wesson patented their metallic cartridge. Three years later, they began to manufacture pistols with patented, bored-through cylinders to go with it. They specialized in .22 revolvers, and their seven-shot pistol became popularly preferred to the Derringer. In the 1870s and 1880s at least fifty companies were producing small cheap revolvers, often with names stamped on the barrel such as Protector, Little All Right, Tramps Terror, and Banker's Pal. Smith and Wesson are still, of course, a major armaments firm; they also manufactured the handcuffs used by the South Vietnamese Government on those of its political opponents held in the notorious 'tiger cages' (a Houston, Texas firm supplied the cages themselves).[29] As Lewis Mumford wrote in *Technics and Civilization* (1934): 'bloodshed kept pace with iron production: in essence, the entire paleotechnic period was ruled, from beginning to end, by the policy of blood and iron.'[30]

As a result of labour shortages and military demands, war also created the conditions for other kinds of technology. The French Navy exploited Nicholas Appert's invention of hermetically-sealed bottles and cans, whilst during the American Civil War the commercial food firms owned by Borden and Armour obtained their footing supplying tinned milk and meat for the Union Army that subsequently made them millionaires.[31] In 1885, the French physiologist E.J. Marey invented a photogun to record the stages of bird flight. The barrel housed a camera lens and the plates were carried on a revolving cylinder and changed by the trigger action at sixteen exposures a minute.[32] On the other hand, we can condense many of the consequences of the repeater-mechanism for more violent political action through Anthony Mann's film *The Tall Man* (1961), in which a detective sergeant tries to foil a plot to assassinate President Lincoln. The action turns on the ability of a pistol to fire one shot and of the addition of a telescopic lens to the rifle. The detective's name is John Kennedy.

III

Walter Prescott Webb's *The Great Plains* described the development of the cattle kingdoms of the American West and of the cowboy who worked the ranches and ranges. The Homestead Law of 1862, the invention of barbed wire in 1874, and the advent of the windmill, the railway, artificial irrigation systems, and the automobile combined to shape – and ultimately displace – the West: 'The life of one man spanned the rise and complete transformation of the ranch; it spanned the rise and fall of the cattle kingdom.'[33] The western man became legendary. 'The ordinary bow-legged human,' the worker on horseback, disappeared 'under the attributes of firearms, belts, cartridges, chaps, slang and horses, all fastened to him by pulp paper and silver screen.' (Not until 1968 would he be analysed back into something nearer fact, however parodied, in Andy Warhol's *Lonesome Cowboys*.) Webb describes the reality of the original life:

Where population is sparse, where the supports of conventions and of laws are withdrawn and men are thrown upon their own resources, courage becomes a fundamental and essential attribute in the individual. The Western man of the old days had little choice but to be courageous. . . . Where men are isolated and in constant danger or even potential danger, they will not tolerate the coward . . . because one coward endangers the whole group. . . . There arises within the group a tradition of courage, and this tradition develops courage in those who come into the group and as surely eliminates those who lack courage. . . .

Throw fifteen or twenty men who have been selected on the basis of proved courage and skilled horsemanship into one camp, let them live all day in the open air and sunshine, ride horseback fifty or a hundred miles, and wear six-shooters as regularly as they wear hats, and you have a social complex that is a thing apart. Such men take few liberties with one another; each depends upon himself, and each is careful to give no orders and to take none save from the recognised authority. There is no place for loquaciousness, for braggadocio, for exhibition of a superlative ego . . .

. . . women were very scarce there. The result was that they were very dear and were much sought after, prized, and protected by every man. The men fitted into the Plains; the life appealed to them, especially to those who were young and in good health. But the Plains – mysterious, desolate, barren, grief-stricken – oppressed the women, drove them to the verge of insanity in many cases, as the writers of realistic fiction have recognised . . .

The cowboy dwelt among horses, cattle, and men. Everything he wore and used – his boots, chaps, spurs, shirt, hat, gloves, and his workbench (the saddle) and his defensive iron (the six-shooter) – was adapted to the horse, to riding, and not so appropriately outside his own domain. These habiliments were picturesque only to those who did not know their uses; they were out of place when the cowboy was in town or on the ground.

As Charles Olson observes in *A Bibliography on America for Ed Dorn*, Webb 'caused the local to yield because at least he applied process, and some millenial sense.'[34]

Out of a cattle economy reliant on huge 'open range' grazing and lengthy cattle trails, a cowboy culture developed from the 1840s onwards. At first, the Texas cowboy penetrated the cattle kingdom of the Great Plains as an itinerant, free-spending, non-permanent resident, and therefore as a threat to whatever family and township stability was possible. Mobility between Texas and Montana kept boundaries fluid for those with a particular set of skills and knowledge of the land. In such an environment, the man from New York, Vermont, Virginia or Kentucky became part of a Texas-originated culture. According to John A. Hawgood's authorities in *The American West*, the word 'cowboy' was from the outset associated with 'cattle rustler' and 'outlaw,' and was a long way from the hero-image later presented in Owen Wister's *The Virginian* (1902).[35] A stabilized cowboy culture in turn moved into lawlessness. In 1867, Joseph C. McCoy of Illinois – 'The Real McCoy' – set up his ranch in Abiline, Kansas, on grass and water. The Kansas Pacific Railroad soon reached him, and by 1872 Abiline had become a cattle town and cowboy culture centre. However, the marshal appointed early in 1871 was trigger-happy Hickok. The railroad continued westwards to boost other centres, and in 1874 McCoy thought it time to write up his memoirs as *Historic Sketches of the Cattle Trade of the West and South West*. Abiline became as lawless as Dodge City, although, according to Andy Adams, the later was not as wild as reputation claims. Local gun law was fairly in control:

> Don't ever get the impression that you can ride your horses into a saloon, or shoot out the lights in Dodge; it may go elsewhere, but it don't go there. . . . You can wear your six-shooters into town, but you'd better leave them at the first place you stop, hotel, livery, or business house. And when you leave town, call for your pistols, but don't ride out shooting; omit that. Most cowboys think it's an infringement of their rights to give up shooting in town; and if it is, it stands, for your six-shooters are no match for Winchesters and buckshot; and Dodge's officers are as game a set of men as ever faced danger.

A large influx of foreign capital aided the cattle boom of the 1880s, but overstocking, low prices during a beef glut, and the severe winter of 1885–86 bankrupted stockmen's corporations. Within one generation the cattle kingdom rose, boomed and slumped. In the 1890s cowboys and cattlemen published memoirs. Mechanization eventually changed the cowboy into a jeep driver who learned his songs from the radio and whose bosses did business by telephone and air. Movies echoed the tale:

> Hoot Gibson, considered the top horse-man of all the Western stars, won the World Championship at Pendleton, Oregon, in 1912 before trekking to Hollywood, and was the first to bull-dog a steer from a car.

> A tragic first: Tom Mix, hailed as the most terrific cowboy in the world – he had fought in the Chinese Boxer Rebellion, had been a Texas Ranger, and had started as a guard with gun in hand in wild animal films – lost his life to his second greatest love on a lonely Arizona road in 1940.[36]

What emerged from the Plains cowboy were the gunman-cowboy, whose methods of self-reliance became more violent as the economic and social supports of range and ranch eroded, and the dude, part of the spectator-sports world of the rodeo, where onlookers dressed in leisure-wear versions of cowboy gear. (By 1961, 542 rodeos offering over three million dollars in prize money were organized annually by the national Rodeo Cowboys' Association).[37] The gunman gained approval as a characteristic western hero: courageous winner, self-reliant and stylish performer, a man who would – sometimes literally – sacrifice himself; or at least the legend needed him in this form. Such criteria of manliness also fleshed out the buckaroo and the broncobuster.[38] Cowboy novels developed the notion of a certain lonely introspection, which may well have been present, and movies familiarized millions with the often vacant, lost eyes of Fonda, James Stewart, Gregory Peck, Glenn Ford, and Audie Murphy. (Paul Newman's Billy the Kid, in Arthur Penn's *The Lefthanded Gun* [1958] was not, however, a cowboy version of David Riesman's inner-directed 1940s hero, but purely impulsive, a prefiguration of Penn's ambivalent gunman in *Bonnie and Clyde* [1967]).[39]

The myth of the villain is encapsulated in the 'desperado,' (with its chauvinistic incorporation of Spaniard and bandit), a figure who is an extreme expression of the American ethic of self-reliance and (in his role as leader) corporate power, and who lives as a lawless force in opposition to social order. The terms applied to the desperado indicate the range of his operations: badman, outlaw, two-gunman, tough guy, gangster, hoodlum, gunman (and gunmoll), trigger man, mobster, thug, high-jacker, vandal, public enemy. Both his agrarian and urban heroism lie in his courage (albeit always with a gun), his independence, and his lack of restraint. He is the figure who can make a fool out of those who hold power or legitimate authority, something always shaky on the frontier or in the *laissez-faire* city. He deflates and debunks. His opponent in the Western is the sheriff or marshal who sets limits to what a man may legitimately get away with in a society of loose law. But the badman also represents hardness in a world which is said to be going soft, yet which continually threatens to define masculinity either through muscle power in unarmed hand-to-hand combat, or through some kind of mental acumen. The gunman lives close to death and maiming in that region of pornographic thrill at the body's vulnerability to breakage and extinction. The villain and hero edge into each other at the point where stoicism and endurance demonstrate how a man can take it, live beyond the worst, and anticipate the inevitable by mocking its approach, as does Robert Jordan at the end of Hemingway's *For Whom the Bell Tolls* (1940).

That there was money in these actions was first blatantly demonstrated by Buffalo Bill, the original dude westerner. William F. Cody (1846–1917), who once defined hmself as having stood 'between savagery and civilization most all my early days,' underwent metamorphosis from scout to pre-movie Western show via the dime novel.[40] In the process, he converted himself into a mythic figure and became the tycoon of a West-as-theatre in which Americans, Indians included, acted out their own recent history. Cody's promoters belonged to both war and fiction: he was backed by General Sheridan, Civil War hero, socializing bachelor and friend of President Grant, and written up by Ned Buntline, dime novelist, ex-actor, jailbird, drunkard, and temperance lecturer, whose Buffalo Bill novels became best-sellers.[41] His show fixed the myth as a universal, far beyond those associated with Kit Carson, Daniel Boone and Davy Crockett. Cody's long hair and white buckskin-fringed jacket established the dude image and its theatre. The Winchester rifle he used lies in the Buffalo Bill Museum of Cody, Wyoming. When, early in 1974, John Ford died, he was surrounded by six Motion Picture Academy Award statuettes, a war bonnet from the Battle of Little Big Horn, and a pair of gloves worn by Buffalo Bill in his Wild West Show.[42]

Another example of the transition from gunman to theatre hero is the Jesse James story. James, a killer who used a Navy Colt .45, was sixteen years on the run. He terrorized weak local officials, enjoyed the protection of the James clan, and was certainly no Robin Hood. His gang's robberies were planned by expert guerrillas, even if their marksmanship seems to have been less accurate than legend prefers (they were not as accurate as, for instance, Harry Lonbaugh, the Sundance Kid.) James was an organizer and a man of nerve whose loneliness bred a streak of cruelty. As the ballad said: 'He was born one day in the

County of Shea / And Came of a solitary race.'[43] His career affected Missouri politics from 1874 onwards, since the state oscillated between ex-Confederate and ex-Union political factions and their supporters. James used the Civil War as an excuse: 'they drove us to it' – 'they' being the Yankees. His parents were from old frontier people in Kentucky. His father, Robert, died as a result of the privations of the California gold-rush of 1849. Jesse himself was assassinated in 1882, at the age of thirty-four and a half, while straightening a picture in his home. The killer, his cousin, Bob Ford, became a wanderer, was treated everywhere with contempt, and (like Cody) took to the stage with *The Outlaws of Missouri*, during the interval of which he told how he killed the outlaw chief, Jesse James. Then he joined P.T. Barnum's circus freak show, began to drink and gamble, and bought a saloon in Las Vegas, New Mexico. But no one would drink the booze of a Judas, so he tried a wild silver town in Colorado. Ed Kelly, a relative of Jesse, finally killed Ford in his fairly successful saloon, while Jesse himself lived on in dime novels and movies.

Few of the gunmen of the West were accurate marksmen. Their weapons were poor or old and their nerves less than steady. So that Burt Kennedy's movie, *Support Your Local Sheriff* (1968), is not only funny but accurate. The aim of his sharp parody of the Western is to debunk the morality of manliness based on guns and fighting; it is appropriate, therefore, that in the final shootout the villainous Danby family are incapable of hitting anything accurately, and that the sheriff – who *is* a marksman – is reluctant, apparently easygoing, accurate with a gun simply in order to survive, and under no illusions that shooting straight brings potency.

The hero-villain of the West is more complex, a hero of *Schadenfreude*, the ambivalence we feel towards successful villains, the Devil himself, Judas (celebrated in Mexico for his function of focussing aggression), and other opponents of law enforcement. In American mythical history he is exemplified by Simon Legree, Billy the Kid, and the traitor Benedict Arnold, figures who gain strength as the Devil wanes, whose villainy psychoanalysis tries to explain by tracing causes, and whose guilt juries find difficult to identify clearly or punish severely.

Education and analysis destroy the idea of the pure villain, the crude ethic of wickedness, and national stereotypes of villainy.

The first recorded victim of the six-shooter 'spin' was Fred White, shot down by Virgil Earp in 1880, according to Eugene Cunningham's *Triggernometry: A Gallery of Gunfighters With Technical Notes, too, on Leather Slapping as a Fine Art, gathered from many a Loose Holstered Expert over the Years*.[44] Warhol's *Lonesome Cowboys* takes up this frontier of fantasy and reality in the cowboy situation, with its emblems, scenes and movements by now reduced to a fixed terminology. The male group bisexuality is explicit without being pornographic, although its object fetishism – through holster, hat, boots, stirrups, and gun – is clear enough. Warhol masters the sense of dressing-up, the assertion of masculinity as freedom, the extralegality and loneliness, the repetitive rituals of work and leisure, the isolation of the sheriff (in this case a transvestite, among his other problems), the latent anarchy and violence, and the endless practice in drawing a gun and holstering it.[45]

IV

The reality and fantasy of Billy the Kid contain the social issues. Sam Peckinpah's *Pat Garrett and Billy the Kid* (1973) needed Bob Dylan and Kris Kristofferson to attract a public, and in 1974 *Dirty Little Billy*, starring the radically unheroic Michael J. Pollard, was advertized at the Hiram College, Ohio, cinema under the rubric: 'Billy the Kid was a Punk.' But by this time Hollywood had made twenty-three Kid movies. Blue-eyed Paul Newman plays the right-handed Kid as a hero in Arthur Penn's *The Left Handed Gun* (1958), finally dying on a cross of wagon shafts. In *The Law and Billy the Kid* (1954), which features Scott Brady as the Kid and James Griffith as Garrett, Billy is shot by one of the sheriff's men while escaping from a visit to his girl friend at Maxwell's house. David Miller's *Billy the Kid* (1941) has Robert Taylor in the leading role. A 1961 TV series, entitled *Robin Hood of the Southwest*, co-starred Garrett and the Kid, with the latter as a Casanova. Walter Noble Burns' *The Saga of Billy the Kid* (1926) transfixed the legends into the formaldehyde of a believer's handbook, and slipped easily into

King Vidor's MGM film of 1930, also called *Billy the Kid*, which starred Johnny Mack Brown, former All-American footballer . . . Aaron Copland's music for Lincoln Kerstein's American Ballet Caravan production in 1938 was part a larger effort during the Depression to create indigenous forms of dance and music. As Wilfred Mellers observes: 'By far the nastiest music is given to Society,' ' "public values" conflict with the fulfillment of private life,' and the music finally makes the Kid 'a tragic figure.'[46]

Facts about the Kid are not easily obtained. The most reliable source is Kent Ladd Steckmesser's *The Western Hero in History and Legend* (1965), in which we see the legend as cover for historical fact, and the legendary figure fusing politics and economics as the desire to be freed from their necessity. The western hero emerges at the intersection of the economy and popular media, themselves already permeated with a belief in permissive conquest as *laissez-faire* in action and lawlessness as natural birthright. John Smith, authoritarian leader of the Jamestown settlement and ruthless manipulator of Indians, becomes the hero of the armchair speculator 'back East' in England. Daniel Boone, 'employee of North Carolina land speculators,' farmer and hunter ejected from his land by lawsuits, becomes the epic founder of Kentucky and the embodiment of man's natural movement across space and into the White God's wilderness. Incompetence in law and business drove Boone west. Law, business, and literature turned him into an executor of the natural, with all its attendant permissions. Steckmesser quotes his resentment: 'Nothing embitters my old age but the circulation of the absurd and ridiculous stories that I retire as civilization advances; that I shun the white man and seek the Indians. . . . You know all this false. Poverty and enterprise excited me to quit my native state, and poverty and despair my native land.'[47] The Boones may have been fearless leaders of westward-moving settlers but they were also part of the exploitative conquest that is the economics of epic.

Billy the Kid was part of both the economics and the fantasy, turned into a stereotypical killer through the agency of the revolver. He lived out the type in the middle of that short period of the West's history exploited by the arts as the Western:

22

'. . . from about 1865 to 1890 or so, a brief final instant in the process. This twilight era was a momentous one: within just its span we can count a number of frontiers in the sudden rash of mining camps, the building of the railways, the Indian Wars, the cattle drives, the coming of the farmer. Together with the last days of the Civil War and the exploits of the bad men, here is the raw material of the western.'[48]

The legendary Kid is a champion shot down in a cowardly manner; the real Kid has been called 'a nineteen-year-old, unpreposessing little assassin.'[49] The facts lie somewhere in-between. The context includes bad men who went bad 'by a process which the West regarded as respectfully as it did religious conversion.' Robbing banks and trains, shooting it out with the law and dying with their boots on, such men were examples of a predatory age quite as much as Jim Fiske and Jay Gould, the financial speculators, 'but rather more easily sentimentalized.' In 1863, William C. Quantrill, operating with his guerrillas under a Confederate captaincy, killed a thousand people and burned numerous buildings, yet the folk ballad says:

> Oh, Quantrill's a fighter, a bold-hearted boy,
> A brave man or woman he'll never annoy,
> He'll take from the wealthy and give to the poor,
> For brave men there's never a bolt to his door.[50]

Billy the Kid, who scared the land-grant potentates of New Mexico, and Jesse James, who robbed the Mid-Western banking and railroad elite, naturally became proletarian heroes. McMurphy undergoes a similar elevation for attacking the combine in Ken Kesey's *One Flew Over the Cuckoo's Nest* (1962). The Kid's reputed birth, in New York City on 23 November 1859, is based on a newspaperman's statement.[51] At the age of three, he left the tenement slum, with his parents, for Kansas. He was certainly in Santa Fé when his mother married for the second time in March, 1873. His father was called William H. Bonney and his mother's maiden name was Catherine McCarty. Catherine's second husband, William Antrim, was a silver miner with whom she moved from Colorado to Silver City, New Mexico, in about 1868 (a photograph shows him in front of the

Confidence Mine, New Mexico, in the 1890s). In the Southwest, Billy picked up the saga of desperadoes like Jesse James, any boy's folk heroes of the 1870s, and learned to use a Colt and a Winchester. Catherine died in 1874, leaving young William H. Bonney, now also known as Henry McCarthy and Henry Antrim, to fend for himself. The following year he was arrested for theft, and two years later killed a blacksmith in some petty feud (legend says he was twelve and defending his mother against an insult – hence his infantilization into the Kid for the rest of his life). Legend: under siege in a ranch-house he saved his protectress's piano from flames as she played 'The Star-Spangled Banner.' Legend: he killed twenty-one men in his twenty-one years, 'not counting Indians,' as Burns writes in his credulous *Saga*.[52] Antrim left Arizona for Mesilla, New Mexico, where in 1877 he was spotted with a gang of rustlers. He escaped to Lincoln County and through his friend George Coe met John Tunstall, who hired him to work on his large ranch. Tunstall also owned a store in Lincoln, and together with his partner, Alexander McSween, a lawyer, was financed by John S. Chisum, cattle baron. In the 'Lincoln County War' they were opposed by the Murphy-Dolan-Riley ranching-trading combine, which was itself backed by the 'Santa Fé Ring,' a powerful monopoly out to control those traders and small farmers represented by Tunstall and McSween. So the Kid was once justified by his boss: 'Most of those he did kill deserved what they got.'[53]

In fact, the gang war obviated justice and justification. As Tunstall remarked in 1877: 'Everything in New Mexico that pays at all . . . is worked by a "ring." . . . I am at work at present making such a ring and I have succeeded admirably so far.' Lincoln County in those days had neither railroad nor barbed wire nor any effective law. It was largely a public domain occupied by settlers, gunslingers (who certainly lacked the sentimentality and wit of Edward Dorn's hero), and feuding cattlemen. The Kid seems to have been hired by both sides in their battle for land rights and economic power. Legend: Billy said of Tunstall, 'he was the only man that ever trusted me like I was free-born and white.' Legend: Tunstall said of Billy 'that's the finest lad I ever met. He's a revelation to me every day and would do anything on earth to please me. I'm going to make a man out of that boy yet.'[54] Whether the mutual devotion of English gentleman rancher and American farmboy is true or not, the Kid's need to avenge Tunstall's murder by the Murphy mob in 1878 seems to be authenticated. At Tunstall's grave he reportedly said: 'I'll get every son-of-a-bitch who helped kill John if it's the last thing I do,' and 'I never expect to let up until I kill the last man who helped kill Tunstall, or die in the act myself.' His furious, vindictive temper became well-known.

The Murphy-Dolan group were powerful enough to make Governor Axtell obtain US troops to defend their interests. The McSweens turned to assassination, and the Kid was regularly named as a killer in reports of the war. On 15 July 1878 they tried to capture Lincoln township, and were defeated after a major shoot-out in Lincoln Plaza and at the McSween fortress-ranch. The boss died, the war was over, and the Kid escaped to the outlaw trail. In Fort Sumner he first met Pat Garrett, then barman in the Beaver Smith saloon. The Kid stole horses from the Chisums in lieu of wages owed, and reassumed the name of Bonney. The President had heard of the shoot-out, as had the new Governor, Lew Wallace, then writing *Ben Hur*. The 1879 Lincoln County War amnesty did not apply to the Kid because he was charged with the murder of William Brady, the Murphy-Dolan sheriff, in 1878; so he wrote to the Governor offering to surrender and gain freedom by testifying against the killers of Huston I. Chapman, Mrs. McSweeney's one-armed lawyer. At the rendezvous, Billy faced Wallace with a Winchester in his right hand and a revolver in his left. He was about nineteen. He lived well in captivity, betraying numerous badmen and being serenaded by the locals. The legend was under way. But Wallace failed to obtain the pardon, and did not put him on trial. The Kid broke jail. In 1880 he killed Joe Grant and Jim Carlyle. The press wanted his blood and blamed him for leading every gang – and it is clear he could lead.

Pat Garrett had worked as cowhand, buffalo hunter, and horse-wrangler for Peter Maxwell, who had also once employed the Kid. In 1880, when he was twenty-eight, Garrett married Polinaria Guiterrey (they had seven children) and the cattle barons elected him sheriff of Lincoln County. It is said that the

Kid befriended Garrett on his arrival in Lincoln – hence the latter's Judas image. In November 1880 Garrett ambushed the Kid at Fort Sumner, but the Kid got away to shoot it out at a deserted farmhouse in Stinking Springs. There he surrendered, along with three allies, after which Garrett took him to Las Vegas, where the *Gazette* interviewed him: '[H]e looked and acted a mere boy . . . a frank open countenance, looking like a school boy, with the traditional silky fuzz on his upper lip. . . . He is, in all, quite a handsome looking fellow, the only imperfection being two prominent front teeth slightly protruding like squirrel's teeth, and he has agreeable and winning ways'.[55]

From jail he had written appealing to Wallace, but the Governor simply released their correspondence to avoid possible scandal. He was tried for Brady's murder at Mesilla in March 1881, the only Lincoln War criminal to be tried and sentenced. (The Kid was to be hung.) He escaped by killing his two guards, one of whom, Robert W. Ollinger, was an ex-gunthrower. Apparently he used a six-shooter hidden in the privy by friends and a Winchester nicked from the prison armoury. His reputation as a ruthless killer was sealed, but he did not attempt to escape to Mexico – one reason may have been a love affair (one name mentioned is 'Dulcinea del Toboso'). To regain any status at all, Garrett had to capture him once and for all. After a three month hunt, he found the Kid at the Maxwell house, half-dressed in the darkness, and shot him down from the head of Maxwell's bed with Maxwell in it, it is said, as Billy entered the bedroom. Neither Garrett nor his deputies could have been sure it was the Kid until Maxwell whispered it was him. It is not clear whether he had only a knife on him or a six-shooter – some reports say he had both. In his report to Wallace, Garrett said that he had wanted him alive but that the Kid had come onto him suddenly, armed to kill. He shot before being shot.

In the context of frontier life, a daily battle for existence where killing was the common outcome of any quarrel and inter-ranch warfare was standard, the Kid's possible five murders out of the legendary twenty-one is small.[56] Frederick Law Olmstead, an early traveller through Texas, wrote that an inventory of the Colt revolvers owned in the state would approximate in numbers the census of the adult males. When

W.W. Mills, brother of Brigadier-General Anson Mills of cartridge-belt fame, came to El Paso in 1858, every male citizen regardless of age or vocation took his six-shooter from beneath his pillow the first thing in the morning, and wore it until he went to bed again.

Garrett lost his badge when the Democrats refused his renomination, and he had to hire a lawyer to get the 500 dollars reward from Wallace. He then went into various ranching concerns, developed a distaste for guns, got a job from President Theodore Roosevelt as customs collector at El Paso, and ended up raising horses. He was killed in a row over property in 1908, and his grave is unmarked: no tombstone and no steel fence to keep off souvenir hunters, unlike the Kid's grave at Fort Sumner. A year after he had killed the Kid, on 14 July 1881, he brought out his *Authentic Life of Billy the Kid*, in order to promote his victory. But by then the legend had thickened. The Philadelphia *Times* had quickly seen the Kid as a cruel sexy leader of two or three hundred men, dressed in Ruritanian quasi-military gear, born in Ireland, and living in an adobe castle. Two dime novels on his career appeared in 1881.[57] In John Woodruff Lewis's *True Life of Billy the Kid*, he signs a writ with the blood of two victims and 'with the laugh of a demon.' In Edmund Fable's *The New Mexican Outlaw* he wears the now customary black buckskin trousers and jewelled hat. In J.C. Cowdrick's *Silver Mask* (1884) he wears 'a rich Mexican suit.' Curiously enough, it is Garrett's book (ghosted by Ash Upson) which began the softening of outlaw into victim of family and society, a Clyde Griffiths without the chemistry of cowardice in Dreiser's *An American Tragedy* (1925). Upson, an imaginative New Mexico newspaperman and once a boarder at the Antrims', needed the legend nearly as much as Garrett, who wrote in his introduction: 'The truth, in the life of young Bonney, needs no pen dipped in blood to thrill the heart and stay its pulsation. This verified history of the Kid's exploits, with all the exaggerations removed, will exhibit him as the peer of any fabled brigand on record, unequalled in his desperate courage, presence of mind, devotion to his allies, generosity to his foes, gallantry, and all the elements which appeal to the holier emotions . . .'[58]

Hence the sacred insulted mother and, in Siringo, the opening killing of 'a Negro soldier at Fort Union' (this book was a best-seller until 1926). But the Kid still had to massacre and rob three Apache Indians and various Mexicans in Sonora and Chihuahua, rescue Texans from Apaches with the James gang, take on twenty 'well-armed savages' in the Guadelupe Mountains with only his six-gun and a dirk, and so on. Garrett-Upson says he was 'polite, cordial and gentlemanly' and cursed in 'the most elegant phraseology.' The farm boy had vanished. In Walter Woods' 1903 play, it is the Kid's father who is the villain, exonerated by being killed in mistake for his son, who thereupon starts a new life 'where the sun shines always.'[59] In 1925 Harvey Furgusson reinforced the Robin Hood association – 'he befriended the poor' – and folklorists ever since have used him to transpose other world myths into American form: Hercules, Faust, Ulysses and other versions of the Clever Hero. He is the little guy in a baron's war, too; a champion of the nonideological: betrayed, shot down, and resurrected.

It is the stereotypical killer, the unchanging star of myth, which Michael McClure dramatizes in his plays and poems about Billy the Kid. In *The Blossom* (1967), Billy moves between Tunstall and Susan and Alexander McSween as part of McClure's involvement in Antonin Artaud and the *acte gratuite* of liberation, the hallucinatory sensation of free action, and the absolute centre of outlawry in madness, the insanity of utter isolation. The play is reprinted in *The Mammals* (1972) along with a section of documents including a tintype of Billy and photographs of Tunstall and the McSweens. *The Beard* (1965) and *The Sermons of Jean Harlow and the Curses of Billy the Kid* (1968) connect the stereotypical gunman with the fixed star of an exploitative Hollywood as repetitive and sterile expressions of American society: partly pathetic, partly monstrous.[60]

In an essay written on the occasion of a reprint of Burns' uncritical biography in 1953, Charles Olson criticizes those who take Billy as 'mere killer' and do not overhear in 'the Kid's question "Quién es?" (with Pat Garrett sitting at the foot of the bed, in the blackness), why El Chivato asked anything, this once, instead of barking, with his gun.' Olson believes Burns' account – 'The Kid had not fired a shot. He lay with his gun still clutched in his left hand and, in his right, Celsa Gutierrez's kitchen butcher knife' – but ambivalently insists that the duty of fiction is to include the 'totality' of history if the characters are not to be 'diminished.'[61] Even less interested in ascertaining the context of the myth is the fifth of Louis Zukofsky's 'Songs of Degrees,' in which the skill of William Carlos Williams provides an analogue for the Kid's abilities: 'The kid / shoots / to / kill,' 'the kid's / self sacrifice,' 'one / sound: / the kid / 's torn, / shot,' and so on.[62] Edward Dorn's *Gunslinger* (1968) begins in the historical location:

> I met in Mesilla
> The Cautious Gunslinger
> of impeccable personal smoothness
> and slender leather encased hands
> folded causually
> to make his knock . . .

But then the gunman rapidly undergoes metamorphosis into Theseus, an 'equilibrium' whose myth is order itself, and a solar god who is man's projection of the single winner. Michael Ondaatje's *The Collected Works of Billy the Kid* (1970) is a less sentimentally mythical compilation of poems and prose towards 'his legend a jungle sleep.' The vision of killing and loneliness is accurate (although the Kid materials rely on Burns), but Deputy John W. Poe's 1919 account of Garrett enables Ondaatje to write: 'Pat Garrett, ideal assassin. Public figure, the mind of a doctor. . . . Ideal assassin for his mind was unwarped. . . . One who has decided what was right and forgot all morals.'

Concerning the Kid, Ondaatje's Pat Garrett recalls: '[H]e never used his left hand for anything except of course to shoot. He wouldn't even pick up a mug of coffee. I saw the hand, it was virgin white. . . . He said he did finger exercises subconsciously, on the average 12 hours a day. . . . I noticed his left hand churning within itself.'[63]

Robert Warshow's 1954 essay 'The Westerner' begins where mythicization must begin: with the gun held by the man, fantasies of the gun, and the importance in both western and gangster mythology of 'guns in the fantasy life of Americans.'[64]

Where the gun is an instrument of self-fulfillment and personal justice on both sides of the law, the willingness to shoot is central. The courage of armed men is like the courage of men under martial law so completely examined in Melville's *White Jacket* (1850): the morality is intersected by coercion. The sheriff and the outlaw are united by their mutual willingness to fire. As Warshow points out: 'What [the gunman] defends, at bottom, is the purity of his own image – in fact his honor. This is what makes him invulnerable.' Defence of honour within the group described by Webb in 1931 becomes an extreme defence against anonymity, a life of labour, a life without gun-power or indeed power of any kind. Reluctance to use a gun becomes the crux for determining courage and cowardice, power and impotence, and it is in these terms that the stereotype takes over and rigidifies a man into a gunman. (In *The Beard*, Jean Harlow and Billy the Kid exist in an eternity of rigid cultural roles; they have become myths, partly during their actual lifetimes). The westerner's values cannot really be extended out of the West. In Warshow's words: 'Those values are in the image of a single man who wears a gun on his thigh. The gun tells us that he lives in a world of violence, and even that he "believes in violence." But the drama is one of self-restraint: the moment of violence must come in its own time and according to its special laws, or else it is valueless.'

As William Burroughs says of his own highly mythical fictions: 'None of the characters in my mythology are free. If they were free they would not still be in the mythological system, that is, the cycle of conditioned action'.[65]

Conditioned action, mythicization and addiction enclose a man in a required role that requisitions his liberty. The myth-user varies the stereotypes but can never fail to expose both the historical actuality and his own preoccupations. In Sam Peckinpah's *Pat Garrett and Billy the Kid*, at least in the version shown in Britain, the feud with Chisum (the cattle baron who employs sadist henchmen) is largely cut, and what remains is a clear nostalgia for manliness defined through guns and male contact. Two men shooting it out to the death is a wierd image of comradeship, a mythical ritual universalized through movies. Garrett refuses to be hired by Chisum and Billy too has to evade such a grouping. The audience is the product of a hundred years' exploitation of land and labour through guns, law and lawlessness. Language is reduced to signals of loyalty, contempt or oppression; the silence is filled by mythic ritual. We compose the film for ourselves out of the group memory of the myth.

Garrett reappears in Billy's life at the point where peace, or rather cold war, has reduced killers to shooting off the heads of chickens. Both Billy and Garrett need the kind of challenge which enables them to establish their manhood in a region whose thin opportunities make for the extreme situation of the fight, a common condition of enclosed societies unable to envisage any other way out. Glory is the prize; the ascent is simplified and appeals to those who fantasize life as the pressure of a finger on a trigger. Billy and Pat are boys who share this adoration, and when Garrett says 'It feels like times have changed,' what he means is 'Leave me out of it.' The interior issue, as usual, is suicide, the death of complex life, the welcoming of a simple absolute. When Billy's two companions allow themselves to be casually shot up, all that's said is: 'Time to take a walk? Hell, yes!' Billy opens his arms to embrace Garrett, death, and his own self-sacrifice or suicide. His guards, too, accept death, smiling with self-satisfaction because they have achieved the only glory available. Of Garrett's two deputies, Pickens clasps his wounds and dies by a sunset river with calm acceptance, and Elam is totally unsurprised to discover that Billy had cheated him from the first; the children and the mother watch the ritual of his end in silence, as immobile as the audience and the myth. The film is authentic but your response will be governed by whether you believe Peckinpah's grotesques retain any value beyond their expert repetition of mythic ritual. The presence of Bob Dylan, a major figure of the American Movement of the 1960s, and the casting of Kris Kristoffersen as Billy suggest that both the sacrifice and the glory may survive into the present. Peckinpah's previous film, *The Getaway* (1972), and *Pat Garrett and Billy the Kid* indicate a director hooked on the manliness of gunning. In *The Getaway*, McQueen does what the advertisements insist is a man's job in a man's world: blasting gang rivals and police cars in order to extricate himself with as large a haul as possible.

Peckinpah's fascination ultimately lies in the conjunction of a man with his instruments of manliness, courage and victory – especially the gun.

V

Samuel R. Delany understands more of the myth in his novel *The Einstein Intersection* (1968), where Billy the Kid appears as a redheaded boy with gold lashes and transparent skin whose eyes 'had no whites, only glittering gold and brown . . . dog's eyes in a human face: "My mother called me Bonny William," the Kid announces. "Now they all call me Kid Death." '[66] Asked why he kills, he replies: "I am more different than any of you. You scare me, and when I'm frightened" – laughing again – "I kill." He blinked. "You're not looking for me, you know. I'm looking for you." ' Kid Death is 'a criminal genius, psychotic, and a totally different creature,' something that was apparent from his tenth year. As a man, he is tied up with what he calls 'their past,' the past of the human race in the West. He is an object other men wish to kill – as if death could be killed, or the impulse to kill could be killed, or ended by killing. He stands at the centre of impotence in western culture. The only figure immune from Kid Death is Green-eye, Delany's image of the Green Man. He is a salvation figure of love 'chary of ritual observances,' and as one character says: 'Everybody blames the business on his parthogenetic birth.' According to Lobey, the narrator-hero of the book, Kid Death seems to be sixteen or seventeen or 'maybe a baby-faced twenty,' although 'his skin was wrinkled at the wrists, neck, and under his arms.' Lobey first asks what the westerns he himself really admires are, and then what a western is. He replies: 'It's an art-form the Old Race, the humans, had before we came.' Within that repetition, Kid Death is himself a killer repetition factor that has to be transcended, not killed. When he tempts Green-eye, it is through the repetitions of old forms of power, old ideas, old technology; insane recoveries of exhausting and exhausted actions and ideologies. ' "There," said Kid Death, "there are the deeds and doings of all the men and women and androgynes on this world to remember the wisdom of the old ones. I can hand you the wealth produced by the hands of them all." Green-eye's green eye widened. "I can guarantee it. You know I can. All you have to do is join me." '

Green-eye refuses the familiar offer to turn 'rock into something to eat,' to accept the luxury of power, to 'turn this mountain-top into a place worthy of you.' Kid Death brings on his thunder but finally makes his getaway: 'Needle teeth snagged the thunder that erupted from behind the mountains as he threw back his head in doomed laughter. Naked on his dragon, he waved a black and silver hat over his head. Two ancient guns hung holstered at his hips, with milky handles glimmering.'

The next section of the book begins with a conversation between the author and Gregory Corso: 'Jean Harlow? Christ, Orpheus, Billy the Kid, those three I can understand. But what's a young spade writer like you doing all caught up with the Great White Bitch?! Of course I guess it's pretty obvious.'

Then Kid Death appears saying 'Howdy, pardners' – 'Where flame slapped his wet skin, steam curled away.' He vanishes into 'wherever he goes.' The next section opens with part of the author's *Journal*, written from Mykonos in December 1965 and concerned with his need to 'excise . . . the images of youth' which plague him – Chatterton, Greenburg, Radiguet; 'By the end of TEI I hope to have excised them. Billy the Kid is the last to go. He staggers through this abstracted novel like one of the mad children in Crete's hills.'

The plot of the hero-narrator, Lobey, is to hunt down Kid Death, since he is the only figure for whom the Kid is not paralyzing. Lobey is the Orpheus of the book, his flute a twenty-holed machete. He is a figure of difference whose difference is not destructive, part of the motion of change leading away from destructive myths and their rigidification of our lives. The traditional figure of law and order, the sheriff agency, is called Spider, a man of strength who is, however, himself caught in unimaginative procedures against death or the statification of men. He defines his job as a limited quest:

' "it demands you take journeys, defines your stopping and

starting points, can propel you with love and hate, even to seek
death for Kid Death –"
"– or make me make music," I finished for him.'

But Spider may acknowledge this double venture, against
creative imagination and against destructive myth, only within
the fixed content of his continuing problem; speaking, as it were,
from the future of the book, he says:

> Wars and chaoses and paradoxes ago, two mathematicians
> between them ended an age and began another for our hosts, our
> ghosts called Man. One was Einstein, who with his Theory of
> Relativity defined the limits of man's perception by expressing
> mathematically just how far the condition of the observer
> influences the thing he perceives. . . . The other was Gödel, a
> contemporary of Einstein, who was the first to bring back a
> mathematically precise statement about the vaster realm beyond
> the limits Einstein had defined: *In any closed mathematical system –*
> you may read 'the real world with its immutable laws of logic' –
> *there are an infinite number of true theorems* – you may read
> 'perceivable, measurable phenomena' – *which, though contained in
> the original system, can not be deduced from it* – read 'proven with
> ordinary or extraordinary logic' . . . At the point of intersection,
> humanity was able to reach the limits of the known universe with
> ships and projection forces that are still available to anyone who
> wants to use them –'

But Lobey's search takes him to the source cave of all earth
caves – that is, to the chthonic teleology within the history of
mythology. The source cave turns out to be 'a net of caves that
wanders beneath most of the planet. . . . The lower levels
contain the source of the radiation by which the villages, when
their populations become too stagnant, can set up a controlled
random jumbling of genes and chromosomes.' Mythology
consists of the forms that source energy takes: Lobey is Ringo as
well as Orpheus, and Spider is Pat Garrett and Iscariot. Lobey
carries a two-edged singing knife. The Kid needs both Orpheus
and Garrett because, although he can change things, he cannot
make something out of nothing. As Spider tells Lobey:

He cannot create something from nothing. He cannot take this skull and leave a vacuum. Green-eye can. And that is why the Kid needs Green-eye. . . . The other thing he needs is music. . . . He needs order. He needs patterning, relation, the knowledge that comes when six notes predict a seventh, when three notes beat against one another and define a mode, a melody defines a scale. Music is the pure language of temporal and co-temporal relation. He knows nothing of this, Lobey. Kid Death can control, but he cannot create, which is why he needs Green-eye. He can control, but he cannot order . . . that is why he needs you.

The final section contains William H. Bonney's letter to Governor Wallace, telling him that he would emerge to give 'the desired information' but is afraid of his enemies. But in this book the Kid, through Spider, has Green-eye strung up. Lobey plays his music and Spider whips the Kid; a flower devours his body. Lobey's music also enables Green-eye's death. The myths are excised and the conclusion is open:

'"It's not going to be what you expect." [Spider] grinned, then turned away.
"It's going to be . . . different?"
He kept walking down the sand . . .'

At least Billy the Kid has been recognized as deadly, a deathly creation of men at a particular time and in a particular place, usable only if those circumstances are made to repeat themselves. There is in Delany's book no question of endless archetypes being divorced from cultures so that they may be perpetuated as images of survival. The cave source can produce only what men wish to need. And certainly a Black American should not need white killer myths.

The gunfighter lived a life of repetitive style dependent on a repeating weapon, the revolver – an ideal, if malignant, way through the problems of both law and stability, creativity and risk. In traditional kung-fu and akaido, at least some training of the whole body-mind is required through apprenticeship and dedication. Henry Fonda may look like a teacher in *The Tin Star* (1957) but he is not. He trains for a simple synchronicity of eye, muscle, and repeater, which is to permit his young pupil – a trainee sheriff – manhood. As Walt Whitman wrote bitterly in his 1856 poem 'Respondez!': 'Let them sleep armed! let none believe in good will!' But armed lack of good will is a response to thinness of opportunity in the latter-day West – and it obviously is in Peckinpah's movie.

In *Piñon Country* (1941), Haniel Long tells how two young men from New York attempted to hold up 'The Apache,' South Pacific No. 11, near Las Cruces, New Mexico, in 1937.[67] They were battered by the passengers and sentenced to serve from fifty to seventy-five years on pleading guilty to second degree murder (a man had been killed). One of the men, Henry Lorenz, had been born in a detention camp in Germany, after his family returned from a failure to settle on a farm colony in Russia. After the mother died, the family emigrated. The father remarried. The stepmother disliked Henry, who took to being 'crazy about the West' and spent his money on western magazines and movies. He ran away from home and tried to save money working in a New York shoe store. When he had accumulated 500 dollars, he invited Harry Dwyer to join him 'to go West and be cowboys.' (Dwyer was of French-Irish descent, and had also been born abroad). Their money ran out on girls, so they held up the train. Just outside the site of their trial, at Old Mesilla, was the Billy the Kid Museum containing the Kid's leg-irons and one of his guns. From the Lincoln County Billy the Kid Museum (housed in the old jail), Haniel Long sent the curator a newspaper cutting of the Las Cruces trial, and suggested 'a museum file under the heading "Results of Hero-Worshipping William Bonney": it is the old story of two eastern boys who wanted to play Billy the Kid.'

VI

Non-violence is related in urban competitive society to inadequate manhood. In an essay entitled 'the Science of Nonviolence,' John Paul Scott begins by pointing out that in Hopi Indian society even the thought of violence is considered wrong, and few weapons are available. A violent man is seen as deranged and people get out of his way. In white society, the damage caused by deranged men is also limited by the availability of weapons. As the earlier part of the present essay noted, most homicides in America are committed with handguns in the hands of people who are not habitual criminals, but who are acting on impulse during quarrels with relatives and friends. Social disorganization among men and animals is a major cause of destructive violence. As John Paul Scott says, 'the principle of multiple causation always holds, and some will escape.'[68] We need to investigate multiple causation, the intersection points of, for example, lack of opportunity, sexual unfulfilment within or outside the family, immigration disruptions, divorce, the boom and depression cycles of capitalism, and the nature of constructively enjoyable behaviour as a counter to other forms of power. Poor pay for a meaningless and menial job, itself at the mercy of economic change, permits the violence of leisure compensations in the form of instant dominance. Personal power, with an easily purchased gun, may shift rapidly into the impersonal scale of war. In fact, under any totalitarian system we are expected to become a soldier or worker or consumer at the next command of authority.

In 'The Triggered, the Obsessed and the Schemers,' Jean Davison reports the results of experiments designed to uncover possible reasons for TV-inspired crimes, mainly research into the cues that trigger attack. She quotes Dr. Robert M. Liebert, a child psychologist and a principal investigator for the Surgeon General's enquiry into TV and social behaviour, who believes that exposure to constant TV violence in the home leads to 'an acceptance of aggression as a mode of behaviour.' He adds: 'Even perfectly normal children will imitate antisocial behaviour they see on television, not out of malice but out of curiosity.' Such exposure is also believed to contribute to bystanders' failure to respond to a victim's need for help, to imitation of TV behaviour, and to the use of TV as a textbook of violent methods. The evidence appears to be overwhelming.[69] In *The Einstein Intersection*, Delany attacks the perpetuation of myths encoding these permissions and intersections, which reach so far down that they are considered to be natural, becoming, as Herbert Marcuse proposes in *An Essay on Liberation*, second nature:

Self-determination, the autonomy of the individual, asserts itself in the right to race his automobile, to handle his power tools, to buy a gun, to communicate to mass audiences his opinion, no matter how ignorant, how aggressive. Organized capitalism has sublimated and turned to socially – productive use frustration and primary aggressiveness on an unprecedented scale – unprecedented not in terms of the quantity of violence but rather in terms of its capacity to produce long-range contentment and satisfaction, to reproduce the 'voluntary servitude.' . . . The established values become the people's own values: adaptation turns into sponteneity, autonomy; and the choice between social necessities appears as freedom.[70]

It is a degeneration of social value of this kind that we observe in the relationships between guns and culture, which this essay has tried to suggest a way of understanding.

*　　　　*　　　　*

We live on the whims of men in custom-tailored suits, who ride in black limousines and whose addition to human insight and knowledge would hardly challenge Billy the Kid.
　　　Walter Lowenfels　*Loving You in the Fallout*

Unless everyone in America owns a handgun there will never be peace in this country [for] no country in the world offers its citizens a greater choice of guns than the United States. . . . We are blessed because anyone in America can have the gun of his choice at a price he can afford. For those who are on relief and unemployed the government could supply surplus weapons from the armed forces at the same time they give out food stamps and unemployment cheques.
　　　There is absolutely no reason why everyone in this country could not be armed by 1973.
　　　Art Buchwald　*Washington Post* 23 May 1972

Billy the Kid said: '*Quién es?*' Pat Garrett killed him. Jesse James said: 'That picture's awful dusty.' He got on the chair to dust off the death of Stonewall Jackson. Bob Ford killed him. Dutch Schultz said: 'I want to pay. Let them leave me alone.' He died two hours later without saying anything else.
　　　William Burroughs　*The Wild Boys*
1976

2

'That Dark Instrument': The American Automobile

Technology throws light upon mental conceptions
  – Louis Zukofsky: '*A*' (8)

In the issue of *Life* magazine for 18 November 1957, the press tycoon Henry Luce exposed his worries about the Soviet *Sputnik* in an editorial criticizing President Eisenhower for leading American complacency. The title was 'Arguing the Case for Being Panicky': 'What, then, should we do? Just this: we should each decide what we really want most in the world . . . What do we want most? A Cadillac? A color television set? Lower income taxes? – Or to live in freedom?'

As if to confirm Luce's confusion, the same issue of his magazine carried a three-page advertisement for the 1958 Cadillac in four colours on a gold background, together with nineteen pages advertizing other cars and a further range of irrational and, in Luce's sense, anti-freedom necessities, ranging from Revlon's Red Caviar Lipstick to Lady Borden's Holiday Bisque Tortoni Ice Cream. The left-liberal *Nation*'s editorial commented that '*Life*, clearly, knows what it wants: freedom *and* the Cadillac account.' Lucius Beebe, in his Virginia City *Territorial Enterprise*, shouted an apocalyptic warning:

For a quarter of a century . . . the most powerful single influence on American taste and its social destinies . . . *Life* has suddenly become aware . . . that the Russians are so far ahead of us in everything that the days of the American Republic are numbered, and very correctly attributes this state of things to the fact that

Americans vastly prefer TV comedians, Cadillacs and pro
football to the dreary precautions of staying alive.

Yet . . . it has lavished billions of dollars worth of space on
rutting Texas cowboys with mandolins and criminal sideburns,
. . . on the mammary glands of Italian actresses, on Detroit motor
car designers, [and] on Hollywood starlets . . . all the things it
now, in the shadow of Judgement Day, is busy renouncing.[1]

But, of course, *Life* had not changed its politics, nor, for many
reasons, was there the slightest chance that its readers would
renounce the automobile in the interests of global survival. In
fact, they needed it for survival nearer home as an urgency of
both transport and the glamours of speed. The car had long
since become prosthetic within that necessity Stéphane Mallarmé
described in 1895 as 'the monotony of winding along the
pavement between one's shin bones, according to the machine
at present in favour, the fiction of continuous dazzling
speedway.'[2]

We need to make an analytical inventory of the rational usages
of any technology, if systems of manipulation of dream and
desire by machine and tool are not to be entirely submissive.
David Mamet's epigraph to his play *American Buffalo* (1975) –
which he says comes from 'a folk tune' – condenses the religious
entrance of the car into American patriotism:

Mine eyes have seen the glory of the coming of the Lord.
He's peeling down the alley in a black and yellow Ford.[3]

Quite a recent folk tune, since Henry Ford resisted having his
cars coloured until 1923. Mamet may use the capital F for that
car, but Gertrude Stein preferred to adopt the lower case,
recognizing as early as 1933 that the Ford object had become
virtually a species, and that, like pets and relatives, it had to be
properly named.[4] Stein drove her first Ford for the American
Fund for French Wounded in 1919 and called it – or her –
Auntie. Her second she called Godiva because 'she had come
naked into the world.' The auto industry has always taken care
to encourage its consumers to locate their products within non-
technological fields, naming them Mustangs, Sabres, and so on.

Pyroxylin enabled cars to have colours called Florentine Cream or Versailles Violet. In the Spring of 1923, Ford gave up his preferred black and launched autos named Niagara Blue and Arabian Sand in order to challenge the dominance of the robin's-egg-blue Chevrolet. The 'new model' fraud was well under way, and desire quickly harnessed to the naming of cars – although owners persisted, heterosexual nomenclature notwithstanding, with the tradition of false feminization of their machines.[5]

The automobile is in fact embedded in whatever is American. The car beneath the skin has to be present, for instance, in innumerable pop and rock music numbers. To take one example: in his 1980 album, *The River*, Bruce Springsteen includes twelve numbers (out of twenty) using cars and the road as a life and death system.[6] The lyrics of 'Cadillac Ranch' modify that line of lyric poetry which addresses itself to the valued life and death object:

> Well, there she sits buddy just a gleaming in the sun
> There to greet a working man when his day is done . . .
>
> Eldorado fins whitewalls and skirts
> Rides just like a little bit of heaven here on earth
> Well buddy when I die throw my body in the back
> And drive me to the junkyard in my Cadillac
>
> Cadillac, Cadillac
> Long and dark, shiny and black
> Open up your engines let 'em roar
> Tearing up the highway like a big dinosaur
>
> James Dean and that Mercury '49
> Junior Johnson runnin' thru the woods of Caroline
> Even Burt Reynolds in that black Trans-Am[7]
> All gonna meet down at the Cadillac Ranch

Springsteen's song calculates a field of mythological effects: the working man's possessive individualism focussed on 'car'; the getaway motif of auto-culture; the feminization of the extension of man called transport[8]; the car's obsolescence in the evolutionary processes of the twentieth century (Marshall McLuhan once reported to the American car industry that the automobile was a technological dinosaur – and got paid for it); the mystic machine of macho Hollywood stars; the last round-up on the range mythically transferred to the automobile graveyard, a major feature of the American landscape; and the girl in tight blue jeans in the last verses (not quoted here), 'drivin' alone through the Wisconsin night' and finally taken off in a death-car, an auto-hearse. This song is part of the world projected and condensed in a 1983 rock number: 'Zodiac, Cadillac, I'm a motor maniac'.

That same year, Stephen King prefaced most of the chapters of his novel *Christine* with quotations from auto-lyrics to provide a context for a story about a vampire–female 1958 Plymouth Fury that seduces the teenage Arnold Cunningham into erotic passions. Cunningham's 'obsessive behaviour' becomes the newest stage in 'possessive individualism' as auto-mania.[9] Christine is a self-renewing factor in American twentieth century culture. She is also a reaction to the male prerogatives of conquest over feminized nature and human femininity by social discipline and technology, whose explicit ingredients of repressed desire are usually consigned to some kind of feminized 'unconscious.' But, as the numerous driverless transport movies (which have since 1960 demonized both inanimate technology and animate energy) reveal, the masks of masculinity continue to dominate.[10] The subject of Eliott Silverstein's *The Car* (1976), for example, is a killer: the black embodiment of manoeuver-ability, noise and aggression on the road. The nature of its power is first recognized by an Amerindian woman still alert to ambivalent forces. In fact, at certain key points, the predominantly white audience for such films is located within the car itself by placing the camera point of view inside the car's orange-tinted glass. After its final explosion into satanic shapes, the auto is reborn, as it has to be in America: charging under the final credits into an easily victimizable city.[11]

As extensions of muscle, nerve and will, technologies become cultural media, a synaesthetic network of desires that not only Detroit but also the visual arts, music, films and literature play on, producing cars, motorcycles and airplanes for any number of purposes besides transport. The point of combustion inside the economy is where industry or basic productivity (finance, services, jobs, transportation systems, and the exploitation of waste of materials and human energies) meets sales, or the consumerist manipulation of desire and rational and irrational 'necessities'. A poisonous cloud is permanently poised over many of America's cities, and this in spite of the nation's lead in de-leading gas.

The first cliché style of the automobile, the horse and wagon with an elevated driving seat, became the archetypal car in America, only reaching nearer the ground as the early twentieth-century stylists imitated boats and planes in an attempt to suggest take-off, land-free acceleration and power. The dashboard increasingly came to resemble a control panel. In the 1930s, Buckminster Fuller's cross-fertilization of car and airplane, which he called Dymaxion transport, was immediately stamped out by Detroit and the oil corporations because his car really did transcend, in manoeuverability and electronics, the stereotyped product.[12] The dream and actuality of democratic mobility in American space proved to be a fertile ground for controls of transportation, including the false idealization of freedom defined as mobility, and various new forms of old powers, those dominant interfaces where pleasure and instrumentality breed.

In his first book of poems, *Discrete Series*, published in 1934, George Oppen wrote:

> The evening, water in a glass
> Thru which our car runs on a higher road
>
> Over what has the air frozen?
>
> Nothing can equal in polish and obscured
>   origin that dark instrument
> A car
>   (Which.
> Ease; the hand on the sword-hilt

Oppen's comment in an interview thirty-four years later augments his vision: 'There is a feeling of something false in overprotection and over-luxury – my idea of categories of realness.'[13] And twelve years earlier, in 1956, at the conclusion of a highly informed and explorative essay on the auto-world, David Riesman and Eric Larrabee wrote of the wider context of song, poem, film and the demonic cults of technology:

> Americans want unconditonal surrender whether they fight a war or seek a market; and lack, for the most part, the flexibility of conduct for limited warfare for limited aims. Thus we come back to . . . the desire to build into every car an inescapable appeal to every whim within the Great American Market, and into the advertizing and sales pitches a rationalization to hold down repressed ambivalences . . .
>
> The Navy, lacking a big stake in strategic bombing and missiles, was once the Chrysler of the Armed Three, backing sobriety and even diplomacy; more recently, it has conceded to the nuclear doctrine of S[trategic] A[ir] C[ommand] in return for being allowed to build big carriers, thus maintaining the principle of 'competition' at the expense of any strategic alternatives to self-destruction . . .
>
> With a whole economy geared to the auto, on what else would we spend our surplus productivity, our surplus energy, were the car suddenly taken away as a central prop? We are no more ready for such a shift than for sudden disarmament.[14]

Other demonstrations of the entrance of the car into American life are offered in Harry Crews' novel, *Car* (1972). As a protest against his enforced inheritance of his father's forty-three acres of wrecked cars known as Auto-Town (the family live on site in Salvage House), Herman Mack decides to express his possessive love for a red Ford Maverick by eating it alive in front of the Sherman Hotel, Jacksonville, Florida – from bumper to bumper on nationwide TV. The best way to possess is to eat, and Mack's commitment also solves what Riesman terms 'the problem of discovering challenge in what Galbraith calls the "affluent society."' Riesman himself reports the experience of living near a park in Kansas City where 'young people from well-to-do homes' repeated at night, in their parents' Buicks and Oldsmobiles, the initiation rites of Nicholas Ray's 1955 film with James Dean, *Rebel Without A Cause*. He concludes: 'Such young people hang suspended between the traditional games of children and those which war and work and some new and old kinds of play provide for adults.'[15]

In such games, women are frequently trophies or motivators: cheer-leaders and chaste goddesses of war caught in a race for dating and partnering frequently centred on the socializing automobile. After researching his three volumes on the history of science and sexuality, Brian Easlea writes: 'Modern science is unique in its repertoire of aggressive sexual and birth imagery.'[16] Productivity out of technology, technology out of science, he proposes as a continual birth obsession, quoting Sir Humphrey Davy at the beginning of the nineteenth century on 'the penetrating genius of Volta' gaining access to the intimate and female secrets of nature's energy – electricity.[16] In late twentieth-century America, Arnie Cunningham and Herman Mack have other acts to perform in the vital theatre of possession, and their company steadily increases. Michael Lang, Vietnam veteran and undercover cop, is remade as Michael Knight for the TV series *Knight Rider* (1981): he is linked to an indestructible car named Knight 2000 through a speaking computer in tune with a sensor implanted in the hero's brain. In 1965, Americans absorbed a sit-com series entitled *My Mother the Car*.

Today, Mary Shelley, author of *Frankenstein, or The Modern Prometheus* (1818), reads like an 'onelie begetter,' and it was Thomas Edison, the very type of the American technological producer, who made the first Frankenstein film in 1910, with Charles Ogle as the Monster. Five years later came the second, Joseph Smiley's *Life without a Soul*, and since then scores of Shelley films have been produced in America. The popularity of such media explorations suggests that Americans dream of a fusion between the desiring body and technics, like astronauts fused with their capsule. The message in the medium is that alchemy and witchcraft never left science, its apparatus, its products or its agents: 'The material aim of all alchemists, the transmutation of metals, has now been realized by science, and the alchemical vessel is the uranium pile. Its success has had precisely the result that the alchemists feared and guarded against.' The words are those of F. Sherwood Taylor, former director of the Science Museum in London.[17]

The transmutational urge is indeed wider and deeper than simple versions of laboratory behaviour. In Thomas Pynchon's novel *V.* (1963), Benny Profane hears Rachel Owlglass talking to her MG as she washes it. Everyone meets Rachel through her car, and she constitutes one of a number of commonplace fusions with the inanimate presented in the text. Pynchon has his eye on the intersections of neurotic need at that point in auto-history when the designer took over from the engineer in the car industry – to be precise, in 1940, when General Motors' Chief Stylist, Harley Earl, became the first designer to reach the position of corporate vice-president. His slogan was 'appearance sells cars.'[18] Rachel addresses her car:

> 'You beautiful stud . . . I love to touch you . . . Do you know what I feel when we're out on the road? Alone, just us?' She was running the sponge caressingly over its front bumper. 'Your funny responses, darling, that I know so well. The way your brakes pull a little to the left, the way you start to shudder around 5000 rpm when you're excited. And you burn oil when you're mad at me, don't you? I know . . . We'll always be together,' running a chamois over the hood, 'and you needn't worry about that black Buick we passed on the road today. Ugh: fat, greasy Mafia car. I expected to see a body come flying out of the back door, didn't you? Besides, you're so angular and proper-English and tweedy – and oh, so Ivy that I couldn't ever leave you, dear.' It occurred to Profane that he might vomit. Public displays of sentiment often affected him this way.[19]

Rachel is soon 'fondl[ing] the gearshift.' In *Christine*, Arnie Cunningham's girlfriend, Leigh, is obsessed as a child with a red Remco racing car, a toy that radiated 'essential illusion . . . magic . . . [and] stole her heart. The illusion, of course, was that the car was driving itself.'[20] In Kenneth Anger's film *Kustom Kar Kommandos* (1965), a group of gays, stripped to their briefs, polish gleaming multi-coloured cars with swansdown puffs to the sounds of the Rolling Stones' 'Satisfaction.' Another kind of erotics obsessed Neal Cassady, the real-life prototype of Dean Moriarty, hero of Jack Kerouac's *On the Road* (1957). In Timothy Leary's autobiography, *Flashbacks* (1984), this self-styled 'auto-pilot outlaw,' who put his life into driving and

parking cars combined with talking and sex, appears in action in
New York in 1960 with a girl called Patty-Belle. Leary walks in.
Cassady talks as he moves:

'. . . if she doesn't get her juicy streamline chassis overhauled
every day, you understand, she gets . . . pouty.' Cassady closed
his eyes to narrate. 'So I gotta grind her sweet soft valves,
lubricate her tubes, fire her spark plugs, you understand, lay
down some tyre-tracks across her rumble-seat, oil her transmission, grease her gearbox, you understand, tune up her soft li'l
cylinders, and jam her throttle to the floor.'[21]

Patty-Belle may thoroughly enjoy this vulgar metonymyzing.
Moreover, like the other instances just quoted, it is not only part
of the car advertiser's dream of consumer-identification with the
product. As Félix Guattari observes in an essay entitled
'Towards a Micro-Politics of Desire': 'Human beings make love
with signs and all kinds of "extra-human" elements – things,
animals, images, looks, machines, and so on – that the sexual
functioning of primates, for instance, had never encoded.'[22]

Neal Cassady also appears in Alan Harrington's study,
Psychopaths (1972): 'According to any medical model ever
devised [he] qualified as a complete psychopath.'[23] But in fact
the Cassady-Moriarty figure is not all that unusual; he is more
of an extreme case of blind self-confidence and exuberance
working at 'the excitement of auto-mobility as a set-breaking
excitement' in the Eisenhower years. Conformist boredom
could, for Cassady, be resisted by motion: 'To save himself he
kept constantly in motion' in both work and leisure. Again, this
is by no means uncommon in a society where obsessive mobility
and speed are not considered fundamentally psychopathic.
Harrington therefore moves his example into a larger context:
'Instant being, not laboring to become. Moving into what you
want immediately, no delay. Free-form, even serene maneuver-
ing, not slowed by sentiment. Thus violence is speed. Motorcycles.
Brutal directness, speed on the uptake. Getting there effortlessly
from one place to another, from one thought to another. Telling
the exact truth is speed. Even more, silence is speed, electric
understanding too swift for words, moving on'.[24] Not surprisingly,

a drug that supplies the sensation in some of these needs is called speed.

Technique, or technology, processes of analysis, synthesis and instrumentality operate always on 'living flesh.' As Jacques Ellul proposed in 1954, therefore, we have to analyze 'the myths of the technicians,' carrying this investigation through today to the irrational career of John DeLorean – from car-designer to alleged cocaine peddlar; the auto-executive who, in Ellul's terms, affords 'the abstraction, Man . . . only [as] an epiphenomenon in the Marxist sense; a natural secretion of technical process.'[25] Interrogation must move, too, between Ellul's analysis of adaptability and the image of Mel Gibson's Max in George Miller's *Mad Max II* (made in Australia in 1981). Clothed in the remnants of biker leathers, with his metal leg-artifice, his car tools as weapon, and his gun, Max survives into a bizarre post-oil crisis age in which bikes and cars have become reconstructed dinosaurs. In *Max Mad II*, late twentieth-century lawlessness has become social norm – a now-familiar terrorism that includes the unscrupulous combat for oil that has controlled American foreign policy for much of the century. In April 1954 *U.S. News and World Report* declared: 'One of the world's richest areas is open to the winner in Indochina . . . Tin, rubber, rice, key strategic raw materials are what the war is really about.' Such motivations thrust towards war, and open a passage towards those pathological responses to Arab oil restrictions instituted by American oil corporations in the 1970s, and the Gulf War in the 1980s.[26]

Max lives by style and in unison with transport in a science fiction future quite like the present,[27] and recognizably part of Ellul's determinist version of present fused to future:

> The psychotechnicians have recognized that adaptation is not possible for everyone. In a completely technicized world, there will be whole categories of men who will have no place at all, because universal adaptation will be required. Those who are adapted will be so rigorously adapted that no play in the complex will be possible. The complete joining of man and machine will have the advantage, however, of making the adaptation painless. And it will assure the technical efficiency of the individuals who survive it.

48

Up to the present, adaptation has been the product of material interaction, with all this implies in laxness, misfitting, and excess. But future adaptation will be calculated according to a strict system . . . it will be impossible to escape . . .[28]

so that the reinforcement of Control from Centre is maintained. The philosophy of such politics is well-known from Jacques Derrida's 1966 essay on 'Structure, Sign and Play in the Discourse of the Human Sciences': '. . . the centre also closes off the play which it opens up and makes possible. . . . And as always, coherence in contradiction expresses the force of desire. The concept of centred structure is in fact the concept of play based on fundamental ground, a play constituted on the basis of a fundamental immobility and a reassuring certitude, which itself is beyond the reach of play'.[29] Ford's dream of the democratic mobility of every American through the advent of the cheap car thus moves towards 'fundamental immobility.'

But the very conditions of work in the Ford factory indicate another origin of automobile immobility: the assembly-line. Since Daedalus worked on the robotic man, science fiction and science have operated as the imaginative source of technology, more recently creating the prosthetically transformed *cyborg*, in Martin Caidin's novel of that name, and its extension in Samuel R. Delany's *Nova* (1968), in which a rocket crew is socketed into a space capsule to provide its energy.[30] Ellul traces the industrial version to the assembly-line worker: first systematized by Philadelphia engineer Frederick Taylor in his 1895 paper, 'A Piece Rate System,' later conceptualized in Europe as Taylorism or Americanism, and then both embraced (by Lenin, in the interests of Soviet productivity, in a *Pravda* article in 1918) and resisted (by Antonio Gramsci, in the name of humanity, in his prison essay, 'Americanism and Fordism').[31] Ellul writes: '[t]o call good the fact that the worker thinks and dreams about matters unrelated to his work while his body carries out certain mechanical activities is to sanction the psychological dissociation between intelligence and action . . . [and to] admit that . . . the ideal state, higher than consciousness, is a dreaming sleep. To acquiesce in the thesis that work is 'neutral' is to acquiesce in this profound rupture'.[32]

The irrationalities of industrial production and the production of consumption can be exemplified by three items in the Riesman and Larrabee article we have cited. The Northeastern Indiana Mennonites favour exclusively twenty-year-old black Plymouth sedans. The station-wagon craze encourages a sense of Bohemian self-reliance its purchasers need in their lives. And for steel workers investigated in Gary, Indiana, 'the car is . . . a decompression chamber in which [they] avoid the bends and the benders in making the transition from the all-male, working-class atmosphere of the plant to the mixed company and middle-class atmosphere of the suburban home.'[33]

But the automobile psychopaths remain active. In 1978 the *International Herald Tribune* reported the following: 'In Sacramento recently, during a fight prompted by a freeway lane change, a passenger in a pickup truck lifted a rifle from a rack in the back window of the truck and fatally shot the driver of the other vehicle'.[34] During the oil shortages of the 1970s the desire for dominance on the freeways even extended into the pit stops, with drivers shooting their way to the pumps. Researching for his film *Rebel Without a Cause* (1955), Nicholas Ray discovered 'a sixteen-year-old boy who ran his car into a group of children just for fun.' (One of Lenny Bruce's salutary one-liners went: 'I hit one of those things in the street – waddya call it? – a kid.') After Ray's star James Dean's auto-death, it was not only teenagers who collected fragments of the true car in which he was killed. The wrecked Spyder became a profitable cult centre: fifty cents to sit behind the wheel.[35]

Such evidences are so numerous that they threaten to become commonplace and taken for granted. But they still show people feeling more powerful in a car, where social controls are assumed and felt to be less present, and in which you can drive off to release tension, explode on the freeway (especially against traffic officers), and show off to an inferior. In *Psychopaths*, Alan Harrington cites a number of revenge dramas involving cars, and one remarkable instance of auto-attachment – more pathetic than murderous for once. An old Plymouth – the car that repeatedly emerges as a key to auto-culture – catches fire on Park Avenue, New York. The bearded driver in a black top hat stops, tries to look under the smoking hood, gives up and begins to run around his car, then stands with other spectators watching it burn. Two fire engines arrive; the driver tries to prevent the firemen hosing and axing his car, crying out while they ignore him. He then goes into a 'forlorn little dance' and calls to a policeman to make the firemen stop. Finally he is left in silence with his savaged automobile. No one has spoken to him in the entire scene. He takes passers-by by the elbow and draws their attention to the wreck: 'They shrug and walk on.' He contemplates 'his dead car, and then he is gone.' At night everything of value is stripped from the hulk, which is towed away three days later. Such is the end of what is – along with the gun – America's main equalizer.[36]

Gradually the American car has been fashioned into the embodiment and container of the living room, jukebox, jet-plane and bathroom, and used in itself as one of many major class props. Ford's 1924 dream of the car as the main populist leveller dissolved as it became part of the class structure; so too did his later dream of 'the ethical car.' He had insisted, with the severity of a Veblen, on putting technology and price first. In the process, however, he created an expanding system of needs. The Ford became an example of Ellul's 'self-augmentation' within technology. As Riesman and Larrabee put it, the assembly-line and the five-dollar a day wage were 'instrumental in creating an economy far too bounteous to be satisfied with the Model T. . . . Machinery . . . redefines aspirations as rapidly as it absorbs them.'[37] Auto-culture would come to include 'new national pastimes . . . [such as] stock car racing, drag racing, [and] demolition derbies,' as well as that anarchic, Emersonian customizing that Tom Wolfe wrote up in *The Kandy-Kolored Tangerine-Flake Streamline Baby* (1965).[38] Auto-names go with the designs and the designers' pathology – Phantom Flasher, Lazarus, Vandal, and so forth. The vanning cult, which took off in the late 1970s, involved the decorative personalization of a common van into a centre of a life-style of self-contained mobility, incidental to travel. As the author of the celebratory report in *Time* magazine put it: 'there's no madness like nomadness.'[39]

Even in the Depression decade, thirty-eight million cars were sold in America, ten million more than in the previous decade.

The industry had begun to dominate the economy, and, as cars became easier to make than to sell, the designer took precedence over the engineer. Colour and shape became major marketing points. The psychology of advertizing dictated sales methods. As Riesman and Larrabee observe, 'the American driver desired to be treated as a passenger on a moving sofa.' Styling was classically exemplified by Harley Earl's wraparound windshield for General Motors in 1954, part of the industry's conception and construction of the car as a gothic edifice in metal and glass, a metallic and plastic sculpture. General Motors immediately commandeered America's laminated glass production. The designer war moved into extravagant waste. In 1950 Chrysler's falling sales were only just rescued by the discovery that their safe and sedate image did not appeal to 'new generations allied to the outgoing life, the two-level ranch house, and the two-tone car.' Their Virgil Exner came up with the jet plane accessories, including 'an intergalactic control panel,' and Chrysler duly returned, with high turnover sales, built-in obsolescence and inflated credit terms, to big three status.[40] The Detroit auto as an exceptional object had ended; the key is now 'model change.' Renault's advertisement in *Rolling Stone* magazine for 1 August 1977 is headed 'Le Car vs. La Competition.' The car carries two bicycles on its roof and the copy promises 'an optional gigantic sun roof which we call a "fun roof."'

So the automobile became part of accelerated time-change, the governance of speed, life as a huge sentence whose fast units stretch before and after in pseudo-inevitable process. The automobile graveyard of Harry Crews' *Car*, sweltering under 'an airy blast of gas and chemicals and stopped-up toilets,' is America's answer to Henry Ford's belief in 'an all-plastic car made out of soya beans and other renewable resources, so that it could be used up and thrown away.' In fact, the car is part of American addiction. In 1961, William S. Burroughs, a major analyst of addictions and metabolic changes, wrote in the *Journal for the Protection of All Beings* – using the slang word for heroin, 'junk': 'Junk is the mold of monopoly and possession . . . the ideal product . . . the ultimate merchandise. No sales talk necessary. The client will crawl through a sewer and beg to buy.

. . . The junk merchant does not sell his product to the consumer, he sells the consumer to his product. . . . Junk yields a basic formula of "evil" virus: *The Algebra of Need*. The face of "evil" is always the face of total need.'[41]

This helplessness extends, for instance, to the replica market – expensive duplicates of classy autos which place their owners safely within what is fondly called the Statusphere.[42] In 1958, John Keats opened his analysis of auto culture, *The Insolent Chariots* (the title derives from a 1957 speech by Lewis Mumford), thus:

> Once upon a time, the American met the automobile and fell in love. Unfortunately, this led him into matrimony, and so he did not live happily ever after . . . He was merely a rustic Merry Andrew with a cowlick and an adolescent tightening of the groin. In his libidinous innocence, he saw the automobile only as curious, exciting – and obviously willing . . . Then, before they were fairly out of the churchyard, she began to demonstrate less enchanting aspects of her character . . .[43]

This kind of application of some ancient myth of sexist helplessness – passivity under the erotic onslaught of wicked technology – has been regularly and severely challenged. But at least Keats gets to the region of desire ignored academically but essential to any consideration of fifty years of automobile alterations in dress, manners, vacation habits, consumer patterns, and what Keats calls 'common tastes and positions of intercourse.' Since traffic has virtually halted in cities, Keats asks, 'will the automobile put man back on his feet?' or will he yield to his vehicle of desire?: 'One crouches to crawl onto an illuminated rolling cave, and then reclines on a sort of couch, there to push buttons and idly wonder what might lie in front of the glittering hood.'[44]

In 1954, Russell Lynes concluded that 'ever since 1905 the automobile industry has been second only to the women's fashion industry in its insistence on the glamour' of model changes; 'in fact, a man clothes himself in his car in much the same spirit as a woman dresses herself in her clothes, and he is subject to the calculated whims of Detroit just as his wife is subject to the equally calculated whims of Paris.'[45] 'Glamour,' the OED informs us, means magic or enchantment: 'a magical or fictitious beauty attaching to any person or object; a delusive or alluring charm.' It quotes a Scottish source: 'When devils, wizards or jugglers deceive the sight, they are said to cast glamour o'er the eyes of the spectator.' The world of Booth Tarkington's trilogy *Growth* (1927) (including *The Magnificent Ambersons*) and his autobiographical *The World Does Move* (1928) show industrial expansion leading to regimes of glamour. Phrases such as 'diabolical glamour' and 'victims of glamour' began to alert consumers to the manipulation of desire – or, to use other and later terms, the internalization of the fashion environment into what Claude Bernard called 'le milieu intérieur,' the internal environment.[46] Tarkington charts a new mobility and a new fashion obsession, from bicycles to cars, in the *fin de siècle* beginnings of speed mania, including the supposedly revolutionary daring of women's bicycle costume and the emergence of the 'fast' woman as the car woman – implying that cars encourage sexual looseness in women, where men were immune. Car bodies and fashion bodies move together in these regimes of fascination, the gaze that controls, the style that addicts, the theatre of power. In 1970, the titular hero of Michael McClure's novel *The Mad Cub* still yields to the required ecstasy:

The car heater makes warmth all the way to the knees . . . I am high – driving into mysterious eternity. I pull the wheel and roll my body turning the sharp bends. Instruction signs about turns never make sense. I am alone in a world of lights and blackness. The smell of the car is the smell of air pipes and gasoline and oil . . . I blank out just a little. It's beautiful but too much to cope with. . . . I flick on the radio knob. Music begins – it is a rich opulent and three-dimensional carpet of sound that fills the car floating and drifting in waves. The car becomes a red four-wheeled chariot in a modern fairy story. I drive into a technicolour infinity. Cars should be honoured and made into creatures with their own sides hammered into patterns of feathers and wings and fur and rich abstract patterns of texture and each one should be unique and loved.[47]

Customizing and vanning achieved just this anthropomorphic individualization.

Cars mobilize America's various private armies, and they featured in the operations of Charles Manson's nomad band: thirty-five men, women and children who travelled in six 'stolen four-wheel-drive dune buggies and camped in a succession of abandoned mining shacks' with 'radio-equipped lookout posts on the mountains.'[48] Manson's power arose at the intersection of automobile, gun, radio and the drug culture, together with his prison studies in post-hypnotic suggestion and transactional psychoanalysis (part of the apparatus of advertizing persuasions): the exact and lethal configuration of consumerist and warfare techniques of rational and irrational manipulation. He operated at the meetingpoint of electronic rock music, guns, televised assassination, Roman Polanski's *Rosemary's Baby* (1968), and his fleet of dune buggies equipped for 'a 1000-mile assault field.' The Family's murders were committed during the summer of 1969, the year after the Lieutenant Calley massacre in Vietnam and the assassination of Martin Luther King, and were partly inspired by The Beatles' *Magical Mystery Tour* and the double album, *The Beatles*, released in December 1967 and 1968 respectively. Their black uniforms were worn in imitation of The Process, one of a number of Los Angeles cults specializing in erotic fears and drugs, the traditional elements of religious control. Manson modelled himself on General Rommel, hero of the international military.[49] By August 1985, black had conquered America far beyond the dreams of Ford and his Model T:

In nearly every culture in every age, after all, the associations have been grim: death, penitence, mysteries of the lower depths and the northern wastes, negation. Suburbanites who hanker after an anodized black aluminium clipboard or a GE fridge with a black plastic front are not quiet closet nihilists or unwitting satanists. But in an insistently multi-colored world, black merchandise is never chosen arbitrarily, and probably not casually: during the 1920s, when nearly every Ford on the road was black, the color may have meant nothing special, but today black signifies. 'It says driving machine, it says high performance, boldness, strictly business,' explains Gerry Thorley, Chrysler's designer in charge of color.

Today's stylish meanings are all severe, unsmiling, sexy but mean. Black as a no-nonsense, high-tech wrapper is the predominant mode. Black stereo components, more deadpan than streamlined, making playing records a serious business. Glossy, all black cars look hermetic, the driver encased and invulnerable. Of all cars, they are also the most unforgiving of blemishes and dirt; like health-club body fetishists, the owners of perfectly polished black cars are out to flaunt the hard work their vanity requires. Even U.S. military engineers have indulged in monumental Darth Vader design: the new Pershing II nuclear missile, solidly black but for a few stripped highlights, may be the first expressionist weapon. . . . The color is gunpowder and midnight; the message is menace and highly private pleasure.[50]

Such is the distance travelled from Muncie, Indiana, in 1925 when Robert and Helen Lynd investigated urban American culture and recorded it in their *Middletown* (1929). In chapter eighteen, 'Inventions Re-Making Leisure,' they provide one of the first sets of data for the auto-era. In 1890, the town had one car; in 1923, 6,221: two for every three families. Forty-one per cent were Fords, fifty-four per cent were models made in 1920 or later. As the number of surfaced roads increased, the car entered 'the equilibrium of habits' and challenged hitherto unquestioned Sunday churchgoing, children's behaviour and pocket money levels, the facts of walking and of living in or outside town, and procedures of shopping, sport and work. In the Lynd's own words: 'Group-sanctioned values are disturbed by the inroads of the automobile upon the family budget.' Homes are mortgaged to buy a car; savings and expenditure deflected to the car as a growing necessity, at the expense of food, clothing and bathrooms. Families are believed to be either held together or dispersed by the car. Speed is believed to increase theft, including theft of automobiles. Cars increase 'sex crimes,' diminish churchgoing and Fourth of July celebration attendances. The 'vacation habit' increases. In 1890 few executives and no workers took a summer vacation; train excursions were major events. By 1925 a few factories closed down for one or two weeks each summer, or workers were allowed off for a vacation – without pay. The radius of holiday trips extended and family fares were cut.[51] James J. Flink believes that 'Henry Ford created a new class of semi-skilled industrial workers and set a new standard of remuneration for manual labour.' '[A]t General Motors under Alfred P. Sloan' during the 1920s, 'the decentralized, multi-divisional structure of the modern industrial corporation, modern management techniques and consumer instalment credit' were all pioneered.[52]

By 1968, about 9.6 million new cars were being sold annually, and one in six jobs was directly related to the industry, which now dominated oil, steel, glass, rubber and lacquer production. Street and highway construction, real estate development, service stations and tourist accommodation (including the motel) had become major controls in the auto-society. Despite the oil crises of the 1970s, by 1974 nearly forty per cent of American's oil went for gas, with 142 million motorists burning record amounts. On 16 July 1979, *Time* magazine reported that the gas shortage was forcing Americans to realize that 'the US lacks a coherent, efficient, and low-cost system of mass-transportation.' Mobility it saw as controlled by a massive lobby of auto-manufacturers, oil companies, construction firms, Teamsters and building trades unions, since ninety per cent of all travel was by private car and seventy-five per cent of all goods were carried by truck. In 1964, the Johnson government had founded the Urban Mass Transit Administration to fund public transport – but its prospects had been vitiated by indecisive squabbles between transport authorities in cities and counties as to who should be responsible for services.[53]

The file on the continuing irrationalities of the auto-industry and the auto-culture is huge and growing ever more absurd. In 1970, the Federal Trade Commission, headed by Caspar Weinberger, concluded a massive study of the automobile companies with a proposal that the industry be regulated as a public utility. A few years later, Weinberger became the very model of advocacy for endless Federal largesse to be handed over to the military-industrial complex, and for the Reagan administration's control of the FTC in order to undo any public service work proposed in the 1970s. One 1984 example can stand for the lot:

The commission settled a suit it had brought in 1980 against

General Motors, alleging that the company had produced more than 21 million cars with defects in transmissions, camshafts, and diesel fuel injectors. Under the settlement, the auto company will not have to reimburse owners for the costs of repairing those cars. Instead, to receive payments each consumer must go before an arbitrator to prove that the car was defective when he or she bought it.[54]

The cover-ups of the absurdities and cruelties of the industry are legion. A blatantly exemplary figure is Lido Anthony 'Lee' Iacocca, head of the ever-failing, ever-bailed out (by state, union and federal government) Chrysler Corporation, who is given to pronouncements such as this one in 1983: 'I was arrogant, but General Motors made a science of goddam arrogance . . . If General Motors and Ford keep thinking that way, we'll run over them.' Iacocca published his life-story in 1984, and denied that he had been considered for the Democratic Vice-Presidential nomination. Republican when he was a Ford executive, he turned Democrat when President Carter bailed out Chrysler with loan guarantees. He became the protégé of Henry Ford II, who later turned jealously against him, ultimately firing him in 1978. Iacocca admits that he put up with Ford's abuse because 'I was . . . greedy. I enjoyed being president . . . I found it impossible to walk away from an annual income of $970,000.' When he took over Chrysler, he fired thirty-five vice-presidents but still needed federal aid to restart the racket, shrewdly taking advantage of the fact that the nation operates under state capitalism and not 'free enterprise.'[55]

The issue for GM and Ford in 1983 was competition between 'the new snappy, four-seat, low-slung G24 sports car' and Ford's performance leader, the 302 HO Mustang GT. When Iacocca announced the launch of the 'minivan' in 1984 – postponed from the days of near-bankruptcy days five years earlier – and called it 'automotive history,' an auto-industry analyst with Vila-Fisher Associates in New York City called it 'a whole new concept to foist on suburbia.' No wonder, then, that in March 1979, 550 industrialists bowed their heads before lunch at the Economic Club of Detroit while a city councillor intoned: 'Almighty God, we thank thee for the wheel. For the person who made it into a vehicle. For those who produce it. And bless us who use it. Amen.' Did they remember those killer tires made by Firestone, investigated by the House Sub-committee on Oversight and Investigations in 1979? Or the killer petrol tanks in the Ford Pinto case? Ford fended off investigation until some 500 people were burned to death, and then fought compensation claims. But the corporation did finally decide to drop the last line of their radio commercial which declared: 'Pinto leaves you with a warm feeling.'[56]

That same year, the Travel Network Corporation imported a German mobile motel called The Snoozer: a 59.4 foot-long 'live-aboard bus' in which a six foot person could walk without stooping. It contained a bar, a kitchen, and eight mahogany-panelled passenger rooms, and offered two beds, a shower and toilet, closets, heating, and air-conditioning. The corporation's president offered the last word on this auto: 'With The Snoozer we're not in the business of transporting people from A to B. The bus is really the destination.'[57] In her novel, *Wise Blood* (1952), Flannery O'Connor already had Hazel Motes, sole incumbent of the Church of Truth without Jesus Christ Crucified, needing a car as house and pulpit. He buys a decrepit Ford Essex, a transaction in which the salesman's hype is central: 'I wouldn't trade over a Chrysler for an Essex like that. That car yonder ain't been built by a bunch of niggers.' The auto world feeds into O'Connor's vision of grotesques in a maniacally religious South: cars exist as irrational instruments in the irrational lives of human beings warped to the demands of the irrational. More recently, the recreational vehicle [RV] has become a centre of controversy and legal predations. An editorial in *The Nation* for 25 May 1985, reads:

The latest depredation against the Fourth Amendment came last week in *California v. Carney*, a case involving the warrantless search of a recreational vehicle. After receiving a tip that a camper parked in a lot in downtown San Diego was being used for pot and sex parties, the police raided it and found quantities of the forbidden weed. Charles Carney, the owner of the vehicle, was arrested and convicted of possessing drugs for sale. On appeal, the California Supreme Court held that his camper was a home and that the cops should have obtained a search warrant before entering . . .

There are eight million RVs like Carney's on the road now . . . most of their owners use them as quasi vacation homes. Should the ability to turn the ignition key entitle them to less privacy than people occupying a fishing shack or a hotel room? (And how about those who live on boats?) We are a mobile society; people must travel long distances to find sylvan settings in which to rest and recreate. Citizens who convey living quarters in the back of the car should not be treated like latter-day Okies. The right of privacy should be as portable as a Coleman stove or an air mattress.

The opening of the Ford Highland Park factory on 1 January 1910 certainly proved to be a symbolic date for the United States. *The 1909–1912 Sears, Roebuck & Co. Motor Buggy Catalogue* has no enclosed cars at all. Driver and passenger are as exposed to the elements as motor-cyclists.[58] Once the car is enclosed, then its massive presence as multiple control begins to take off. The search for 'the ethical car' begins with Ford's 1909 advertisement: 'I will build a motor car for the great multitude. It will be large enough for the family but small enough for the individual to run and care for. . . . it will be so low in price that no man making a good salary will be unable to own one – and enjoy with his family the blessing of hours of pleasure in God's great open spaces.'

That car entered Ford's Heraclitean philosophy of perpetual change, and necessarily lost out in the process: 'Everything is in flux, and was meant to be. . . . We fortunately did not inherit any traditions, and we are not founding any.'[59] The auto-industry became 'a desiring machine' within a society constructed as 'deplacements and metamorphoses of energy that never stops decomposing and recomposing sub-units.'[60] America became *the* major site of a twentieth-century coalition. As Félix Guattari puts it: 'A society which overcodes product through the law of capitalist profit tends to create an inescapable split between desiring production and social production. Desire is thrown upon private life while sociality recedes into profit-making labour'.[61]

'Production of desire, a dream, a passion' takes place within 'the variable investment of work forces and the constant investment of technical means.' Acceptance and rejection of these investments depend on the connections of machines to desire – explicitly, the desiring body. In Guattari's terms:

> At the heart of the industrial machines there are desiring machines which are split, separated, and tapped by the dominant system. The point at issue is whether this division which is considered to be legitimate and human . . . can or cannot be overcome . . .
>
> A social chemistry of desire . . . runs not only through history, but also through the whole social space . . . . It is never a man who works – the same can be said for desire – but a combination of organs and machines. . . . It is because the production forces of today cause the explosion of traditional human territorialities, that they are capable of liberating the atomic energy of desire.[62]

Ford's belief in the elimination of traditions and the need for them leaves an endless obsession with newness, a form of mobility in itself. Theodor Adorno writes: ' "History is bunk," an expression attributed to Henry Ford, relegates to the junkpile everything not in line with the most recent methods of industrial production, including ultimately, all continuity of life.' But in fact this is a new continuity: the continuity of the new, a sense of accelerated change through pseudo-new events and models. The state becomes an automobile state – the inner sense of the old tag: 'What's good for General Motors is good for America.' The car is the state: 'Once capital itself has become its own myth, or rather the interminable machine, aleatory, something like a *social genetic code*, it no longer leaves any room for a planned reversal; and this is true violence'.[63]

1983

3

Blood on the Nash Ambassador: Cars in American Films

I

Decoding the automobile in American movies is part of the study of interactions between culture and technology, between the human body, its extensions in tools and machines, and their presentation in the 'multivocal and polysemous' structures of America or any society. The intervention of a new machine 'alters the sense ratios or patterns of perception' and restructures both the environment and what Claude Bernard called the *milieu intérieur*, translated by Hans Selye as 'the internal environment.'[1] Cars are used for other purposes besides transport. The large black 1920s limousines in Roger Corman's *The St Valentine's Day Massacre* (1967) register the use of vehicles for submachine guns in the hands of gangsters; their violin cases did not protect violins (Billy Wilder had fun with this in 1959 at the beginning of *Some Like It Hot*). The car as transport is parodied, just as the mob's boardroom meetings around large polished tables parody the gangster operations of corporation directors. As Michael Corleone explains to Tom Hagan in *Godfather II* (Coppola, 1974), 'all our people are businessmen.' In Corman's film, Jason Robards' Al Capone is a Carnegie who stretches the law only a stage further than the 'legitimate' millionaire. In the interchange of cars and motorcycles, the police and the criminal share their violations within the elasticized interfaces of law and permission. In Peckinpah's *The Getaway* (1973), the car which harbours Steve McQueen and Ali McGraw parodies home as the only enclosure their love on the run is afforded, a usage which in turn parodies the usual function of the getaway car in gangster films. In these and related ways, the automobile's mobility frequently indicates the amorality and immorality of human needs in action, and the sheer adjustability of American social codes to requirements of the thrusting self – in a society which has hardly begun to consider seriously the nature of peaceful relationships between vertical personal projection and lateral community coherence. Expedient mobility evades rigid oedipal obediences as far as possible. Ever since the 1929 crash and the subsequent patching recovery, the key event of disillusionment overlaid with moral perfidy in recent American history, American films have endlessly paralleled the dramas in Stanley Milgram's *Obedience to Authority*.[2] The car has been a major instrument in the battle to establish levels of popular morality in an endlessly collapsing and recovering hegemony. Necessarily, American films have shown an insatiable appetite for this continual state of emergency.

The combined weaponry of car and gun dominates law, and thereby enables the challenge and response structure in both the elaborately timed attacks of Don Siegel's *The Killers* (1964) and Arthur Penn's *Bonnie and Clyde* (1967), the classic evasory movie of the South-east Asia War and domestic Civil Rights period. Such capers invariably parody free enterprise and warfare, the main preoccupations of official America; as Edward G. Robinson says in *The Biggest Bundle of Them All* (Annakin, 1966), 'Timing, planning and, above all, daring and it's ours.' So that there are few surprises in American films, outside cutting and editing effects. Recognition patterns dominate, generating an audience with, as William Gaddis puts it, 'the unhealthy expectancy of someone who has seen a number of American moving pictures.'[3] In the history of Hollywood conventions certain 'situations are as recurrent in movies as the set themes of speeches in Seneca's plays.'[4] Even technology in science fiction films generates the unknown – a blob, a Thing, a gorilla, an ant – so that it can be dealt with in customary categories. In *Planet of the Apes* (Schaffner, 1968), it is the apes who use minimal technology rationally, playing the Houyhnhnms to the astronauts, not the technologically superior but emotional humans. Cool Buster Keaton never actually triumphs over the machine he is caught up with: it becomes instrumental, since *he* is the ape on the planet of *The General* (Keaton and Clyde Bruckman, 1926) and *The Navigator* (Keaton and Donald Crisp, 1924), surviving the train and the liner and – in other films – the steamboat, camera, film projector, car and motorcycle. But in doing so he becomes a machine himself, hence the emotionless mask, very nearly the mask of a 'bachelor machine'[5]:

> . . . each 'meet' with Machine some 'sport' with larger and more emphatically playful Gods.
>
> The chronological trace of his whole careering shows Buster growing smaller and – finally tiny . . . insect-like – in relation to Deus Ex Machinaes. They use him much as much as he Them. He has become a wildly flexible cog in Their destination. His is an involution sizewise back thru the whole of childhood to himself as Cosmic Hero: Tom Thumb.[6]

In comparison Jerry Lewis appears as a surreal extension of Mack Sennett's escapers in cars. In *The Family Jewels* (Lewis, 1965) he comes on as the idiot who falls out of a plane and disarms a torpedo, a fantasy comic-strip character in a world whose violence cannot violate or seriously injure. The Kid/Idiot triumphs through luck and rapid instinct rather than intelligence and understanding. Frank Sinatra's cop in *The Detective* (Douglas, 1968) uses the car to think in, and the Joad family in *The Grapes of Wrath* (Ford, 1940) escape Dust Bowl extermination in a Model T and make for the orange groves of California and a new life within the capitalist structure. The Joad trek is parodistically prefigured in the exodus of W.C. Fields and his family in *It's a Gift* (McLeod, 1934) and itself provides the model for one kind of road-movie to come. Their battered jalopy becomes the archetype of American automobile usage during the Depression and later. Survival by car is a fixed motif in American films.

But the sparagmatic dismemberment or utter demolition of the car is equally obsessive, and nowhere more so than in the Laurel and Hardy classic *Big Business* (Horne, 1929), where car demolition is paralleled by house-smashing. Brakhage takes its implications further: '. . . the subject of "war" itself . . . Xmas trees in Los Angeles – that was a start! . . . a joke perhaps –

along with a house that was due to be wrecked . . . a destructable prop.'[7]

But 'war' in Laurel and Hardy's scenario is divided between the sheer fun of smashing a house and the sheer fun of competitive revenge through the vulnerability of the car's parts: a dream, in fact, of violence fulfilled within the limits of a dream movie. Cars, and any other familiar object, re-function in transformatory situations in dream and waking life alike. Hitchcock's car dream tells him a scene he can use: 'In one of my dreams I was standing on Sunset Boulevard, where the trees are, and I was waiting for a Yellow Cab to take me to lunch. But no Yellow Cab came by; all the automobiles that drove by me were of 1916 vintage. And I said to myself, "It's no good standing here waiting for a Yellow Cab because this is a 1916 dream!" So I walked to lunch instead.'[8]

The eminent practicality of Hitchcock's films demands the treatment of technology as apparatus for dream and murder. So that the sinking of the car in *Psycho* (1960) is not only Norman Bates's method of eliminating evidence against his 'mother'; the bubbling, sucking sound is the sound of traumatic experience *and* of the overcoming of any fetishistic clinging to the auto. Car-owners in the audience for *Psycho* watch the type of their beloved, paid-for, intimate object being taken over, wastefully, by nature. Two years later, in *Guns of Darkness* (Asquith, 1962), Leslie Caron and David Niven escape from a swamp in which their 1957 Ford station-wagon is vanishing. Movies imitate the information processing of dreams in their semantics. The car's resurrection under the end-titles of *Psycho* adds to the perturbation, especially since it is so muddied. For those to whom the car is a partly vicious, partly lethal instrument, the scenes afford peculiar satisfaction. Ambivalently placed within the rest of the film's coding, they lead to involvement in a certain poetry:

> Whereas the instruments of poetic or philosophical communication are already extremely perfected, truly form a historically complex system which has reached its maturity, those of the visual communication which is at the basis of cinematic language are altogether brute, instinctive. Indeed, gestures, the surrounding reality, as much as dreams and the mechanisms of memory, are

of a virtually pre-human order, or at least at the limits of humanity – in any case pre-grammatical and even premorphological (dreams are unconscious phenomena, as are mnemonic mechanisms; the gesture is an altogether elementary sign, etc.).[9]

Hitchcock has once again involved us in the re-enaction of secret desire. The decoded scene speaks volumes about obsession with the car, the conversion of transport into libidinous impulse. The accumulation of such effects is in fact the cinema: 'Each film is not only structural but also structuring. . . . The viewer is forming an equal and possibly more or less opposite "film" in her/his head, constantly anticipating, correcting, re-correcting – constantly intervening in the arena of confrontation with the given reality, i.e. the isolated chosen area of each film's work, of each film's production.'[10] Simplistic structural separations into natural and cultural, denotative image and connotative composition, primary and secondary 'levels' – as for example in the work of Christian Metz – weaken complex reception of the simultaneities in Hitchcock's vision, or indeed practically any important car images used in a film.[11] For the director who understands the film image, the sign is never, as Saussure claims, arbitary; the object is never a metaphor; 'no symbols.'[12] Each film requires the kind of 'collective text' produced by the editors of *Cahiers du Cinéma* for Ford's *Young Mr Lincoln* (No. 223, 1970), so that what Pasolini calls 'the profoundly oneiric nature of cinema, as also its absolutely and inevitably concrete nature' can be read. The oneiric and concrete constitute a poetics rather than a semantics: the artist's necessity precedes the parasitism of the theorist; the society of the audience precedes the critic's journalistic needs to hold his ego-column within whatever bit of the Press has afforded him a ledge. The relationship of image to reality – arbitrary terms since the reality is itself a construct – is usefully described by Umberto Eco as an 'iconic sign,' which reproduces 'some of the conditions of perception, correlated with normal perceptive codes . . . we perceive the image as a message referred to a given code, but this is the normal perceptive code which presides over our every act of cognition.'[13] John Wayne big-game hunting by car in *Hatari* (Hawks, 1962) or W.C. Fields golfing from a 1930

Bantam called 'Spirit of South Brooklyn' in *The 300 Yard Drive* (Monte Brice, 1930) set up complex systems of memory and anticipation.

II

Raymond Lee's *Fit For the Chase* provides us with excellent iconic information on Hollywood's absorption of the automobile from the beginning (in fact film, car and jazz grew together as a key twentieth century triad).[14] But although cars are evident in very many movies, their use is often for purposes other than transport. Clara Bow, Joan Crawford and Jean Harlow were the first girls to have love scenes in cars, parallel to Bogart, Cagney and Robinson using cars as wheels for guns. Andy Hardy/ Mickey Rooney fell in love with a car. Miss Bow took a California football team riding in the early hours in her Kessel. Valentino raced his Isotta Fraschini and 1925 Avion Voisin. Miss Harlow vamped it up in her black V-12 Cadillac. Jackie Coogan kept two Rolls Royces, even if he had to maintain a kid-star image, and his father bought the first Rolls agency to Southern California. Dolores del Rio drove a Model A Ford. But then Cecil B. DeMille mounted a camera on the back seat of a car; Hoot Gibson bulldogged a steer from a car; and back in 1910 or 1913 – reports vary – Mack Sennett quoted Ezekiel x. 10 – 'As if a wheel had been in the midst of a wheel' – and the Tin Lizzie became a star: chased, caught, chasing, and choreographed. Raymond Lee's stills and snaps tell the story of the car-star-director interchange, with informative captions such as 'Adolphe Menjou tempts Constance Bennett with a 1930 Cadillac, which introduced the V-16 engine. The car, which cost over $8,000, is today considered a true classic.' (A quarter of a century later Judy Holliday will realise her dreams of wealth in *The Solid Gold Cadillac* (Quine, 1956)). Of Cagney's wound in *Each Dawn I Die* (Keighley, 1939) Lee writes: 'The blood is being spilled on a 1930 Nash Ambassador.'

The fantasizing of cars began at the birth of the movies, and since both were distributed throughout the class system, fantasy proliferated according to class need. The car has never become entirely alien, even if it is a major energy waster and environmental polluter, and was by 1960 out of date according to every rational standard. The Keystone Model T Fords were, along with the police, implements of farce and the grotesque in the national imagination. The outsize uniforms worn by Sennett's cops suited both the destroyed fetish of the auto-mobile *and* the sense that law enforcement was acrobatics. As recently as 1963 the Model T is being fantasized – Fred MacMurray flies a 1915 version in Robert Stevenson's *Son of Flubber* (1963) – and cars are gag props in *The Great Race* (Blake Edwards, 1965), the exemplary parody of Grand Prix and road movie genres. Laurel and Hardy tore apart a 1919 Model T in *Two Tars* (Parrott, 1928), and so did Harry Langdon and W.C. Fields in *It's the Old Army Game* (Edward Sutherland, 1926). In *Giant* (Stevens, 1956), James Dean drives a 1926 Ford pickup and is seduced by Elizabeth Taylor in a 1932 Duesenberg; the rich Texans own Rolls Royces and Lincolns. Dean's own Porsche Spyder came later and still exists as sacred fragments in various parts of America. The Three Stooges used a Model T for fun, but in the 1930s cars began to bear the brunt of gangster action or were crashed for nemesis. The 1942 Ford Jeep came of age as a shield for Spencer Tracy in *Bad Day at Black Rock* (John Sturges, 1955) – although there had already been *Four Men in a Jeep* (Lindtberg, 1951), *Four Jills in a Jeep* (Seiter, 1944), and the Dean Martin and Jerry Lee Lewis vehicle, *At War With the Army* (Hal Walker, 1950).

Cars on fire are standard joys, especially once colour tinged the screen: the examples are too numerous to mention. But among other uses can be cited John Wayne fighting off a rhinoceros from a 1948 Chevrolet truck in *Hatari!* (Howard Hawks, 1962), John Conte caught between a 1958 Thunderbird and a 1958 Mercedes in *Ocean's Eleven* (Milestone, 1960), and probably the first car to be driven into a shop – the 1914 Model T in a 1917 Keystone comedy (this is now a cliché of course). Drunken driving for fun is established in Chaplin's *City Lights* (1931) – the car is a Rolls Royce. W.C. Fields's driving in *The Bank Dick* (Eddie Cline, 1940) terrifies a bank bandit into a dead feint, while the gays polishing cars with swansdown puffs to the sound of the Rolling Stones's 'Satisfaction' in *Kustom Kar Kommandos* (Anger, 1965) provide other sensuous pleasures (the film was started when Anger received a Ford grant).

Taxi Driver (Scorsese, 1976) is the most recent in a long series exploiting the vulnerability and opportunities of the trade. Joan Crawford starred in *The Taxi Dancer* in 1927 and Cagney was a cabbie in *Taxi* (Roy del Ruth, 1932). 'Follow that car!' is a command convention, and so is the private eye's friendly cabbie (notably in *The Maltese Falcon* (Huston, 1941)). Scorsese's Travis Bickle investigates city life through his cab, and prepares for moralistic vengeance with fetishistic guns, becoming a national hero by rescuing an under-age junkie hooker by slaughtering her pimps. His fellow taxi drivers either fantasize his sexual powers and his bravery in taking fares all over New York, or, like Wizard, grant him a sham reputation for knowledge and insight. In fact he moves out, through his cab, into the alien world of Times Square and the political upper middle class. He works nights anywhere, as the opening scene makes clear, because he cannot sleep, the indication being that he fears masturbation and that this relates back to an experience with the Marines. His life lies between tablets and guns in a squalid bedsitter and his taxi, between an enclosed private life and a social life dominated by the exigencies of taxi driving – so that the huge opening close-up of the yellow cab and the closing shot of the same cab in the same downtown streets are appropriate. Travis is a male degenerate loose on the night streets, a soldier living a myth of violence with an ignorance appalling in its rabid self-generation. *Taxi Driver* is a war film: Travis needs to intervene in other people's lives out of inadequate knowledge and a desire to dominate – hence the Cherokee haircut. His gun-ridden invasion of the brothel and his subsequent heroism constitute an analysis of war and its glorification in a society which still refuses to understand its intervention in South-east Asia.

Between the city gangster and taxi films and the road films lies the major genre of the race movie. Examples are legion. They range from an early Christie Comedy, *Race Caper*, and the 1927 *Fast and Furious* (not Busby Berkeley's 1939 film of the same name) to Hawks's *The Crowd Roars* (1932), using an actual race track (as does *Devil on Wheels* (1939)) and Cagney as a racing driver, and Clarence Brown's *To Please a Lady* (1950), like *The Green Helmet* and *Road Racers* and *The Racers* to Corman's *The Young Racers*. In Paul Newman's *Winning* (Goldstone, 1969) the hero is a victory maniac, and the work features footage of a seventeen-car smash-up on the Indianapolis track. Stars' personal involvement in racing is well documented. James Dean's morbid desire to race probably began with the making of Nicholas Ray's *Rebel Without a Cause* in 1955, conceived as 'a pool of information gathered from police, parents and kids.' The 'chickie run' scene, in which Dean drove a 1946 Ford, records a commonplace challenge structure within the corrupt morality of competitive society:

> [Irving] Shulman remembered a newspaper item about a 'chickie run' at night on Pacific Palisades. A group of adolescents had assembled in stolen cars on the clifftop plateau. Drivers were to race each other towards the edge. The first to jump clear before the rim of the cliff, the drop to the sea, was a 'chickie.' On this night one of the boys failed to jump in time. The 'chickie run' on the plateau replaced the original blind run through the tunnel.[15]

(*The Blind Run* had initially been considered as a script for a film on children and adolescents; Ray chose Shulman as his scriptwriter because he had been a high-school teacher and was deeply interested in sports cars.) Dean researched his role by mixing with teenagers and gangs who modelled themselves on movies, until the film became a personal responsibility, a deliberate counteraction to Marlon Brando's *The Wild One* (Benedek, 1953). Incidentally, Brando contemplated narrating a documentary on Dean, 'maybe as a kind of expiation for some of my own sins. Like making *The Wild One*.'

Dean used cars for the risks of speed, as a philobat's need to draw near to death, first driving an MG, two Porsches, and a Ford station wagon, and then racing cars in 1955, working on his own machine, and reaching a level sufficient to be entered in the California Sports Car Club races: 'It's the only time I feel whole.'[16] He also loved bullfighting, kept a Colt .45 on the film lot, entertained Aztec fantasies, posed in a coffin, kept a model gallows in his New York hotel room, was known – according to Kenneth Anger – as 'the human ashtray' for his sexual proclivities, and used to repeat a line from Ray's *Knock On Any Door*: 'Live fast, die young, and have a good-looking corpse.'[17] He died at the wheel of his Porsche Spyder after being ticketed for driving at 65 in a 45 mph speed zone. He had driven into a Ford sedan which he could not avoid. The car enabled Dean to be self-accountable, an extension of Emerson's cowboy self-reliance which remains so central to the American male. In *Giant* his cowboy hat and old car exemplify his mobility. After his death, the James Dean death club lit candles, played Wagner, and discussed their cult object. For fifty cents you could sit at the wheel of the wrecked Spyder, and bits of its metal were sold as relics. Frank O'Hara celebrated him twice as the sacrificed hubristic hero of the gods, 'racing towards your heights.' Dos Passos placed him as an age type in *Mid Century* in 1961, one of 'the Sinister Adolescents' who were 'box office.' And Dean features among both the dedicatees of Kenneth Anger's *Scorpio Rising* (1966) and the star devotees of bondage in Anger's *Hollywood Babylon*.[18]

Steve McQueen's less morbid obsession is documented in McCoy's biography.[19] After military service, he partly supported himself by racing motorcycles, but in 1960 he hung a sign on his bike reading 'The Mild One,' in protest against his Hollywood reputation, and transferred his speed addiction to cars: 'speed rivals making love.' Facial plastic surgery, broken limbs and deafness were no obstacle. By 1965 he had gained a good reputation as a racing driver and owned a glittering stable of cars. He maintained that his dedication was without 'any death wish like Jimmy Dean.' For *Bullitt* (Peter Yates, 1968), he carried out his own stunts – under licence from a generously paid city – and his role as police lieutenant chasing criminals came second to the car smashing, reminiscent for him of 'the old Keystone Cops.' The over-rated speed sequences in *Bullitt* were followed by the dullness of *Le Mans* (Lee H. Katz, 1971) and the quieter pleasures of *The Reivers* (Mark Rydell, 1969), in which McQueen played Faulkner's Boon Hogganbeck, driving a 1905 Winston Flier. In *Junior Bonner* (Peckinpah, 1972), his old car and horse trailer take him round the dwindling rodeo circuit in an excess of nostalgia related to the car and plane killing of the last mustangs in *The Misfits* (Huston, 1961), with its receding dream of independent male life free from wage-slavery.[20]

The difficulties of creating race movies without boring duplications of car scenes are only partly overcome in John Frankenheimer's *Grand Prix* (1966), in which cars are choreographed and their engines orchestrated in pastoral and track scenes presented in split-screen images. But the aim is still to document speed in a bizarre macho drama that leads to maiming, suicide and virtual murder. The drivers are junkies of speed hurtling towards ambivalent apocalypse.

For the car chase obsessions in *The French Connection* (Friedkin, 1971), city permission was again received to clear traffic and 'use real pedestrians and traffic.'[21] The director was supplied with 'members of the New York City tactical police force to help control' the streets, and maintained that 'murderous and illegal actions' in the film were justified because they were those of 'an obsessive, self-righteous, driving, driven cop.'

Disaster dominates American films as much as it governs British news bulletins on radio and television. A wrecked or flaming car evokes desire. The murder of Glenn Ford's wife in an exploding car near the beginning of Lang's *The Big Heat* (1953) is therefore ambiguously moralised as the destruction of a police family unit by a crime-business syndicate (as Emmerich remarks in Huston's *The Asphalt Jungle* (1950), 'after all, crime is only a lefthanded form of human endeavour'). To be uncertain is to be involved. Lang's skill depends on the fact – one of the reasons why Godard places him centrally in *Le Mépris* (1963). If a police or syndicate car crashes, pleasure is unalloyed. This is a mainspring of, for instance, Brian de Palma's *The Fury* (1978), in which superior scientific and occult information is hardly challenged by the old-fashioned technology of a police car. As McLuhan once observed, in connection with 'our intensely technological and, therefore, narcotic culture,' 'at the heart of the car industry there are men who know that the car is passing.'[22] Obsolescence must be speeded up. Simultaneously the junkie needs another vein. The choreographic film crash continues the dream of inevitable casual disaster on which the renewal of the State is based: social and economic recovery is as inevitable as the Crash itself.

Films maintain the characteristic western confusion of human

72

life with machine energy, a personal and social neurosis increasingly destructive of well-being in cultures dominated by engines and electronics. We are for ever putting on and plugging into machines and circuitry. Michel Carrouges' *Les Machines célibataires* identifies the typical networks of pleasure and pain. Men and women have always been connected to machines for torture, and *Grand Prix* is an invitation to a feast of tortured pleasure in search of heroics, money, and the deadly limits of masculinity. Its auto-erotic and automatic games are 'the nuptial celebration' of a curious but accepted alliance which produces only 'intensive quantities . . . to a point that is almost unbearable – a celibate misery and glory experienced to the fullest.'[23] By ecstatic example, *Grand Prix* increases death on the American roads by intensifying the desire to turn them into tracks of hallucinatory power whose final equilibrium is the production of stereotypical suicide and murder. The human breaking point obsesses the twentieth century, and cars in films are frequently instruments for this process of testing and climax. *Grand Prix* and the rest indicate the tolerance level for gun and car violence quite as much as the more commonly cited *Rebel Without a Cause* or *Bonnie and Clyde* (Penn, 1967), the latter with its joyful getaways in a 1930 Model A Ford, a 1931 Plymouth, a 1931 Graham, and so on. 'The observation of aggression is more likely to induce hostile behaviour than to drain off aggressive inclinations' is Leonard Berkowitz' research conclusion.[24] The range of cars and stars in Blake Edwards' *The Great Race* (1964) – a film almost devoid of brutality and suicidal climax – is the exception to the rule.

In *Bonnie and Clyde*, which combined the chase and road genres, violence results from the use of cars to challenge the status quo. The criminal pair act, in the words of Arthur Penn (perpetrator of this ambivalently focused, if not muddled, film), as 'retaliators for the people.' The 1930s cars on country roads and in fields parallel the pastoral effects in *Grand Prix* as the Barrow gang enters its own civil war, backed by the jaunty banjo-picking sounds of Earl Scruggs' 'Foggy Mountain Breakdown.' The Joads appear, as it were, in the form of a sharecropper family invited to fire at the expropriation notice the bank has placed on their old wooden house, and as Bonnie's family and the camp-site travellers who give C.W. Moss water towards the end of the trek. These are supposed to be the 'poor folks' – Clyde's phrase – who justify robbery and murder. In fact the car wars focus this country-gangster movie, with the sheriff's posse of the Western regrouped in counter-vehicles. Certainly, Penn's car-consciousness made the film:

> At that time there was no national police force: they were all state-confined police forces. When Ford made the V-8, which was sufficiently powerful to out-run the local police automobiles, gangs began to spring up. And that was literally the genesis of the Clyde and Bonnie gang. What happened was that they lived in their automobile – it was not unusual for them to drive seven and eight hundred miles in a night, in one of those old automobiles. They literally spent their lives in the confines of the car. It was really where they lived. Bonnie wrote her poetry in the car, they ate ginger snaps in the car, they played checkers in the car – that was their place of abode. In American Western mythology, the automobile replaced the horse in terms of the renegade figure. This was the transformation of the Western into the gangster.[25]

But Bonnie and Clyde spoke contemporaneously, since the car remains the American's second home. This is the plot gist of scores of films, and a reason why a work as critical of car usage as Godard's *Weekend* (1968) has been virtually impossible in America. Directors concentrate on car as menace (Robert Mitchum in *Cape Fear* (J. Lee Thompson, 1961)), car anxiety (classically in *Duel* (Spielberg, 1971)), and the car as the centre of intense energy (*Point Blank* (Boorman, 1967); *Chinatown* (Polanski, 1974); and Barry Newman meeting death in a road block of dredger tractors in *Vanishing Point* (Richard C. Sarafian, 1971)). A major part of the car's effect emerges from the common identity of cars used by gangsters, diplomats, police, millionaires and the mafia. But it is in *The Detective* (Gordon Douglas, 1968) that Sinatra's Joe Leland uses the car for private self-consideration. It is the only place he can be alone, think back, between the domestic apartment (the female) and the precinct building (the male job); driving in city streets is the arena of flashback. and it is only in Dreyer's accident prevention film, *They Came to a Ferry* (1948) that death actually appears as a fact in driving itself, in the shape of a car driver before the victim's moment of truth; and he steers, of course, an antique car. Nor is Guido's escape in Fellini's *8½* (1963) American. The film begins, in absolute silence, with a shot of the back of his head as he sits in his car surrounded by traffic jammed in a low tunnel. Then the camera pans out of the darkness, over the cars, and into the over-exposed light, looking for an exit. Guido's nervous breathing breaks the silence as his car fills with steam. Other car people look dead. He pounds the window. One driver strokes a woman's breasts. Guido climbs out, *flies* from the tunnel, over the sea. Similarly, in another film by a European, Antonioni's *Zabriskie Point* (1970), Mark walks down a Los Angeles street to phone within a dense technological space, which includes cars. He escapes it in a stolen plane, rising up into clear space. Beneath him, a middle-class camper driving through Death Valley is covered with tourist labels, signs of false mobility, limited change within the urban density. Bresson's *Le Diable probablement* (1977) reverses the action: suicide takes place amid the technology of record player, phone, guns, river boats, television and cars.

III

In contrast, the car contest in *Rebel Without a Cause*, the car versus train contest in *The French Connection*, the car chase in Siegel's *The Line Up* (1958), and the cars, helicopters, motorcycles and horses entangled in the chase sequence of Arthur Marks's *Detroit 9000* (1973), all accept the perverse exhilarations of technological destiny. American directors freely manipulate audiences' possessive affection for their cars. In *Castle Keep* (Sidney Pollack, 1969), Corporal Clearboy is deeply attached to a Volkswagen, one of the most popular cars in the world. He envisages VW's populating the Earth after men have died out, and when his fellow soldiers fail to sink his car ('it's just showing off'), one of them shouts 'Jesus Christ, it's still alive!' Clearboy's response is 'they're drowning her.' In Woody Allen's *Sleeper* (1973), a VW has survived into the future, but it has to be pushed over a cliff and into history. In Bogdanovich's *The Last Picture Show* (1971) a car is presented as a deeply felt gift between youngsters; it acts as a courting apparatus and as a major alleviator of drudgery, loneliness and isolation in rural America. Cars are courting and testing apparatus again in *American Graffiti* (1973), about which director George Lucas has said: 'That was my life. I spent four years driving around the main street of Modesto, chasing girls. It was the mating ritual of my times, before it disappeared and everybody got into psychedelia and drugs.'[26] In the film itself cars therefore function nostalgically in a vision of a barely existent, uncorrupted America before rock went political. The cars are choreographed to the 45s of the era – the age from Ike to JFK, which was the heydey of radio programmes featuring mystic disc jockeys (here it is Wolfman Jack) playing minimal unseen gurus and fixers for the kids. As in *The Last Picture Show*, this world has to be relinquished for manhood and America's wars.

Lucas' soundtrack is mainly an acoustic environment of motors and radio songs. But the car sounds are repeatedly reduced to an over-all monotone, the sound of putting on cars like clothing. Cars are homes, once again; there are no scenes inside homes, and only two buildings are entered: a drive-in restaurant with waitresses on roller skates and the college hall with a commencement dance in progress. The film's style itself is consistently mobile, speeded up only for action against the cops (a police car's back axle is wrenched away) and a disastrous macho race at the end (much less solemnly stylised than in *Rebel Without a Cause* nearly twenty years earlier). The necessity of cars to life is as accepted here as in Michael Pressman's *Boulevard Nights* (1979), where cars are places of work and the burnt car is a personal violation. In Lucas' *THX 1138* (1970), Americans have become complete and highly technologized zombies, reminiscent of the workers in Fritz Lang's *Metropolis* (only uniformed in white, not black). God is a televised picture (based on the blown-up reproduction of a Dürer self-portrait), and the acoustic environment is as white, dehumanized and electronic as the clothing and decor. Where Curt Henderson escapes small-time America by plane in Lucas' later film, here THX reverts to a racing car to avoid total enslavement; although it is an emphatically futuristic vehicle, it images sufficient nostalgia to suggest that the automobile never entirely died. Even in *Close Encounters of the Third Kind* (Spielberg, 1977) roadside peasants react to early sightings of spacecraft with something like 'They can put rings round the moon but we sure as hell got 'em beat on the roads.'

So much attachment to the car is culturally assumed that it must hurt in Walter Hill's *The Streetfighter* (1978), not only when James Coburn's new car – a real sign of wealth in the 1930s – is smashed by a livid thug as a warning that he must pay his debts; but also when the streetfighter himself expresses his detachment from corruption by refusing a car. The sheer retentiveness of car life began controlling vocabulary early in the twentieth century: in *Skateboard Kings* (Horace Ové, 1977), the cult design of clothing, pads, dance routines, and the defiance of gravity by skate-boarding in a desert water-pipe section are described in terms drawn largely from car and bike language – for example, movements are labelled grinder, front side-car, aerial edge, extreme tail top, and so on.

Film therefore reflects America as a nearly century-old car culture of remarkable tenacity. *Psycho*, a film dominated by women and cars, plays with the facts. A car switch enables a sensual and repentant thief from Phoenix, Arizona, with a bird's name – Marion Crane – to escape discovery. After her murder, Norman Bates sinks her getaway car to the same bubbling sounds we heard earlier in the shower as he cleaned up. Between its opening voyeuristic penetration of fugitive bedroom sex and the final retrieval of the muddied car, the film collects policemen and a car salesman, a private detective, Marion's boyfriend and Bates, like cars, to sink them. Marion is killed 'because' she acted male and trapped herself in Bates's male trap, a motel for car travellers; victory comes from the thrust of Marion's sister Lila and the woman in Bates. Back in 1932 *The Times* pointed up the ambiguities of car-obsession in *The Crowd Roars*: 'The various episodes of this romance of the American motor racing track are at least as painful as they are exciting . . . The ugly emotions of the crowd which delights in such disasters are represented with some accuracy, but it is not explained what we are to think of ourselves if we enjoy this film.' Years later Hitchcock tells Truffaut: 'the placing of the images on the screen, in terms of what you're expressing, should never be dealt with in a factual manner.' And as Lawrence Alloway observes, violence 'is still a part of general taste, embodied elsewhere in the styling of American automobiles, which have not fundamentally altered during the same period. The annual style changes were sufficient to entertain us with a comedy of newness but not radical enough to disrupt continuity with earlier models.'[27] In his useful compilation on the 1950s, Jay Berman indicates the first climax of car culture in the United States:

> Automobiles boomed in the fifties. A combination of new found leisure time and money for luxuries created a demand for more elaborate and specialised vehicles; and production facilities, swollen by the defense jobs of World War II, shifted to fulfil the demand.
>
> The auto, formerly a mode of transportation, sought to be a total environment on wheels, rivalling home for comfort and luxury. The auto was heaped with adornment, worn as a badge of status, and admired as a piece of jewelry. It filled those empty hours with a new activity, 'motoring.'[28]

Film language using cars has likewise changed. In *The Man on the Flying Trapeze* (Bruckman, 1935), Ambrose Wolfinger's need to drive quickly to the wrestling match is interrupted and reduced to stasis by a cop, a chauffeur and a runaway tyre, but for the 1960s and 1970s such action is largely archaic. So too is the pessimism in Welles's *The Magnificent Ambersons* (1942), in which 'The Original Morgan Invincible' begins to undermine a bourgeois America founded in the horse city. But by then, as Colin McArthur shows, cars had become murder weapons in 'repeated patterns' which 'might be called the iconography of the genre . . . the means whereby primary definitions are made.'[29] Once Sergeant Bannion's car is blown up in *The Big Heat*, repetition of the same scene instills anxiety. As Christian Metz says, 'the cinema is language, *above and beyond any particular effect of montage*' (although the five bathtub images reproduced in Monaco's *How to Read a Film* indicate the limitations of the idea).[30] Gangsters use city and industrial technology – guns, cars, phones – automatically (the Kojak series is dull because it repeats the genre like a doggerel of slick conservative morality, which a lollypop-sucking officer does nothing to modify). McArthur usefully quotes Andrew Sinclair, saying that the gun-cars 'created a satanic mythology of the automobile which bid fair to rival the demonism of the saloon.' But it should be added that by the 1950s the car had become the potentially lethal weapon of any 'average person,' voluntary or not. The gangster film's 'symbol of . . . unbridled aggressiveness,' so strong that 'characters may respond with fear to an automobile without seeing the men within it,' is repeated in general usage as much as it is in, say, the car images from *The New Centurions*, where cars are used as if they were private weapons by men committed to law-enforcement and self-enforcement in a society structured for leadership and competiton.[31] The prowl car is a weapon on both sides of the law – if indeed that distinction still holds effective meaning. The Volstead Act of 1919, which declared the manufacture and sale of alcoholic drinks except for medicinal purposes illegal (hence the term 'medicine' for booze), not only gave crime its 1920s impulse, but brought death to the roads as a common daily occurence.

Changes in the sides of law are manifest in John Carpenter's *Assault on Precinct 13* (1976). By this time the car-hunt has become commonplace – revived effectively in, for instance, *The Savages* (Lee H. Katzin, 1974), in which Andy Griffith plays a lame sadist hunting a young guide through the desert. Hunter cars are casual in American action. In Reisz's *Who'll Stop the Rain* (or *The Dog Soldiers*, 1978) cars are used as thoughtlessly as helicopters and armoured vehicles in South-east Asian warfare, in an America given as a combat state where FBI methods are indistinguishable from those of any other terrorist order. In Carpenter's film, cars are used as vehicles of attack by urban guerrillas terrorizing a police station. Their initial prowl car parodies the police, and their siege parodies *Rio Bravo* (Hawks, 1959), pointing up changes as much as using nostalgia as technique. A small girl protests to the ice-cream man that she has the wrong flavour; she is gunned down from the prowl car. There are no innocent bystanders in America, 1976. And when Julie cries 'Why would anybody shoot at a police station?' the audience knows exactly why. The black limousine besiegers are the 1970s equivalent of gangsters or, in Hawks's terms, rustlers from out of town. Ethan Bishop, a black police lieutenant, is named after John Wayne's character in *Rio Bravo*, but it is real blood that drips – not on to a Nash Ambassador but on to a police patrol car – from the murdered telephone linesman.

In Walter Hill's *The Driver* (1978), the nature of the professional getaway driver is examined for the first time. But Hill – who wrote the script for *The Getaway* – sets Bruce Dern's obsessed cop against Ryan O'Neal's getaway man. Dern's lip-smiling cop admits to no difference between police and criminal, except that he is better at his job; the scene is a game. O'Neal, a homeless, girl-less, gun-toting maniac killer, poses as a cool, sane man at play in the only game, which is also his job. Having established these contemporary facts, Hill concentrates on the sound and accelerating rapidity of the car in the hands of a maniac driver, the dream speedster inside all automobile owners. He does so with the same kind of abuse of technology that characterizes Peter Bogdanovich's *Targets* (1967). Beginning with the opening printed example of berserk murders, Bogdanovich's film ostensibly promotes enquiry into the uncontrolled ownership of firearms. But he lovingly shows us that the car boot also harbours the arsenal of weapons with which Bobby Thompson will pick off motorists on the highway and in a drive-in cinema. His target is the average secure American in his car home and movie seat. The film's strength is precisely this intersection of guns, cars and film at the point of maximum personal vulnerability, with Boris Karloff as the retiring horror movie actor who understands exactly what action has to be taken against a terrorist to disarm him.

The average car owner considers himself a secure citizen, as secure as the old lady nourishing herself on rape fantasies and obscene phone calls in the trailer park of Don Siegel's *Charley Varrick* (1973). But there is no privacy in the sacrificial combat state. Siegel plays variations on the city mafia extortion movie, but the genre scene is shifted to a small-change business played out in provincial trailer parks, and the action is filmed mostly in sunlit woods and fields. Like Rubber Duck and Dirty Lyle in *Convoy* (Peckinpah, 1978), Varrick is one more 'Last of the Independents' – a crop-duster and small-town bank robber. He discovers that some money he has stolen is part of an out-of-state Mafia drop. In one scene Molly, the Mafia hit-man, repossesses a car from a terrorized black family; so that Varrick's final victory over Molly is a vindication of the victimized – and it takes place in a huge used car dump, ironically re-used as a barricade against technology and terrorism. Varrick's independence, as well as his sidekick Harman's vulnerability, are exemplified by his trailer home: mobile and anonymous. This combination is neatly exploited in Howard Zieff's *Slither* (1973), where a collection of loose-moraled egoists battling for embezzled money are enclosed in a red car hauling a trailer in which Peter Boyle's wife is permanently housed. The trailer has been converted from a quarantine tank used by astronauts returning from the moon. They are followed by two huge black, quasi-military armoured vehicles (labelled for a children's camp) whose drivers are most of the time as invisible as the aggressive truck driver in Spielberg's *Duel* (1971), the classic road movie exemplifying driving as combat between temporary psychopaths.

In Hitchcock's *North by Northwest* (1959), Roger Thornhill is hunted across an empty stubble field by a crop-duster plane flown by a faceless assassin. In Richard Matheson's screenplay for *Duel*, Frankenstein's monster has become a 1970s truck, the standard road menace for millions of American – and British – drivers. But the work is more complex than the singularity of the action suggests. The exhaust stack of the tanker (labelled or named 'Flammable') pollutes the air stream in which advertizing executive David Mann is compelled to drive. Mann responds to the jungle demands of a male-dominated society. His car radio broadcasts part of a phone-in which includes a wife-dominated, impotent man attacking marriage. During a phone call it is clear that Mann's wife believes he failed as a man in not challenging a man who, she alleges, 'practically raped' her at a party. His sense of inferiority becomes pathologically obvious when confronted by working-class truckers in a roadside café. But it is the tanker which gives the broken-down school bus a helping push, and then, while attempting to kill Mann, wrecks an old lady's Snakerama. Mann accepts the unseen Goliath's challenge but, since he had failed to renew a damaged radiator hose, does so at the risk of burning his own car out. He ultimately sacrifices the car rather than himself, but the final shots show him whimpering and crying hysterically while tossing stones down the cliff where the two vehicles lie grostesquely entangled. The blazing sun seems to emphasize the futility of the whole episode.

The police are not involved as they customarily are, for example, in *Convoy*, and in *Vanishing Point* (Sarafian, 1971). The police-hunted driver in Sarafian's remarkable film is named Kowalski, ex-Marine hero with an honourable discharge after fighting in the Vietnam War, ex-police (detective) hero with a dishonourable discharge (drugs and general attitude towards the force), and ex-racing biker who now delivers cars faster than anyone else. Sarafian's hero is a man involved in America's official law and technology, who is now at large in the huge spaces of the South-west. Kowalski arrives in Denver urgently wishing to return to California; his contract entrusts him with a super-charged Dodge Challenger of exceptional performance. The ensuing chase is used to contain brief flashbacks of his life – a crash, a tender love affair, the rescue of a young girl from mauling narcotics cops, and so on – and to refer him to various people who attack or help him on the road, the latter including Super Soul (Cleavon Little), a blind black disc-jockey operating from a local Colorado station, who transmits messages between rock and country music. Hostility comes largely from small town people and from various States' police, and the man-hunt is energized by helicopter and taken up by CB radio. Police bikes and cars duel with Kowalski (no Christian name is found by the police) on the roads of Colorado, Nevada, and California; he is handed on from force to force with no explicit criminal charges except fast driving (in each crash he stops to see if the other driver is alive and walking). So that the main theme, as in *Convoy*, is official aggression on the roads. All of these films are in fact analogues of American official aggression, both imperialist and domestic. Kowalski's friends are a black biker, a white biker and his girl (who motorbikes nude around their patch of ground in mid-Nevada), and Super Soul, who informs of police action until his station is smashed by local white thugs. In the hyped-up DJ language of Super Soul, and like the heroes of so many of these road movies, Kowalski is 'the last beautiful free soul on the planet.' Super Soul renames his station after him as it returns to the airwaves. The internal plot of *Vanishing Point* (like that of Tennessee Williams' *The Fugitive Kind*, made by Sidney Lumet in 1959) concerns not only the flight of the independent but the possibilities of salvation. The latter may take the form of a revivalist group, police law, or small-town aggression against a pair of homosexual men who fake a breakdown in their car and turn on Kowalski with a gun; or it may result from various forms of individualism: Kowalski himself, the lone snake-catcher in his broken down old car, Super Soul, and the two white hippies. Kowalski finally accepts defeat and crashes his car to explode in a police barricade of huge yellow clearage vehicles. He has used up his resources. There is no place for his courage, energy and driving skills. He takes his place with the men of *The Misfits*, *Convoy*, *Two Lane Blacktop* and *J.W. Coop*.

The road movie of the 1970s became a major vehicle for a primary and traditional American hero, translated from the West, the backwoods and the prospecting sites, and the battle fronts. Cliff Robertson's J.W. Coop (he starred in and directed his own script in 1971) copes with the same field as Junior Bonner but with less despair and more technique. After a ten-year sentence he resumes a rodeo career and challenges the reigning national champion, Billy Hawkins. The latter flies a Beechcraft to his rodeos, and Coop has to graduate from a 1949 Hudson to his own monoplane. Transport technology enables old-fashioned masculinity games to survive. Coop ends up broken by a huge bull, but he is still lone and independent. He is also rich and has had a love affair with an intelligent hippie, with whom he has formed a core of value against the corrupt rodeo world and the aggression of the 'silent majority,' exemplified by a middle-aged farmer driving a Ford truck and the middle-aged driver of a colossal oil tanker, both of whom identify the enemy as the unions and the 'commies.'

The three drivers and the hippie girl in Monte Hellman's *Two Lane Blacktop* (1971) are nameless, credited simply as the Driver, the Mechanic, G.T.O., and the Girl. They are also homeless. But the cars *are* named in the cast list: Chevrolet, Pontiac and so on. Human lives are dominated by the road, the characters travelling across America as if it were a plain with halts for gas, or an infinite race track. G.T.O., a dreamer and liar, a drifter and a car-proud speed-freak, meets the challenge he needs in the driver and mechanic (a certain class opposition is only identified in the cost of G.T.O.'s car). He races them to the futile end – beyond which the film itself burns out. Hellman creates a fable of expended energy in competition without end, the search for imagined and never achieved satisfactions and victories. In fact the Girl sings 'Can't get no satisfaction' – once again – while playing a pinball machine. Behind the forlorn elegance of this elegiac film lies the car door banged endlessly on Stan Laurel's bandaged foot, Jackson Pollock photographed on the running board of his old Ford, the used car dump in William Wyler's last film, *The Liberation of L.B. Jones* (1970), and scores of Westerns. *Two Lane Blacktop* is the penultimate parody of the core American movie. The ultimate is Peckinpah's effort to bring Rubber Duck and his woman through the obstacle race of *Convoy* (1978) without too much sentimentality and nose-thumbing.

The softness of Peckinpah's nostalgia can be contrasted with Spielberg's *Sugarland Express* (1973) and, more sharply, with Harvey Laidman's *Steel Cowboy* (1978). The former is based on an actual event, in 1969, when a young Texan couple hijacked a police car and forced the patrolman to drive them three hundred miles to Sugerland, where the girl was to reclaim her baby, taken by the State from his foster parents. The film is one long chase by a convoy of police cars over several days. The cars talk to each other by loudspeaker, the cops trying to protect their colleague from the inevitable final bullet. The humour is more corrosive and less good-natured than in the Peckinpah, but both films are nostalgic for independence against the State. *Convoy* is nearer in spirit to Raoul Walsh's *They Drive by Night* (1940), a rig melodrama in which two truckers (Bogart and Raft) fight for their money within the competitive violence of the trucking racket. But Peckinpah is more ambitious: 'the purpose of the convoy is to keep moving' says Rubber Duck, the leading trucker. In fact this south-west road convoy is an allegorical procession, a process which deliberately collects the nation's problems of leadership, direction and law. 'Keep moving and the complaints will need no serious analysis' is the traditional motto built into the film. The status quo – combat – is maintained in a traditional 'Western' equilibrium in which Dirty Lyle Wallace, the patrolman-sheriff who claims 'I am the law,' stands against the truckers, who explicitly dramatize themselves as cowboys. Mobility within conflict is both the tradition and the very substance of American capitalism. To maintain that order, the Army is introduced to crush Rubber Duck: 'the State, its police, and its army form a gigantic enterprise of antiproduction.'[32] When, at one point, Lyle's car increases mobility and charges over an embankment, the effect is dreamlike, as if it were an invention of the unconscious.

C.W. McCall's trucking ballad is used to manipulate the cowboy-law elements into a safety jargon, but the convoy music itself is military rather than country, emphasizing combat leading to final confrontation. *Convoy* summarizes trucker and road movies right down to its repetition of the scene in John Sturges' *McQ* (1974) where John Wayne's car is crushed between two trucks. Observing Lyle's squeezing, one trucker remarks: 'They're making a sandwich out of the sheriff!' But *Convoy* is as much a war film as *Who'll Stop the Rain* or *The Deerhunter*: when, at the end of the film, the Army and the police blow up Duck's high explosive tanker on a bridge, the scene is duplicated and parodied from endless war movies. Ernest Borgnine's presence as Lyle ensures the stereotyping. Conflict between the trucker fraternity and the cops undermines the mutual individualist understanding between Lyle and Duck (the CB name of Martin Penwald). Pig Pen, Spider Mike, and the rest of the CB code-named truckers are finally trapped in the strict coding of American society, which they, like millions of others, believe supports independence rather than State intervention. Lyle easily obtains his bribes from the fraternity, which knows very well he will continue to demand more and that beating him up in the café makes no substantial difference. Duck faces Lyle with 'there aren't many of us left' – the Junior Bonner and J.W. Coop theme – but it is the racist issue that brings out the latent tension between law and cowboy. Smashing the jail with trucks to release black comrade Spider Mike is a minimal act of chivalrous despair in this male, police-ridden world (a world in which women have babies, are seduced by casual male glances, are eminently beddable, or themselves become forcible truckers – like the black fraternity member named Widow Woman).

Peckinpah's café brawl is violent and farcical, in line with his need to make the film a victorious comedy for Duck and the fashionable photographer Melissa. The absurdity of the angry situation and its parodies of macho confrontations is not lost on the director. But the convoy still has to contain the anarchic emotions, protests and frustrations of the south-west community and, by implication, 1970s America, as it keeps moving against police, politicians, and Teamsters' union alike. Governor Haskins proposes taking Duck's protest against police harassment to Washington as a national cause, a move which will also help him politically. But Duck refuses because the immediate issue is Spider held in a Texas jail, a black trapped in the rigidities of American racism. At this point the trucker breaks with both Melissa and some members of the trucker fraternity in order to chase 'the Devil . . . Dirty Lyle,' as the ballad has it. When Melissa asks why they follow him, Duck replies: 'I'm just in front.' So the discrediting of American leaders will not be corrected by the independent loner. The politician panics when the people choose Duck as a popular hero – he is, in fact, practically manufactured by the media – but the mobility plot is easily allowed to take over: it is the civil war story, without the élitist, samurai overtones of *The Magnificent Seven*. As in *Vanishing Point*, radio communication aids the hero, although CB technology and code are devices cop and cowboy have to share. But, as in *Who'll Stop the Rain* and *The Deerhunter*, helicopters intervene, in an attempt to arrest by air the trucker's leader on the road: as Duck leads the convoy through the police cars, 'the bear in the air' extends the bear in the patrol car.

But Peckinpah's last-minute rescue of his independent is comic-strip stuff – no wonder he has Lyle laughing at Duck's escape! Once again sentimental anarchy wins in American fiction: law and army lose out to the miraculous resurrection of Duck from the final holocaust. But if law is defied, manic law has the last laugh, as extra-legal as it was in the old Keystone movies. America remains a perpetually destructive comic society – at least in its favourite myths. Peckinpah reassembles his dismembered hero and the film ends with an old couple in an old car left in the dust of the victorious convoy, gently kissing. Spider has presumably reached his wife. Melissa has Duck. And the car and the truck have enabled Americans to evade law, the will of the people, politics and the unions. Capra rides again. Peckinpah inherits the Mr Deeds hero, the man without dogma or scripture, and asks us to accept his equation of the laughing cop and the laughing cowboy driver. Americans repeat themselves for the nth time as farce: 'Like car-stylists, film-makers have to work for the satisfaction of a half-known future audience. . . . This is one source of the extraordinary quality that films have of being topical while being at the same time conservative and folkloric. A successful film representing a mutation of a current convention will be imitated because it introduces vital information about previously unknown audience interests.'[33]

But a skilful director can cut the sentimentality and put the realism back into a convention. Laidman's *Steel Cowboy* modifies Walsh's 1940 simplifications while using at least some of the old myths. Clayton Pfanner's truck is called 'Outlaw,' and both he and his partner K.W. ('I always wanted to be a cowboy') wear cowboy hats and speak in a south-west manner, using a language layered with exotic images and, in K.W.'s case, literary instances ('You're harder to find than Richard the Third's horse'). Clayton's wife, Jesse, has an unfinished university degree course to return to; she is both beautiful and intelligent, and finally leaves the husband she loves because his cussed independence keeps them in constant financial anxiety. The increased 1970s cost of living is explicitly the context of Clayton's outlaw sense. When K.W. says 'we're about a week away from wearing uniforms' – company uniforms – Clayton responds as if his manhood were at stake. He drives across a picket line of strikers, smashing through two parked cars outside the depot in order to drive through a payload.

Laidman indulges in little of Peckinpah's fantasy and is concerned continually with the practical matter of living as a trucker and with the loneliness of a trucker's wife: Jesse's response to her husband's plans for gaining an extra buck is 'And what am I?' Being steadily in debt in the 1970s is pointless;

she might as well go back to college. The boss villain, Pinkie Pincus – pink shirt or, like Gatsby, pink suit, and pink custom-decorated car (with cattle horns) – offers fast money for cattle rustling by truck. K.W.'s scruples and his influence on Clayton are eliminated by Pinkie's hit men: he joins Western trucking (wears a uniform) and is blown up in one of their trucks carrying oil drums. K.W. had functioned as the male equivalent of Jesse's necessary normal perceptiveness of what the financial situation really is ('old Clint Eastwood didn't have to wait this long'). Clayton has to deny he ever had this buddy relationship in order to maintain his independence, but eventually – and utterly alone – he can only assert that independence by driving his Outlaw through Pinkie's houseful of Meissen china, crystal glass, and other expensive knick-knacks: 'this is for you, K.W.!' The scene is recorded in loving and, for once, justified slow motion. Clayton hands over his truck to a driver whose own has burnt out, and fades out of the movie by thumbing a truck lift and by a long shot of reunion with his wife – a touch of sentiment which does not weaken the treatment of transport cowboy independence at all, since Jesse is the point of realism rather than rear-view mirror nostalgia.

The road saga will continue for the same reasons that America cannot solve its fuel-consumption greed: the automobile culture is coterminous with Americanism.[34] The process has been lengthy – at least from the smiling Cagney nursing a submachine gun in his limousine in *G-Men* (Wiliam Keighley, 1935) to the two neurotic cops in *The New Centurions* (Richard Fleischer, 1972) driving a patrol car inscribed 'to protect and to serve.' The pile-up of cop cars and bikes at the end of *Scarface* (Hawks, 1932), the car advancing on you in a blind alley, the face in the windscreen wipers, the exploding car – still lovingly exploited by Coppola – have long been stereotypes. The Joads of *The Grapes of Wrath* are relegated to the margins of *Bonnie and Clyde*, a film which attempts to make fun out of murder by reverting to Keystone Kop chase methods. The Sennett system made farce out of what Ivan Illich, years later, would dub 'industrial violence such as the speed of cars.'[35] The suicidal games continue to imitate Fields's drive to the maternity hospital – his car gets stuck in a fire-engine ladder. The

Princess will continue to entice Orpheus to Hell in her Rolls Royce.

1981

4

The Metallic Necessity and the New American: Culture and Technology in America, 1850–1900

'Nature made me blind and would have kept me so. My oculist counterplotted her.'

Herman Melville *The Confidence Man* (1857)

In a letter to Cid Corman on 13 June 1952, the American poet and teacher Charles Olson considered design and method as techniques of coherence for a society:

((A propos art and technology:

techne as root means 'an art'! adj.
   and *technic/*
(meaning # 3 reads: *Stock Exchange*. Designating
or pert, to, a market in which prices are
mainly determined by manipulation or
speculative conditions!

technics, n., reads:
'The doctrine of arts in general; branches of
learning relating to the arts'

and (to round off these incredible cross-shoots) *technology* is
literally the science of the arts.[1]

From this, Olson deduces that neither art nor science, in the customary formulations of these terms, 'can be given the special respect' – nor can technology, 'or it will run straight ahead into super-science as organization of man.' We still need a word, he says, 'to cover the process by which form is accomplished to the degree that it is deeper than technique – to the degree that there is a will to form, an initiation in us to express "forms," to bring them into being.' Olson then defines the term methodology as 'the necessities that the execution of form involves . . . a branch of logic dealing with the principles of procedure.' It ensures that totality, or the 'cluster' of the forces in a culture, is recognized, and that invention is not isolated from society. Methodology is 'the science which describes and evaluates arrangements of materials and instruction.'

Olson emphasizes the future tense of technology, as against 'prior concepts of coherence,' and 'the will to disperse' countering 'the will to limit.'[2] Leadership is the product of '*organization*, the principle of *efficiency*, the characteristic of the machine,' and the quantity of resources – a totality which is 'a cluster of force.' Method is not so much a path as 'the way the path is discovered,' a process grounded in 'the habitual practice of orderliness and regularity', but not trained towards a rigid 'consistency condition.'[3]

Olson's is in many ways a deeply American enquiry and assertion. Behind it lies at least 150 years of enquiry into the engineering method through which society – or what Olson would call the *polis*, the idea of a city rather than what 'pejorocracy' had made of the city – might be inaugurated.[4] But it is a type of American empiricism taken up into the democratic process only with considerable difficulty. Olson's desire for leadership reminds us that just over 100 years earlier Americans were already excited and perturbed by the apparently inevitable ascendancy of the exceptional man in a supposedly egalitarian republic, and by the role of any manipulatory human power within social organization.

Like most of the influential Romantics of the early nineteenth century, Emerson held Napoleon to be the ambivalent image of social engineering leadership – a man both exhilarating and abhorrent. Napoleon, and not Thomas Jefferson, would be Emerson's 'incarnate Democrat': selfish, encroaching, bold, self-reliant, a member of that class which 'desires it keep open every avenue to the competition of all, and to multiply avenues: the class of business men in America, in England, in France and throughout Europe; the class of industry and skill.'[5] The line of that admiration passes through the ambivalent suspicions of Melville in *Moby-Dick* (1851) and the clear hostility of Ignatius Donnelly in *Caesar's Column* (1891), into the blessing of Thorstein Veblen at the turn of the century, the manic dreams of managerial empire in the twentieth century, and that mad vision of world government by international corporations which is today being fulfilled. Emerson wrote in 1845: '[M]en saw in [Napoleon] combined the natural and the intellectual power, as if sea and land had taken flesh and begun to cipher . . . This ciphering operative knows what he is working with and what is the product. He knew the properties of gold and iron, of wheels and ships, of troops and diplomatists, and required that each should do after its kind.'

As a result of this knowledge, 'the old, iron-bound, feudal France was changed into a young Ohio or New York.' But Napoleon's system of efficiency was necessarily military, and on such organizations the middle class thrives, especially in America: 'I call Napoleon the agent or attorney of the middle class of modern society; of the throng who fill the markets, shops, counting-houses, manufactories, ships, of the modern world, aiming to be rich. He was the agitator, the destroyer of prescription, the internal improver, the liberal, the radical, the inventor of means, the opener of doors and markets, the subverter of monopoly and abuse.' Emerson then uses two technological images for the Emperor's energy. He was the 'strong steam-engine [which] does our work,' and the generator of electricity: the 'success of grand talent . . . enlists a universal sympathy . . . we feel the air purified by the electric shock.' Unfortunately, Emerson admits, Napoleon was also 'singularly destitute of generous sentiments,' 'egotistic and monopolizing,' 'a boundless liar,' and so on – not, in fact, a gentleman but '*Jupiter Scapin*, or a sort of Scamp Jupiter.' This title could be applied to most of America's leaders, who uphold democracy and the class system with such breathtaking simultaneity. Emerson's essay, as much as Olson's letter, takes us into not only a primary American respect for the engineer, the social

92

engineer, the mechanic and the opportunist, but also the uncertain alarm generated by their morality. Ambivalent and irritated intellectuals have at once acknowledged their power and dissented from their determining sway over technology; they have not exactly refused to partake in the middle class benefits and profits from their marketed patents, products, and securities. Once Moby Dick is imaged as 'the modern railway' and Ahab's energy as electricity, the *Pequod* crew become workers subservient to capitalist technology.[6] It is a short step to the bridge, the tunnel and the plane together comprising 'the gigantic power house' for Hart Crane in *The Bridge* (1930), and to the industrial war machine of Moloch that is the focus of damnation in Allen Ginsberg's *Howl* (1956).

In his inaugural address to the American Society of Mechanical Engineers in 1880, Robert H. Thurston declared that invention and engineering were 'the only real civilization.' The true Founding Father was Samuel Slater, builder of the first successful power-driven cotton-spinning mill at Pawtucket, Rhode Island. There may be beggars in the cities, Thurston claims, but at least they wore 'a finer fabric than kings could boast a century ago.' In 1891, Senator Platt of Connecticut celebrated a hundred years of American patents with a paper entitled 'Invention and Advancement' in which he asserted: 'the spirit of invention' had brought about '[c]hange, improvement, advancement . . . to be so large a part of our history that we should the rather wonder if they ceased to go forward with accelerated motion. We are satisfied with nothing else.' Above Alexander and Napoleon, James Watt is Platt's true hero, since it was he who 'developed the world's capacity to produce.'[7] Throughout the century and through to Thorstein Veblen's *The Engineers and the Price System* (1921), accounts of technicians and engineers as managerial 'carriers of social transformations' increased.[8] Thoreau could sneer that the proposed Atlantic cable would transmit nothing but trivia, such as the intelligence that Princess Adelaide had whooping cough.[9] But few of those who controlled America took any notice, either of him or of his fellow critics. As Perry Miller writes: 'By 1835 . . . scientific materialism had become so strong that many were convinced that the nation had now surpassed all Europe put together.'[10]

Since engineering controls Nature it is a part of that exploration of the possibilities of exploitation which haunts the guardians of democratic principle. The movement from study and laboratory to the machine, from the theory of Nature to the making of a tool, from machine production to mechanized human nature, is watched constantly by the humanists. Changes in the environment predicate changes in the organization of human nature. The model of nature and the model of human nature interchange. The theme is conquest. The pursuit of knowledge may not turn out to be part of that pursuit of happiness announced in the Declaration of Independence, either for the community or for the isolated inventor. In the eighteen-fifties, Nathaniel Hawthorne's fiction repeatedly returns to the pressures exerted on the exceptional man in a democratic society. His contemporary, Ralph Waldo Emerson, may have asserted men were adaptive, plastic and made for harmony: 'By his machines man can dive and remain under water like a shark; can fly like a hawk in the air; can see atoms like a gnat; can see the system of the universe like Uriel, the angel of the sun; can carry whatever loads a ton of coal can lift; can knock down cities with his fist of gunpowder. . . . his body a chest of tools, and he making himself comfortable in every climate, in every condition.'[11] And he could even assert that 'machinery and transcendentalism agree well.' But Hawthorne's chemists, doctors, physicists and inventors offer much less social hope as they work at the interface btween verified and imagined facts. In a notebook entry he once proposed the story of 'a steam engine in a factory to be supposed to possess a malignant spirit; it catches one man's arm, pulls it off . . . catches a girl by the hair, and scalps her; and finally draws a man, and crushes him to death.'[12] His 1843 story 'The Birthmark' concerns a scientist who mistakes science for a religion of which he is the priest, and who therefore gives himself permission to tinker with a human body (his wife's) in order to produce a perfection which is not found in nature – except in the replication of crystals – and which is death to human life. Hawthorne refers to the diorama (1822), the stereoscope (1832) and the daguerrotype (1835), but the main issue is 'faith in man's ultimate control over Nature,' a desire that has taken possession even of the scientist's dreams.

In 'The Artist of the Beautiful' (1844), Owen Warland's desire is to imitate Nature's ingenuity by producing a perfect butterfly machine. This 'exquisite mechanism' is intended to bridge the gap between imaginative vision and 'the practical,' but it is taken by Hawthorne as a transgression of Nature's limits, through which 'a man of genius' is 'thrown off the balance to which Providence had so nicely adjusted it.' Warland reduces himself to an isolated loveless eccentric. In 'Rappaccini's Daughter' (1844), Hawthorne's theme is the technology of plant breeding and the discovery of medicinal fluids – that is, the issue of cultivation within Nature that may, as it does in this story, result in a deathly over-extension of human powers.

But conquest of nature is endemic in the expansive history of America. In Henry Nash Smith's *Virgin Land*, Americans are shown transforming wilderness into a garden: 'The image of this vast and constantly growing agricultural society in the interior of the continent became one of the dominant symbols of American society . . . that defined the promise of American life . . . all centering about the heroic figure of the idealized frontier farmer armed with that supreme agrarian weapon, the sacred plow.'[13]

Hawthorn's apprehensiveness went against the grain of American technological confidence. To the conservative professor Baglioni in 'Rappaccini's Daughter,' the biologist and pharmacist of the title is 'a wonderful man indeed; a vile empiric, however, in his practice, and therefore not to be tolerated by those who respect the good old rules of the medical profession.' In fact, the conquest of Nature and of human nature as the destiny of man had arrived in the New World as Renaissance and Enlightenment programmes of expansion, extensions of the Christian capitalist permission to exploit the Earth and Man described in Lynn White's essay, 'The Historical Roots of our Ecological Crisis' (1967): '[M]odern technology is at least partly to be explained as an Occidental, voluntarist realization of the Christian dogma of man's transcendence of, and rightful mastery over, nature.'[14] If, in White's terms, 'modern western science was cast in the matrix of Christian theology,' the mere permission to apply technology to nature could be taken for granted. The conquest defined its own morality. Applied to human nature, this could provide a cover for both the eradication of the Indians and the institution of slavery; it could likewise provide grounds for the invention of the mechanized slave, the robot that haunts the technological imagination throughout the century as an answer to the cheap labour force of slaves and immigrants so urgently required by capitalism for developing the huge continent.

In 'Economy,' the opening section of *Walden*, Thoreau criticizes the Puritan standard which maintained labour as a criterion of life itself as no better than 'the gross but somewhat foreign form of servitude called Negro Slavery.' In the following year, 1855, Herman Melville published his criticism of the factory system and its hubristic engineers in two stories in *Harper's Weekly* and *Putnam's Magazine*. The context is the long dream of a figure whose energy is never exhausted, whose force is under total control, and who is an absolute slave employable without moral opprobrium or technological entropy. In the *Politics* (1253 b), Aristotle cites the statues of Daedalus as slave substitutes, and this is the historical field of Melville's 'The Bell-Tower' and 'The Tartarus of Maids.' In 1954, the cyberneticist Norbert Wiener observed that 'the automatic machine, whatever we think of any feelings it may or may not have, is the precise economic equivalent of slave labor.'[15] The myths of the prototypical engineer – Daedalus, the overreaching inventor, and Prometheus, the thief of energy from Nature or Jupiter – are active in nineteenth century America. Behind Wiener's sense of the body as an applicable system lies Emerson's statement in 'Works and Days' (1870): '[This is] the age of tools in which the human body is the magazine of inventions, the patent-office, where are the models from which every hint was taken. All the tools and engines on earth are only extensions of its limbs and senses.'[16] The following year, Walt Whitman's 'Passage to India' celebrated the Suez Canal of 1869, the joining of the main American railroads in the same year, and the laying of the Atlantic cable in 1866, as part of the healing euphoria of the nation emerging from Civil War. But Emerson by this late date also urged a warning: 'Machinery is aggressive. The weaver becomes the web, the machinist the machine. If you do not use tools, they use you. . . . The machine unmakes the man. Now that the machine is perfect, the engineer is nobody' – a belief he also used in more generalized language in his 'Ode to W.H. Channing' back in 1846: 'Things are in the saddle,/And ride mankind.' The full meaning of his words is suggested by Siegfried Giedion's *Mechanization Takes Command* in 1948, an enquiry into 'how mechanization corresponds with and to what extent it contradicts the unalterable laws of human nature.'[17] During the nineteenth century the machine moved radically into both labour and home life, while intellectuals – among them Melville – continued to voice their anxieties.

In 'The Bell-Tower' the engineer-architect of the bell-mechanism in a high tower dies from a blow to the forehead, the place of rational ambition, delivered by his robot, Talus. Named after a Greek thief of energy from the Sky God, and therefore a Promethean figure, Talus is described as a 'new serf.' His creator, the engineer with the prohibitive name of Bannadonna, is not a Faustian idealist but a practical man of 'vice-bench and hammer,' ambitious to rival Nature, 'outstrip her, and rule her.' His name is therefore active in his domination of the female principle of natural energy. 'With him,' writes Melville, 'common sense was theurgy' – that is, a modern magic, since the word combines *theos* or god and *ergos* or working energy. But in another Greek myth Talus is the brilliant apprentice who surpasses his master, the engineer-inventor Daedalus. For Melville, the logic of engineering progress is hubristic. Bannadonna's robot moves on 'a grooved way, like a railway' in order to strike the bell or kill the master; in *Moby Dick*, indeed, Melville had already imaged Ahab as a man on rails: 'Swerve me? The path to my fixed purpose is laid with iron rails, whereon my soul is grooved to run. Over unsounded gorges, through the rifled hearts of mountains, under torrents' beds, unerringly I rush! Naught's an obstacle, naught's an angle to the iron way!'

The killer-machine appears in a different form in 'The Tartarus of Maids,' this time as a paper mill, a hell for the girl workers whose function is to service the machinery for making competitively cheaper paper. They feed the machine and their energy is devoured by its continuous action. Speech is replaced by machine noise: 'Machinery – that vaunted slave of humanity – here stood menially served by human beings, who served

97

mutely and cringingly as the slave serves the Sultan.' Melville is clearly aware of the implications for democracy of the developing American factory system: the machine's control of the labour force analogues the engineering of human life as a social hierarchy, a process common in the positivist thought stemming from August Comte at the beginning of the century. The rag section of the hellish mill is the very image of industrial pollution: 'The air swam with the fine, poisonous particles, which from all sides darted subtilely, as motes in sun-beams, into the lungs.' The factory is controlled by clock time and clock work – in Melville's phrase, 'the metallic necessity.' As Marvin Fisher's *Workshops in the Wilderness* shows, he did not invent his regulated Tartarus, the model of what Thoreau sardonically called 'an improved means to an unimproved end.'[18]

Debate on technology and labour conditions later in the century can be exemplified by two documents from the 1880s. In 1883, Carroll D. Wright, head of the Massachusetts Bureau of Labour Statistics, testified to the Senate Committee on Education and Labour that the factory system did not degrade, but constantly elevated unskilled labour to skilled work, and was in every way beneficial.[19] Two years earlier, in 1881, George M. Beard published *American Nervousness, Its Causes and Consequences*, part of his pioneering work in psychosomatic medicine and the effects of the industrial environment.[20] In it he makes an analogy between the human nervous system supplying the body's organs, and Edison's electrical supply to the light bulb. Energy is limited, and when 'new functions are interposed in the circuit, as modern civilization is constantly requiring us to do,' the energy supply weakens or fails. Among the causes of debilitating nervousness and anxiety, Beard examines the concentration of mind and muscle on one mode of action, the over-heated and ill-ventilated work place, compulsory punctuality, constant information by telegraph (33,155,991 messages were transmitted across 170,103 miles of line in 1880), and travelling by or working on railways.

Beard's book is part of a widespread resentment of clocks in late nineteenth century America, present in 'The Tartarus of Maids,' as we have noticed, but also in Mark Twain's story 'My Watch,' in which the erratic time-telling of an ill-repaired watch wrecks the narrator's life. It dates from 1870, at about the same time the ballad of John Henry appeared:

> The man that invented the steam drill,
> He thought he was mighty fine,
> But John Henry he made sixteen feet,
> And the steam drill only made nine, Lawd, Lawd,
> And the steam drill only made nine.
>
> John Henry hammered on the mountain
> Till his hammer was strikin' fire.
> He drove so hard he broke his pore heart,
> Then he laid down his hammer and died, Lawd, Lawd,
> He laid down his hammer and died.
>
> They took John Henry to the graveyard,
> And they buried him in the sand,
> And every locomotive comes roarin' by,
> Says 'There lies a steel-drivin' man, Lawd, Lawd,
> There lies a steel-drivin man.'[21]

The Pendulum in Edgar Allen Poe's 1843 story, 'The Pit and the Pendulum,' was aimed at the heart of a political prisoner held within an elaborate machine, the analogue of the enclosed systems of religion and industrial society. As the cell space contracts, so mechanical time becomes the instrument of death. The hero's clock, in Charles Brockden Brown's 1798 novel, *Wieland*, controls life across two generations of worship, and measures catastrophe in the life of the heroine, Clara. The time mechanism becomes the figure of authoritarian control. The rationalization of industry accelerated, and in the 1880s Frederick Taylor, a Philadelphia engineer who had introduced high speed steel, transformed production lines for 'scientific management.'[22] His 1895 paper, 'A Piece Rate System,' systematized the lives of the John Henrys. Production would be measured through 'time-study' in which a stop-watch determined essential operations and enabled management to fix rates of pay accordingly.

Taylor recognized that the worker was part of industrial process efficiency: 'an attitude toward production which involved a complete mental revolution on the part of both workers and management.'[23] Increased surplus depended on Taylor's 'exact scientific investigation and knowledge.' Naturally, labour believed that such systematization increased worker exploitation, but Taylor himself seems to have held the kind of crude notion of social harmony between workers and rulers exposed at the conclusion of Fritz Lang's *Metropolis* (1926). In *The Principles of Scientific Management* (1911), he wrote that 'the rights of the people are greater than those of either employer or employee,' but he envisaged no change in the hierarchical structure of power which might give meaning to his belief. In 1918, Lenin published an article in *Pravda* stating that Russia should 'try out every scientific and progressive suggestion of the Taylor system.' As Antonio Gramsci pointed out, writing 'Americanism and Fordism' in a Fascist prison in the 1930s, state capitalism and democratic capitalism differ little in their treatment of the worker as part of an engineered system.[24] His essay is a detailed analysis of the significance of Taylorism as a form of totalitarian government.[25]

Once the wooden clock mechanism was replaced by metal parts it could regulate factories and railroads.[26] Hawthorne suspects the impulses of Owen Warland, but Thoreau is ambivalent about the railroad which ran near his Walden Pond cabin. 'We do not ride upon the railroad,' he writes, 'it rides upon us.' But then he euphorically calls the train itself 'this travelling demigod, this cloud-compeller,' as well as the more conventional 'iron horse.' The railroad is as regular as the rising sun and as such a sign of rebirth: 'we live the steadier for it.' By the 1850s, however, railway engineering's penetration into the wilderness already synthesized the interrelated elements of America's new technological culture. It transformed the law by enabling a gunman to make his getaway at high speed across state boundaries. In the form of tunnels, embankments and bridges it controlled nature and challenged Amerindians to renewed tribal struggle right through to the wars of the 1870s. Provincialism was eroded. National unification took on a different urgency. Conservatives feared that, along with the electric telegraph, the railroad would spread liberalism through the rapid exchange of goods, people and information.[27] Jeffersonian images of an agrarian America entered a phase of pastoral nostalgia until social Darwinism gave them a new twist of aggressive survivalism. The conflict between ranchers and railroaders in Frank Norris's *The Octopus* (1901), for instance, turns between technological choice and evolutionary determinism. The hero is not a nature-hero or a landscape and the villain is not the city. The railroad brings wheat to people who need it, even if the Pacific and South Western Railroad acts as much against social justice as the Southern Pacific did in reality. But Norris's animal images translate engineering into natural selection. The 'iron horse' becomes a monster, a thing of darkness associated with death at night, part of civilization's 'second nature,' and therefore misunderstood by most of the characters in the novel. The exception is the artist-hero, Presley, who at least rejects the idea of Nature itself as 'a gigantic engine . . . a leviathan with a heart of steel,' and accepts wheat as an example of truth working for good. But, unfortunately, the hold of the ship which carries him out to sea conceals the corpse of S. Behrman, the railroad agent, accidentally buried under a landslide of wheat.

In 1867, *The North American Review* wrote up the railroad as one of 'the most tremendous and far-reaching engine[s] of social revolution which has ever either blessed or cursed the earth.'[28] The next stage, according to Winwood Read in *The Martyrdom of Man* (1872), would be migration into space. We 'will cross the airless Saharas which separate planet from planet, and sun from sun. The earth will become a Holy Land which will be visited by pilgrims from all quarters of the universe.' Writing in Bret Harte's *Overland Monthly* in 1868, Henry George, in a piece entitled 'What the Railroads Will Bring Us,' was not so sanguine:

> [I]t will be the means of converting a wilderness into a populous empire in less time than many of the cathedrals and palaces of Europe were building, and in unlocking treasure vaults which will flood the world with precious metals.[29]

California will be infinitely wealthy, George goes on, but will the riches be 'evenly distributed'? Children in Massachusetts 'are being literally worked to death.' The old cosmopolitan charm of California – 'a feeling of personal independence and equality,' high wages, and the reckless, generous spirit of mining communities based on chance and trusting to luck – would vanish.

But by the 1870s the superiority of Owen Warland and Bannadonna had become the commonplace of the engineering social group (itself a major addition to the traditional power professions of law, university, government, and the military) – a bonding which continually challenged what Thomas Parke Hughes calls the permanent 'technological frontier':

> The most extreme result of technological frontier penetration is the creation of a man-made environment and the rendering of nature imperceptible. . . . The front edge of technological advance delineates the border between the natural and the man-made world.[30]

The railway was an archetype: 'the engineer obliterated nature's earth surface undulations as he had bored through mountains and spanned great depressions to maintain his unnatural level.' In 1870, the Sheffield Science School at Yale offered civil engineering courses which exactly reflected the needs of the technological frontier as the engineer moved towards predominant power and the American wilderness became 'a building site.'[31] 'The ancient deification of natural forces' became unthinkable in America, even if the language with which technology was described included nostalgia for a sacramental earth.

In a sermon of 1872, the popular moralist Henry Ward Beecher – who was once greeted in Memphis with a twenty-one gun salute[32] – declared that the energies of the Civil War could now be directed 'against nature.' Americans were to be 'warriors for peace' until they 'subdue[d] the nations to the blessed condition of industry, as well as social and civil conquest. . . . The higher instincts, then, when civilized, become engineer's forces, and not military forces.'[33]

The engineering forces encountered resistance from other than intellectual naturists. In Independence Square, during the Philadelphia Centennial, Americans had recovered 'the main prop of authority, the great instinct of obedience.' Yet in the following year, civil war developed between railroad strikers and the militia, the first nation-wide American strike, and the beginning of an industrial strife stretching into the next century.[34] The growing counter-philosophy of governing Americans is clearly expressed by Andrew Carnegie, writing in the *North American Review* in 1889: 'the law of competition [is] not only beneficial but essential for the future of the race.'[35] The mass of emigrants from Europe were to be rapidly engineered into a proletariat. As Alfred North Whitehead once stated the position: 'The self-sufficing independent man, with his peculiar property which concerns no one else, is a concept without any validity for modern civilization.'[36]

But Europe, still occasionally seen as the home of liberalism and the eighteenth century revolutionary impulse, was usually believed to be a barely-modified ancient feudalism and, in retrospect, an absurd receptacle of tyranny and mysticism which engineering technology could have corrected and would now conquer. The message is clear in *A Connecticut Yankee in King Arthur's Court* (1889), in which Mark Twain, reacting directly to the pastoralism of Thoreau and the anxieties of Hawthorne and Melville, rewrites history as a dream of know-how engineering in Arthurian Britain. In his 'Speech on Accident Insurance,' delivered at Hartford, Connecticut, in 1875, Twain had begun:

> Gentlemen, I am glad, indeed, to assist in welcoming the distinguished guests of this occasion to a city whose fame as an insurance centre has extended to all lands, and given us the name of being a quadruple band of brothers working sweetly hand in hand – the Colt's Arms Company making the destruction of our race easy and convenient, our life-insurance citizens paying for their victims when they pass away, Mr. Batterson perpetuating their memory in his stately monuments, and our fire-insurance comrades taking care of their hereafter.[37]

Twain's transplanted Yankee hero, Hank Morgan, is foreman at the Hartford Colt Factory and an all-purpose mechanic: the new employee developed by the mass-production line. The factory had developed considerably beyond the manufacture of celebrated revolvers into a famous centre of scientific technology and new manufacturing methods.[38] The making of firearms required increasingly precise machinery: the Colt armoury improved the turret lathe (a lathe on which tools were held on a vertical axis), and former Colt employee Christopher Spencer (inventor of the Spencer repeating rifle) developed a machine for turning sewing-maching spools, methods of making metal screws automatically, and the automatic turret lathe.[39]

Hank Morgan would therefore be a recent urban variation on the old frontier saying that 'God created men; Colonel Colt made them equal.'[40] His real trade is 'to make everything: guns, revolvers, cannon, boilers, engines, all sorts of labour-saving machinery . . . anything in the world, it didn't make any difference what.' By this time, 'vile empiricism' and 'metallic necessity' had conquered the earlier American traditions of pastoral aristocratism. Thomas Jefferson may have wished Americans to be farmers in order to avoid the moral taint of European workshops. 'It is better,' he wrote, 'to carry provisions and materials to workmen there, than to bring them to the provisions and materials, and with them their manners and principles.' But by 1860 America ranked fourth in the world's manufacturing nations, and by 1894 the value of American manufactures nearly equalled those of Britain, France and Germany combined.[41] Hank Morgan is part of the reversal of Jefferson's desire. In Twain's novel, moreover, the quest for the Holy Grail is replaced by the foreman's founding of a colony in Britain, a factory which turns 'groping and grubbing automata into *men*.' In this managerial revolution, self in a state of competition is aided by engineering: 'training is all there is *to* a person. We speak of nature; it is a folly; there is no such thing as nature.' Hank's 'peaceful revolution' is engineered through a number of machines through whose operations men would be modified: the sewing machine, a major transformer of American society and example of 'technological convergence' (its technical requirements further enabled changes in the boot and shoe and clothing industries, and in the manufacture of tents, sails, harnesses, rubber and elastic goods, and much else[42]); a telephone system (a machine patented by the Scots-American Bell in 1876 and a feature of the Philadelphia Centennial Exposition); the mass-produced newspaper distributed on time;

104

bombs and cheap guns available democratically to all[43]; the typewriter, the steamboat, the railway, the telegraph and the phonograph; barbed wire, which had transformed the interior of America after its invention in 1874[44]; bicycles, which had captured America after 1885. High-wheeled English bicycles had been exhibited at the Philadelphia Centennial, but spectacular growth occured only in the 1890s after the invention of the 'safety' form. By 1900, twelve firms produced them, and their manufacture in turn became instrumental in changing machine-tool industries, in lubrication, and in the development of ball-bearings, the flat-link chain, light tubular steel, and high tensility wire. A great deal of this expansion contributed to the rapid manufacture of automobiles from 1900 onwards.[45]

In addition, Hank transfers to Britain American baseball, the team game which both democratizes and trains for team labour. In fact, he brings to what Hawthorne thought of as 'Our Old Home' the core of American power: the structure of the machine and machine-tool industries, and by implication the dream of American imperial conquest through economic expansion.

Initially, Hank organizes the knights for utilitarian purposes, rather than the metaphysical waste of chivalric elitism. But the Church and the chivalric order finally defeat him. He retreats to a defensive base and prepares to 'blow up civilization.' His weapons include an electrified fence, thirteen Gatling guns (invented in 1861) and 'glass cylinder dynamite torpedoes' (invented during the Civil War, in 1864, by Robert Whitehead). Merlin's cave becomes a dynamic source of electricity, like Richard Hunt's Machinery Building at the Chicago Exposition of 1893, which Henry Adams envisioned as 'a step in evolution to startle Darwin.'[46] Twain's novel does indeed end in technological holocaust: 'I touched a button and set fifty electric suns aflame on top of our precipice.'[47]

While writing *A Connecticut Yankee*, Twain infatuated himself with financial speculation in support of John W. Paige's typesetting machine.[48] On the occasion of Whitman's seventieth birthday in 1889, he wrote that engineering 'marvels' had brought 'man [to] almost his full stature at last! – and still growing, visibly growing, while you look.' Such hysteria influenced his writing and contributed to his failure as a capitalist tycoon. The Paige machine was outdated as early as 1881 by the rotary type caster, whose metal moulds were not only faster than the machine Twain saw at the Colt factory, but also reusable. Paige may have been, according to Twain, 'the Shakespeare of mechanical invention,' but his machine afforded no technocratic power to its backers. The successful model of the engineer–businessman would be Bell, who in 1880 founded the Volta laboratories, a centre for applied scientific discovery whose manufacturing section, Western Electric, in turn established its own research laboratories. The engineer had entered the system of mechanized research and marketing, and had become the all-powerful technocrat, the engineer who ruled through industry based on controlled science. The ideal society for many Americans became the expanding technocracy.[49]

Between 1886 and 1896 alone, over one hundred works of utopian fiction were published. One of the most popular, Edward Bellamy's *Looking Backward, 2000–1887*, issued the year before Twain's novel, in 1888, was among the first totally technological utopias, and offered a vision of a mechanized America as an engineered state, organized for 'the limits of human facility.' Over one million copies were sold in the first ten years of publication. In 1883 Lester F. Ward coined the phrase 'social telesis' for the engineering of means to ends; in *Dynamic Sociology* (1883) he wrote out the terms for a society endlessly frontiered, endlessly unstable as a 'resource-intensive' culture; a society in which the mind should 'preserve the dynamic and prevent the statical condition of the social forces [and] prevent the restoration of equilibrium between the social forces and the natural forces operating outside of them.'[50] He believed, that is, that the processes of nature were planless, and that the human mind should not be natural but should instead engineer its society. Knowledge, for Ward, is to be 'the piston of civilization.'[51] The reversal of Jefferson's propositions is complete, and the state of cultural entropy remains a major subject for speculation, not least in Thomas Pynchon's fictions of totalitarian system in the later twentieth century.[52]

Between 1859 and 1870 steel production was shaped by Siemen's gas-fired furnace (1869), Nobel invented dynamite

(1869), the Atlantic cable was laid (1866); Armour opened his meat-packing factory in Chicago (1888), the transcontinental railroad was completed (1869), and John D. Rockefeller founded Standard Oil. In 1870 the first through train from Boston to the Pacific carried eight cars equipped with melodions – musak became part of the communications system at an early date.[53] In 1877 a Boston hotel installed running hot and cold water in all rooms.[54] By the 1880s the 'sacred plow' would be mechanized on the prairies, and between 1871 and 1881 Edison perfected the duplex telegraph, the phonograph, and the incandescent electric bulb; Scholes designed the Remington Company's typewriter (1873); Solomon introduced pressure-cooking for canned foods (1874), and A.A. Pope manufactured the first American bicycle (1878).[55] Incidentally, in the 'Conclusion' of *Walden* (1854), Thoreau had envisaged something of the multiple effects of canned food as America expanded her empire, and of the more local needs and results nearer home – what he called 'the private sea':

> Be rather the Mungo Park, the Lewis and Clark and Frobisher, of your own streams and oceans; explore your own higher latitudes – with shiploads of preserved meats to support you, if they be necessary; and pile the empty cans sky-high for a sign. Were preserved meats invented to preserve meat merely?

Today we would want to know where Thoreau suggested the cans be piled – the beer can on the highway has become the very image of pollution.

Between 1882 and 1892 Daimler built his petrol engine, the Northern Pacific Railroad was constructed, Maxim invented his recoil-operated gun, Edison patented his kinetoscope, Eastman produced the 'Kodak' box camera using celluloid film, the Wainwright building rose in St. Louis using a steel skeleton, Burroughs invented the keyboard electric calculator, and Judson invented the zip-fastener – and the first automatic telephone switchboard was built. Between 1893 and the end of the century society began to adjust to wireless telegraphy, X-rays, the monotype setting machine, the first petrol tractor at Marion, Ohio (the mechanization of the 'sacred plow'), the acetylene lamp, wireless transmission of speech, and – none too soon – aspirin. Three years later, in 1903, Ford founded his automobile company, the Wrights were flying, and the first sensitive electroscope and the ultramicroscope had been invented.[56]

In 1883 President Arthur and Governor Cleveland opened Brooklyn Bridge, conceived back in 1857 by John Roebling as a work of engineered art which would 'forever testify to the energy, enterprise and wealth of that community which shall secure its erection.'[57] Hart Crane was to celebrate Roebling's creation as the euphoric arc of expanding enterprise within the myth of American prowess in his 1930 poem, *The Bridge*, in which Edgar Allen Poe is found strap-hanging beneath the bridge and the East River in the New York subway – an artifact which by 1902 already exemplified that rapid obsolescence of technology characteristic of America in the twentieth century.[58] In 1899 a ten thousand horsepower (steam powered) unit had been built for the subway; it had to be scrapped in 1902 because it was too large (forty feet high) and uneconomical. It was replaced by a steam turbine a tenth its size. The days of the steam engine were drawing to a close.[59]

But engineering euphoria still flourished. For the Philadelphia Centennial, Erastus Salisbury Field made a thirteen foot by nine foot canvas entitled 'Historical Monument of the American Republic.' Eight enormous towers rose high into the air, encrusted with depictions of national events and heroes; near their tops connecting steel bridges carried communicating steam trains. The centre tower was dedicated to Lincoln and the Constitution.[60] This enthusiastic work combined bridge and train with exactly that sense of American engineering that Walt Whitman gives in his poems 'To a Locomotive in Winter' (1876), 'Passage to India' (1871) and 'Years of the Modern' (1865); a belief he summarized in 'The United States to Old World Critics' (1888):

> Here first the duties of to-day, the lessons of the concrete,
> Wealth, order, travel, shelter, products, plenty;
> As of the building of some varied, vast, perpetual edifice,
> Whence arise inevitable in time, the towering roofs, the lamps,
> The solid-planted spires tall shooting to the stars.

After visiting the Centennial, W.D. Howells observed:

> It is still in these things of iron and steel that the national genius most freely speaks; by and by the inspired marbles, the breathing canvases . . . for the present America is voluble in the strong metals and their infinite uses.[61]

That feeling was also evident in the recorded responses to the Corliss Engine at the Centennial.

But within the sense of expansive power, some of the old apprehensiveness about the dark machinations of the scientist and heroic inventor remained. The portrait of the Mississippi river boat pilot, Horace Bixby, in Twain's *Life on the Mississippi* (1883) looks back nostalgically to a hero as complete controller of technology acting unmistakably for the benefit of society. Pilotage is 'an "exact" science' operating in the interface between nature (the river) and the machine (the engines of the boat):

> His movements were entirely free; he consulted no one, he received commands from nobody. . . . Indeed, the law of the United States forbade him to listen to commands and suggestions.

As both free hero and national figure, Edison generated a certain anxiety. In 1879, the cover of *Harper's Weekly* carried a full-page drawing of 'the Wizard of Menlo Park' at work alone in his midnight tower – a folklore image of mysterious control. The editorial describes him as 'a midnight workman with supernal forces whose mysterious phenomena have taught men their largest idea of elemental power; a modern alchemist, who finds the philosopher's stone to be made of carbon, and with his magnetic wand changes everyday knowledge into the pure gold of new applications and original uses . . . deep in his conjurings of Nature while the world sleeps.' Then the writer tries to dispel the anxiety by portraying Edison as an ordinary American who sold newspapers as a boy, tinkered with gadgets, invented *useful* things like the telephone, and crowned his acceptability by becoming a successful businessman. The wizard is countered by the engineer-tycoon, the technocrat of New Jersey.[62]

The potential tyranny within Edison's mysterious power is dramatized in Christopher Davis's *A Peep into the Twentieth Century*, a novel based on the relationships between electrical engineers of the late nineteenth century.[63] Working with Edison, Nikola Tesla made alterating current a practical fact, inventing both transformers to reduce the loss of electricity travelling in wire and the motors through which to run them on A.C. But Edison, with his usual fanaticism, committed himself to direct current, lobbying New York State into adopting A.C. for the first electric chair in order to dramatize the campaign against its vicious nature. Tesla in turn enlisted the help of George Westinghouse, the New York engineer who in 1888 invented the brake using compressed air rather than muscle. Together they defeated Edison in 1893 with an A.C. contract to develop Niagara Falls' hydro-electric power. Christopher Davis's novel concerns the electric chair struggle and the combatant's complete absorption in the need for control. As a prison official tells the first victim of the chair: 'Your quick death represents money to [Edison]. . . . Control over men, over all for the benefit of the few . . . it's control they're after in all things large or small, but where you see it is in the prison system.'[64]

Despite this defeat, Edison's tenacity enabled him in the space of four years to patent three hundred inventions which modified the technology of communications and thereby changed the nature of the extensions of the human body. When in 1877 the Emperor of Brazil cried 'It talks!' and dropped the telephone at the Centennial, Queen Victoria promptly ordered one for the palace; Edison had improved on Bell's prototype. In 1881 he invented a metal-locator to find the bullet in the body of the assassinated President Garfield, but the initial procedure failed because Edison forgot the steel springs in the death-bed mattress. In 1899 he perfected the process of filming successive images on Eastman's film; this resulted in his own company producing *The Great Train Robbery* in 1903, directed by Edwin S. Porter and inspired by an actual railroad robbery staged on 29 August 1900[65]

Control through social engineering is certainly the overall issue at stake. In Chapter 23 of Theodore Dreiser's *The Titan* (1914), Frank Cowperwood's tycoon dream of being 'the sole master of street-railway traffic in Chicago' is hardly interrupted by the Haymarket bombing in 1886:

> He did not believe in either the strength of the masses or their ultimate rights, though he sympathized with the condition of individuals, and did believe that men like himself were sent into the world to better perfect its mechanism and habitable order.

It is despair of both the ruling oligarchy and the masses' capacity for leadership that motivates Ignatius Donnelly's *Caesar's Column* (1891), a novel which projects a Europe and America whose workers are enslaved by a capitalist aristocracy and whose revolt itself becomes an anarchic bloodbath. The 'gigantic abnormal selfishness which ruins millions for the benefit of thousands' is countered by an underground organization, the Brotherhood of Destruction. The resultant civil war results in the suicide of civilization with the aid of advanced technology: 'an age of bribery terminates in one colossal crime of corruption' and technological control culminates in aerial bombardment:

> I can see, like a great black rain of gigantic drops, the lines of the falling bombs against the clear blue sky.

The self-appointed nucleus of a future in Africa is rescued from a roof in ruined New York by a Demon, the mythical – even Faustian – name given to a hovering aircraft:

> The engineer touched the lever of the electric engine; the great bird swayed for an instant, and then began to rise, like a veritable Phoenix from its nest of flame, surrounded by cataracts of sparks.

The structure of the new order developed in the African mountains is distinctly unlike Hank Morgan's technologized Britain. It refuses to 'give any encouragement to labour-saving inventions.' It tries to convert 'metallic necessity' into an agrarian Phoenix state in which 'the ingenuity of man,' which had 'conquered the forces of steam and electricity,' is applied to 'the great adjustments of society, on which the happiness of millions depends.' The result is a class-structured isolationism, 'a garden of peace and beauty' with a distinctly Jeffersonian tionality. History repeats itself, for the nth time as nostalgic utopian fiction.

In Chapter 6 of *The New Empire* (1902), Brooks Adams summarizes the historical position of America's material power:

> In March 1897 America completed her reorganization, for in that month the consolidation at Pittsburg undersold the world in steel, and forthwith the signs of distress multiplied.[66]

In an essay of 1955, Charles Olson prefaces this passage with words which still echo those of Lester F. Ward in 1883:

> In civilization nothing is at rest, the movement is trade, the necessity is metals, and the consequent centralization of power also moves.[67]

For Adams' brother, Henry, the prevention of distress could come only from a unifying understanding of the nature of energy under power – sexual as well as electric. Americans would have to be educated from an early age that morality without training in science and technology, without active comprehension of the historical and potential role of women in society, and without a proper grasp of power politics, would be a continuous disaster. In 1905 he wrote, in the final chapter of *The Education of Henry Adams*:

> The new American must either be the child of the new forces or the chance sport of nature.[68]

1978

5

Living Mythically: The Thirties

In May 1932 the Museum of Modern Art opened on 53rd Street in New York in an old mansion. A number of artists associated with *New Masses*, the leftist magazine founded in 1925, showed a collection of political murals commenting sharply on the economic imbalance and social cruelty of the times. Hugo Gellert's mural was entitled 'Us fellas gotta stick together,' a phrase drawn from an already notorious conversation between a member of the Vanderbilt family, who had obtained a reporting job on a Hearst newspaper, and his equally rich interviewee, Al Capone, then in gaol. Capone, as usual, knew the score and told the young capitalist heir: 'Us fellas gotta stick together.'[1] Gellert's mural neatly encapsulated the Hearst-gangsterdom axis, since the centre of corruption in America, then as now, was the interlocking of business and crime. Naturally, President Hoover, Henry Ford, J.P. Morgan and J.D. Rockefeller found the exhibition offensive: they were the 'fellas' in the mural with Capone. Another picture, by the great political artist Ben Shahn, showed figures in the Sacco and Vanzetti case; one by William Gropper, another fine political artist, showed the notorious millionaires J.P. Morgan and Andrew Mellon eating tickertape with two pigs, protected by militiamen. The Gropper was entitled, with little subtlety but quite accurately, 'The Writing on the Wall.'

Louis Adamic has a nice example of business hypocrisy at the height of the Depression:

Daniel Willard, president of the Baltimore and Ohio Railroad (on which began the bloody riots of 1877), stated . . . that, to his mind, 'those who manage our large industries, whatever be the character of their output, should recognize the importance and necessity of planning their work so as to furnish as steady employment as possible to those in their service, [for that was] an obligation connected with our economic system.'

As Adamic says, these tycoons spoke as though business, the most important factor in American lives, was not 'largely dehumanized and . . . indifferent to vital human and social questions; that, by its very nature, business could have no spontaneous and direct, no intelligent, "Christian," or benevolent interest in Society.'[2]

The broad poster–effects of the *New Masses* artists may be placed behind the more detailed analysis of James Agee's study of the southern poor, *Let Us Now Praise Famous Men* (1936), a commission from *Fortune* magazine which turned into one of the most compassionate indictments of callous degradation ever written. Agee's words are complemented by Walker Evans' terrifyingly beautiful photographs – immediately effective images of the conditions capitalism had imposed on its victims. (The Farm Security Administration was to use Dorothea Lange's photographs to similar effect.) The minimal entertainment available to alienated workers throughout America, the movies, played a major part in guiding values in the nation's state of decline; Hollywood had emerged as the disseminating centre of consumer manipulations, controlling not only patterns of family and sexual life, but also clothing and household properties, a process documented in Margaret Thorpe's *America at the Movies* (1946). But it is Nathanael West's *The Day of the Locust* (1939) which more fully examines the tensions between consumer art and consumer frustrations, and it is striking how West's novels resist ideological dogmas rife in the 1930s. Neither he nor Agee, with their shared knowledge of the waste of life in America, was politically committed to any myth. West's satire, both here and in *Miss Lonelyhearts* (1933) and *A Cool Million* (1934), is radical in its disillusion and refusal of compromise, untempted by short cuts into either communism or conservatism or liberal-reformist fence-sitting.

114

Thirties intellectuals and artists made too many decisions with Stalinist communism as their paradigm of vitality. Certainly, it can be argued that the Depression and the Communist example 'gave focus to the unformulated radicalism of the 1930s and influenced, directly or indirectly, almost every American writer of any importance.'[3] A large part of the intellectual middle class seized a viable point of view, 'a direction for anger, a code of excited humanitarianism.'[4] The idea of being 'on the left' enabled a person to live mythically without committing him- or herself to revolutionary change and without being considered pathological or doctrinaire. A writer might obtain a shot of vitality beyond mere compassion, as Clifford Odets did, resulting in his plays of 1935–6. When the Left turned inquisitorial, writers were submitted to the Stalinist pressures characteristic of any totalitarianism.

Upton Sinclair dragged Sergei Eisenstein into a classic case of bogus leftism. Stan Brakhage gives it the right dimensions:

> Upton Sinclair – one of the so-called 'cocktail communists' of the American thirties . . . these men, living in hellish contradiction of being wealthy proletarians – rich 'poor folk' . . . or some such – thus hack idealists . . . these men, then, proving more destructive to any possible art or, even, human understanding than the worst materialist business man that dishonest commerce had ever created – Sinclair finally taking all Sergei's Mexican footage away from him and selling it piecemeal to 'Castle Films,' etc., for travelogue movies.[5]

Kenneth Rexroth recalls an episode on a movie star's yacht in which he and others, some of them top Communists, tried to persuade Eisenstein to remain in America. He feared that the Russians would expose his homosexuality. When someone said, 'Well, so what?' Eisenstein replied: 'It would kill my mother.' Caught within the network of stereotypes, he opted for Stalinist Russia and his own artistic destruction. Rexroth says he does not understand it;[6] but Hollywood would have destroyed Eisenstein. Sooner or later the situation portrayed in Norman Mailer's *The Deer Park* (1953), where film director Charley Eitel comes under pressure from the House UnAmerican Activities Committee, would have emaciated his ability to develop his genius.

115

But it is untrue simply to claim, as Robert Warshow did in *Commentary* in 1947, that the influence of the Left caused 'a disastrous vulgarization of intellectual life, in which the character of American liberalism and radicalism was decisively – and perhaps permanently – corrupted.'[7] Awareness of 'some "larger consideration"' did not just result in what he calls 'organized mass disingenuousness' destroying honesty and meaning, although it did cause the over-estimation of a novel like *The Grapes of Wrath* in 1939. Intellectuals, writers and critics distanced themselves from the New Deal. Warshow puts it straightforwardly:

> for most Americans [the atmosphere of the Thirties] was expressed most clearly in the personality of President Roosevelt and the social-intellectual-political climate of the New Deal. For the intellectual, however, the Communist movement was the fact of central importance: the New Deal remained an external phenomenon, part of that 'larger' world of American public life from which he had long separated himself – he might 'support' the New Deal . . . but he never identified himself with it. One way or another, he did identify with the Communist movement.

It was the middle class intellectual who decided what was and what was not 'proletarian' literature or art. 'Mass culture' became, once again, a set of alibis through which to simplify men's lives so that they could be manipulated by the entertainment, film, book and radio industries. Some poets celebratedly resorted to paradox and irony – a new 'orthodoxy,' to use T.S. Eliot's favourite theological term. Warshow's indictment of Left literature is not borne out by the work in Joseph Freeman's *Proletarian Literature in the United States* (1935) – which contains Caldwell, Dos Passos, Farrell, Fearing, Patchen, Rukeyser, Odets and John Wexley – nor by Joseph North's *New Masses* anthology (1969) – which includes some of the same writers, together with Agee, Lorca, Saroyan, Hemingway (a remarkable piece on the death of worker-veterans in a Florida hurricane in 1935), William Carlos Williams, Dreiser and Perelman.

II

Eliot is the primary example of the writer of the period who combined formal literary ability with social decadence, a nexus also worked out through his magazine *Criterion* between 1922 and 1939. The context is the use in American literature of urban and agrarian–realist techniques to tackle experiences of social collapse, the thorough weakening of moderate solutions, and the perpetual veering towards myths of Right and Left as substitutes for discriminating analysis. Communist, Fascist and capitalist-Christian movements such as the *Action Française* forced bourgeois liberalism to become an agency weakening democratic controls. The liberalism of the New Deal was no way to curb the power of capitalism. On such issues the intelligentsia were notoriously careless. As George Orwell pointed out in his essay on W.B. Yeats in 1943: 'the best writers of our time have been reactionary in tendency, and though Fascism does not offer any real return to the past, those who yearn for the past will accept Fascism sooner than its probable alternatives.'

In the American South, William Faulkner wrote up a hostile environment as an archetype of permanence – his fiction and his personal utterances indicate a sensibility to which even liberal reform was repugnant.[8] The twelve aristocratic southern writers who contributed to the Whig Jeffersonian reaction of *I'll Take My Stand* in 1930 included critics who would influence American university literature departments for the next three decades – Allen Tate, John Crowe Ransom, Stark Young and Robert Penn Warren. Their 'stand' advocated authoritarian disciplines, strong order, hierarchical religion, scholasticism (that is, knowledge and taste organized as laws), and the cult of the Byzantine (in part lifted from T.E. Hulme and Yeats). It is not surprising that T.S. Eliot's 1934 lectures, later printed as *After Strange Gods: A Primer of Heresy*, were delivered at the University of Virginia. Eliot's targets included D.H. Lawrence, Thomas Hardy and James Joyce, and although his criticism has long since become of merely academic interest, it is worth pointing out that he understood neither those artists' account of personal relationships nor their ideologies. Eliot, like many writers of the time, had been panicked by Oswald Spengler's

The Decline of the West (the English translation appeared in 1926, although the work had been around in German since 1917). Spengler's neo-Hegelian prophecies of inevitable cycles of civilization and barbarism gave writers and politicians who needed it a neat alibi for authoritarianism. Not least, they provided a sanction for that cult of managerialism and amoral engineering efficiency which, gilded with a paternalism out of Carlyle's notions of vitalist destiny, still forms a strong pattern in American sociology and academic political thought.

Charateristically, Ortega y Gasset's *The Revolt of the Masses* (1932) could be used as a whip *against* the masses, blaming them for the thinning and alienation of culture, as if the rich upper classes really did stand for culture as well as loot. It was not only Eliot and his friends the southerners and the *Action Française* for whom the ideal was an unhistorical myth of neo-medieval church and state designed to counter 'bolshevism' (a 1930s word meaning panic at the slightest thought of a redistribution of income and power down the social pyramid, rather than the historical party concept). Hollywood, too, dreamed of a return to feudal structures. Its medieval 'costume dramas' barely concealed the inclinations of 'us fellas' and enabled producers in particular to indulge their fantasies. Making *Marie Antoinette* in 1938 they found that the *Galérie des Glaces* at Versailles was not big enough, so they built a larger and better palace for Norma Shearer to parade in. A fan in China sent her a hundred-dollar embroidered handkerchief because Marie Antionette apparently introduced handkerchiefs. The museum set up in New York to display artifacts used in the film opened its doors on Bastille Day, but it was a private affair. The mob were let in free next day.[9]

As Muriel Rukeyser's poem 'Movie' (1934) says:

> We goggle at the screen: look   they tell us
> you are a nation of similar whores   remember the Maine
> remember you have a democracy of champagne –

> And slowly the female face kisses the young man,
> over his face the twelve-foot female head
> the yard-long mouth enlarges and yawns
> The End . . .[10]

Eliot's *The Idea of a Christian Society* appeared in 1939, the year after *Marie Antoinette*, and already contained those opinions which led the Conservative Party's Political Centre to publish his 1955 pamphlet as part of their propaganda, complete with an introduction by the subsequent hero of Suez, whose name is neatly mythological – Eden. The former work speaks of schemes to manipulate the masses in their mediocre sluggishness, and of pastoral units 'attached to the soil' as a norm for societies. In 1932, his 'Modern Education and the Classics' gave us the 'uneducated man with an empty mind . . . as well equipped to fill his leisure contentedly as is the educated man,' but no programme of economic or class reform.

The social divisions are described by John Tipple in his *Crisis of the American Dream*:

> While national planning, to an assertive individualist such as President Hoover, was 'national regimentation,' to socially-minded thinkers such as Lewis Mumford and John Dewey it was more than an emergency measure, it was an inevitable consequence of the advance of technology. Invincible technological trends, declared Dewey, made the social control of economic forces necessary if the goals of democracy were to be realized. Those who shouted 'regimentation' had failed to see that effective liberty was a function of the social conditions existing at any time.[11]

The academic-literary Left in *Partisan Review* sat tight and ambivalent on Eliot's *After Strange Gods*. Its second issue carried a review by William Phillips denouncing its reactionary attitudes, a combination of Catholicism and feudalism, and stating bluntly: 'Only the blind would hesitate to call Eliot a fascist.'[12] But *Partisan Review* was stuck with an 'incomplete understanding of what the literary tradition meant,' and its attitudes were riven with contradictions, not entirely fruitful, which caused Dwight Macdonald to leave the editorial staff in 1943.[13] When it came to *The Idea of a Christian Society*, the centrality of Eliot, the Harvard expatriate American, to the ideologies of *Partisan Review* was clear: Trilling absolved him from reactionary inhumanity.[14] Eliot's commitment to intellectual life, to an élite of Christian aristos, made him a culture hero for the Columbia University-*Partisan Review* axis.

Some of the major 1930s writers were content to place their inhumanity within elegant structures, and the cultural aristocrats of politics and the universities gladly maintained the evasion. Robert Frost opposed his extreme *laissez-faire* libertarianism against even Roosevelt's efforts to prevent total capitalist collapse. In *Build Soil*, a pastoral poem delivered, not unnaturally, at Columbia University on 31 May 1932, at a time when Roosevelt needed support for election, and when a quarter of the entire labour force was unemployed, and the suicide rate higher even than in 1931, Frost came out for oligarchy and 'monarchic socialism,' adding: 'I'd let things take their course. And then I'd claim the credit for the outcome.' Small wonder, therefore, that John F. Kennedy asked Frost to read a poem at his inaugural ceremony three decades later. Us New Englanders gotta stick together.

Many of the writers on the Left, however, wrote flabbily: mediocrity stifled the vitality of socialists in the 1930s. The stronger writing lay in the urban realism of James T. Farrell's Chicago novels (their accuracy vouched for by Kenneth Rexroth in his *Autobiographical Novel*) and Clifford Odets' work for the Group Theatre in New York. But even finer power came with the severity of West, the compassion of Agee, and the understanding of carelessness in Fitzgerald. Under the tutelage of Edmund Wilson, Scott Fitzgerald read Henry James and Karl Marx as well as Spengler, and learned something of the sociology and psychology of money and the historical logic that led to the Depression. He learned from Freud that psychoanalysis had to be played into Marx and Lenin in order to understand the suicidal nature of inter-war societies and why 'the ability to function' had collapsed in the 1930s. He was too early for Wilheim Reich's diagnosis, but he would have understood Reich's rejection of the rigidities of psychoanalysis, communism and liberal humanism. Put another way, his was a need to resolve the impasse documented by Orwell's 'Inside the Whale' (1940), in which Orwell looks back to his argument with Henry Miller at the end of 1936.[15] The collision of Orwell's anarchism and Miller's Spenglerism affords a hold on the period. Miller told Orwell that going to Spain was 'the act of an idiot': 'He could understand anyone going there from purely selfish motives, out of curiosity, for instance, but to mix oneself up in such things *from a sense of obligation* was sheer stupidity. . . . Our civilization was destined to be swept away and replaced by something so different that we should scarcely regard it as human – a prospect that did not bother him, he said. And some such outlook is implicit throughout his work.' Orwell recalls a reply Miller had sent to a questionnaire circulated by the American *Marxist Quarterly*: 'Miller replied in terms of extreme pacifism, an individual refusal to fight, with no apparent wish to convert others to the same opinion – practically, in fact, a declaration of irresponsibility.'

But Orwell understood Miller's position between the yea-saying progressives and those who ignored immediate politics:

> [Miller] is neither pushing the world-process forward nor trying to drag it back, but on the other hand he is by no means ignoring it. I should say that he believes in the impending ruin of Western Civilization much more firmly than the majority of 'revolutionary' writers; only he does not feel called upon to do anything about it . . . he feels no impulse to alter or control the process that he is undergoing. He has performed the essential Jonah act of allowing himself to be swallowed, remaining passive, *accepting*.

But *Tropic of Cancer* (1934) and *Tropic of Capricorn* (1939) criticised the assumptions that life had to be governed by labour, and the primacy they gave to erotic life – not as the centre of sexual productivity or anti-puritanism, nor as theorized into Freudian schematics, but as a Dionysian force that could take energetic forms and, in Georges Bataille's sense, transgress and break taboos continually – had a liberating effect on readers that would extend and develop through the century. Miller's dense cloud chambers of language exactly articulated that erotic inescapability, not so much a release as an immersion, without resort to oedipal resistances, mysticism of blood, and cults of ganglia.

III

Intellectuals leapt into Freudian schematics, as they leapt into the schematics of political ideology, and there submitted. West, Agee, and Fitzgerald did not succumb to 'the disastrous vulgarization of intellectual life.' But the possible effect on a young black American is partly recorded in Ralph Ellison's *Invisible Man* (1952) – that is, betrayal by both the Communists and the Garveyites. After the Harlem Renaissance of the 1920s, blacks could do little but consolidate their small cultural gains and steady levels of protest, on the one hand acting as part of the degradations of the poor in Agee's terms, and on the other exploding into the impotent violence depicted in Richard Wright's Chicago novels. Wright's poem 'I Have Seen Black Hands' (1934) begins with the conditions of black exploitation by industry and commerce, and has black Americans caught in 'the revelries of sadism.' Yet it concludes with the only action that sustains him – black and white fists raised in unison: 'Some day there shall be millions and millions of them, / On some red day in a burst of fists on a new horizon!'.[16]

The equivalents of Louis Armstrong and Duke Ellington had yet to emerge in literature, and these two artists had reached the second stage of their mature performances only against a background of that ambivalent Prohibition prosperity summarized by the pianist Sammy Price: 'There was no depression for the gangsters.'[17] The music of Earl Hines and his orchestra in Chicago in 1934 and New York in 1935 is the sound of *art deco*, of gangster-owned night clubs. The size and density of the sound – a hard, sophisticated version of earlier jazz inventions using dehumanized vocals – denotes value. It is a musical commodity, one which comes across now almost as pure style, whose energy is tightly controlled surface fitted over elementary dance structure. It places itself at the disposal of patrons, so the emotion is never subtle or illuminating but modernistic and predictable.[18] Jazz bands provided popular entertainment; jazz was something else, since it has never been a popular art. Jazz artists survived by going to Europe or taking other jobs. Prosperity came with 'the high-pressure tactics of modern publicity' that sold swing from 1935 onwards; but, again, Guy

Lombardo was show-biz to Ellington's creative individualism.[19]

One way of estimating the black cultural condition is through Eugene O'Neill's *The Emperor Jones*, written in 1920. In *The Big Sea* (1945), Langston Hughes recalled how, when it was performed at the Lincoln Theatre on 135th Street in Harlem, the black audience responded to Jones's naked forest panics: 'naturally they howled with laughter. "Them ain't no ghosts, fool!" the spectators cried from the orchestra. "Why don't you come on out o' that jungle – back to Harlem where you belong?"'[20] But it was only in 1971 that the film of O'Neill's play, made in 1932, was distributed. The script had the help of DuBose Heyward, author of *Porgy* (which Gershwin adapted from the play of the novel into his opera in 1935). The film did best in Harlem, and, curiously, in the southern states, where the censors only 'clipped the two murders and a shot of a woman smoking.' But it differed from O'Neill's original considerably. As Marie Seton pointed out, the members of Jones's court were more like minstrels, and the underworld was that of the standard movie gangsterlands in *Little Caesar* (1930) and *The Public Enemy* (1931). At least the film is a step away from the ghetto movies which, ever since the first all-black pictures in 1916, had generally displayed self-contempt, dark and therefore lower caste 'Negroes' marrying upper class lighter blacks, heroines killing themselves because they were black, and the rest of the degraded life that only began to change significantly in 1960. The *Emperor Jones* hero does not die because he is black; he deals with blacks and whites in a power relationship that reduces colour to relative irrelevance.[21]

But the context of this significant film was the rapid decay of Harlem, of local employment, and of faith in 'Negro' autonomy during the 1930s.[22] The Harlem Renaissance remained a promise of awakening, one which gave way under the sterilities of proletarian uplift and Leftist rhetoric, both alibis for inaction. The Communist Party conned Negroes into believing they were the spearhead of the American proletarian revolution. Negroes in Moscow said so, and poems appeared to match the sound of the politics – veneer without any analysis of facts. Enlightened conservatives under Roosevelt encouraged 'Negroes' to contribute their abilities to the New Deal. The results can be seen in the Works Progress Administration's project to document the history and present condition of New York Negroes. Reporters on the project included Ralph Ellison, Claude McKay and Roi Ottley; they completed their research in 1940 and the product, *The Negro in New York*, is a major work of the 1930s, suggesting the necessity of radical social changes. It was not published until 1967 because, according to Jean Blackwell Houston, curator of the Schomberg Collection of Negro Literature and History of New York Public Library, 'information contained in it was too startling for conservative taste.'[23]

IV

The ground base of the decade's essential conservatism is clearly evident in the comic strips. Chester Gould created Dick Tracy in 1931 as a character moving through the gang warfare of the 1920s with the profile of a 'young Sherlock Holmes' and the costume of the modern G-man; the image of the non-professional professional so beloved of the detective–story world. The year 1938 is memorable for – among other events – the arrival of Superman into the American Pantheon of *Action Comics*, there joining Abe Lincoln, Davy Crockett and Tom Mix. Superman's unlimited supernatural power is only impotent against Kryptonite, and his aim is to rid the world of something called 'evil.' His costume is a kind of 'drag,' consisting of skin-tight blue fleshings with a red and gold shield badge (and a capital S for himself), scarlet briefs, a golden belt and a scarlet cape. This image of assertive masculinity, with its usual complement of homoerotic energy, is a flight dream of sex energy that channelled America's insurgent dream of itself as world cop, sex hero and moral terminus. Superman's daily life disguise, Clark Kent, is an ordinary newspaperman on the *Daily Planet* (the name seems to have stimulated his cosmic conscious-ness). He therefore represents a metamorphosis of the hero as reporter maintained in the films and fiction of the inter-war period, beginning with Ben Hecht and Charles MacArthur's play *The Front Page*, which had been written in 1920 and filmed by Lewis Milestone in 1931. Clark Kent himself wears spectacles (generally a sign of weakness in popular art), cringes before danger, fails with his girlfriend Lois Lane, and on the whole represents a level of failure to measure up to the current images of manliness and easy solutions. Marshall McLuhan encapsulates him adequately in *The Mechanical Bride*:

> The attitudes of Superman to current social problems . . . reflect the strong-arm totalitarian methods of the immature and barbaric mind. . . . Superman is ruthlessly efficient in carrying on a one-man crusade against crooks and anti-social forces [without] appeal to [the] process of law. Justice is represented as an affair of personal strength alone. [He therefore suggests] that today the dreams of youths and adults alike seem to embody a mounting impatience with the laborious processes of civilized life and a restless eagerness to embrace violent solutions. . . . Unconsciously, it must be assumed, the anonymous oppression by our impersonal and mechanized ways has piled up a bitterness that seeks fantasy outlets in the flood of fictional violence which is now being gulped in such a variety of forms.[24]

Superman is a 'necessary angel,' superior to time and space, requiring neither education nor experience and possessed of natural flawless intelligence. But fallen angels may become devils and the comics are full of such cases. As Milton Caniff, creator of Steve Canyon, once remarked: 'Whatever it is that makes popular art effective – escape, or the appeal to basic emotions, or 'audience-identification' – the funnies have it, and they have more of it than any of us ever suspected.'[25]

In World War II chaplains were said to be alarmed that GI's had more faith in Superman than Jesus Christ. The year after Superman, in 1939, came Batman, followed by Captain America, Captain Marvel and Wonder Woman; in 1965, Magicman appeared, clothed in a black leotard, the uniform of sexual violence and mephistophelean body-sheathing.

The funnies gave access to the word and image history of Americans in training for world power, maintaining that 'evil' is a formulated, conquerable enemy unable to resist American magic. But this iconographic mythology proved as impotent against local Depression problems in the 1930s as it was to be against Asians in the 1960s. The interior myth maintains that problems can be solved without radical changes in basic assumptions and social structures. Superman and his immediate antecedents and successors appeared in dozens of daily papers, miles of comic books, endless movies and radio shows – it was the heyday of radio, as Roosevelt well understood. They also helped to sell consumer goods, the consumption of food with myths being particularly effective in cults of power, as the Christians have long known. Superman is a fantasy of power, Matthew Arnold's 'best self' become super-self, and the epitome of the liberal secret dream in which strength is privately and violently employed for social purpose without changing the social structure. At the end of the 1930s, when World War II came and his instruments of orgasmic explosion between in-fighting authoritarian groups became the general global norm, Superman did not immediately join the army. But in 1940 he did destroy the West Wall and an article in *Das Schwarz Korps* branded him – of all fates for the Super-American – a Jew.[26] Thereafter, television reduced much of his original power by making him visibly an actor. Camera tricks made him ridiculous, and 'camp' recognitions reduced his credibility.

Similar insights can be retrieved, of course, from Blondie, Mandrake, The Spirit, Dogpatch and the rest. As a guide to popular presentations of the over-all culture they can be correlated with the best-seller lists of the 1930s.[27] The directions are obvious. The annual leading best-seller between 1931 and 1938 was either an Ellery Queen detective thriller or an Erle Stanley Gardner. The close runners-up were equally sinister or trashy: Pearl Buck's *The Good Earth* in 1931; Hervey Allen's *Anthony Adverse* and James Hilton's *Lost Horizon* (1933); Dale Carnegie's *How to Win Friends and Influence People* and Margaret Mitchell's *Gone With the Wind* (1936); Marco Page's *Fast Company* – a 'mystery' – in 1938. The exceptions were *The Best of Damon Runyon* in 1938 and *The Grapes of Wrath* in 1939. Steinbeck's work sold well because, as Robert Warshow says, it 'had all the surface characteristics of serious literature and it made all the 'advanced' assumptions.'[28] But it is fundamentally confused, does not examine its social assumptions, approves of capitalist paternalism, and places at its centre a form of Emersonian transcendental self-reliance which, in the context of the Depression, is both pathetic and dangerous.

The best-seller is a sociological event, controlled partly by the book trade's need to instigate a structure of flourishing and dying (thereby ensuring consumer competitiveness), partly by critics writing advertizing copy for the trade, partly by public libraries selecting from lists, criticisms, advertisements and demand, and partly by day-to-day changes in society. What this list of best-sellers does show clearly is that any author who cooks up new ways to murder becomes rich, while any author who described the act of sex and love could be jailed. Henry Miller was ostracized while power-mad detectives ravaged the land. Speculating on this phenomenon, Edmund Wilson concluded that the 1930s were 'ridden with an all-pervasive feeling of guilt and by a fear of impending disaster which it seemed hopeless to try to avert because it never seemed conclusively possible to pin down the responsibility.'[29] Spengler's destiny—programming abetted the helplessness. Nobody was guiltless, nobody was safe. The murderer is a villain but is caught by 'an Infallible Power, the supercilious and omniscient detective, who knows exactly where to fix the guilt.' Responsibility is not fixed in the structure of social controls that influence personal psychology, but in a villain, a person unlike you or me or the detective. Such pure fantasy exerts great power, and it is no wonder that T.S. Eliot was, on his own admission, a detective–novel addict.

Analysis of magazine fiction in the 1930s reveals a characteristic also to be found in the funnies – that is, both their fulfilment and instigation of popular requirements. 'Americans' meant English-speaking Wasps, who formed 90.8 per cent of characters and 80 per cent of the characters offered for approval and who generally have far more positive roles and values, and much more money. As one study concludes, 'the world belongs to them, and they run it.' Characteristically, 'their goals were more frequently pleasant and idealistic and "pure"' – 'pure' meaning not calculating and mundane. The rest of the characters vary only in degree of subservience and villainy. Negroes are lazy and/or ignorant, Jews sly, the Irish violent and superstitious, the Italians criminal, and so on. Problems of ethnic groups are 'never exposed to serious and direct presentation. . . . Minority representatives are consistently deprived within an atmosphere which acknowledges no basis for such deprivation.'[30] Stereotypes dominate; the message is the permanence of racism and the class structure. The fears of white workers and the white middle classes are dramatized as endless strip fantasy.

V

There is probably even less radical diagnosis in the commercial cinema. The situation is accurately portrayed through the intersections of finance, faith in the morally educative value of films, personal idealism and the star system in Fitzgerald's *The Last Tycoon* (1941). Hollywood is the index of images that Americans were afforded of their own lives in the Depression. Repeatedly, the plots turn on a belief in personal opportunity within a society where mobility tends naturally upward, challenged by a catastrophe not admitted as a possibility in textbook historiography. The myth of opportunity, a sustaining vision for millions of Americans, was once and for all intersected by opportunism, the Spencerian principle of survival that had for decades supplied the standard alibi for crude evolutionary economics: namely, that 'us fellas' governed by divine right of Nature. The most muck-raking rhetoric of Hollywood movies, ostensibly presented in documentary fashion, falsified social issues. Pare Lorentz' *The Plow That Broke The Plains* (1936) concerns the long-term and radical misuse of the Great Plains that led to the Dust Bowl of the mid-1930s (and is complementary to Walter Prescott Webb's *The Great Plains*, published five years earlier in 1931). But it was made by the Resettlement Administration, a New Deal agency. The free verse commentary, the fine poetic images, the compassion and the grand scale cohere to the point where it is clear why government intervention was necessary; but that free enterprise at various levels was responsible for the neglect and ruin, and that the system of America was itself exploitative and immoral in its anti-ecological wastefulness of life, are issues barely even broached. The New Deal was, after all, an emergency measure.

Frank Capra is nearer the centre of conservatism. *Mr Deeds Goes To Town* (released in 1936, the same year as Lorentz' film) dramatizes the liberal belief that personal integrity and class dialogue can succeed. Gary Cooper plays a man of simple-hearted innocence, who has little intellectual skill beyond arithmetic; a man close to the common people. He gives his wealth away to the unemployed which his wealth had created because he suddenly discovers the immortality of business. After the beloved parable, the system remains and 'us fellas' win again. Capra consistently employed Cooper and James Stewart in fake reformist roles of this kind. The equivalent in the field of musicals was Mervyn Le Roy's *Gold Diggers of 1933*. The action here is ostensibly reformist: four girls looking for work, a producer for money, and a playboy songwriter for outlets in which to invest money and talent. Money wins and the decor demonstrates glamorous opportunism, while the words try to suggest the energy wasted. Busby Berkeley's dance-routine designs parallel Earl Hines's dehumanized brilliance, using large abstract patterns of light and shade with human bodies and costumes as the instruments of mechanized lavishness. The world of *Public Enemy*, directed by William Wellman in 1931, endured. Wellman offers the rise and fall of a gangster guided by inevitable fate, associating virility with the saloon and poolroom existence of James Cagney, a life of loot without labour whose enemy is not the law and its agents but other gangsters. The direction's emphasis on anxiety and excitement, whatever the script's other aims, frequently produced romantic audience reactions.[31] Gangsters enacted the whole society's possessive individualism, and at least lived it up before the final slaughter. 'The shame of the cities' remained untouched. Intimations of the epic in Wellman were grotesquely extended in Cecil B. DeMille's reprograming of American history as an epic of fists and finance, with the box-office attraction of 'sensational sinning' slotted into self-righteous moral conclusions.[32]

One of Hollywood's central mythical figures in the 1930s is Spencer Tracy. Featured in twenty-five films between 1931 and 1935, his image is the calculated creation of a man of force and integrity who dramatizes tensions between physical power, limited intelligence, personal honour and social-political position. If the plot called for dubious or criminal behaviour, redemption shaped the denouement, however broken the Tracy character had to be. His stoicism, in various forms, became the characteristic stance of a man in a depressed, non-revolutionary society, and the basis of his stardom. Tracy was Hollywood's counterpart of the stoically-enduring Hemingway hero and the very embodiment of Roosevelt's first inaugural address: 'This great nation will endure as it has endured, will revive and will prosper.'

But Hemingway's endurance ended in *nada* and Roosevelt's endurance is not much more than Faulkner's advice to Negroes; endure. The common centre is impotence. The boy heroes of Odets' *Awake and Sing!* (1935) and Kingsley's *Dead End* (1935), like the boys in Tracey's *Captains Courageous* (1937) and *Boy's Town* (1938), are products of capitalist paternalism who are cruelly expected to make out in a merely pseudo-reformist social structure. In 1936 the stage version of Erskine Caldwell's *Tobacco Road* (later filmed by John Ford) began its decade-long, successful run, reducing the original statement on poverty to the myth the middle class could tolerate: that the rural poor were grotesque hicks, sexually bestial and comically drunk. Similarly, the characters of Capra's *You Can't Take It With You* (1936) are quirky individualists fighting for life in a system careless of their well-being. Anarchistic self-reliance, the great curse of the American Dream, programmed self-respect, hoggish selfishness and unemployment into a stoicism nearer to self-abuse. Dashiell Hammett's Sam Spade and the Thin Man stoically opposed crime where city law and its agencies had broken down; as Duke Mantee in *The Petrified Forest* (1936), Humphrey Bogart began to shape his image of the hipster prior to Mailer's formulation of the White Negro in 1957: the wary survival of the cynic without ideology, the desire to resist impotence in the face of degrading and recalcitrant conditions, the acceptance of some measure of outlawry if cunning and chivalry were not to corrupt absolutely or become the smugly self-righteous figure John Wayne stereotyped from *Stagecoach* (1939) onwards. Meanwhile, Hollywood existed as it was exposed in Kenneth Anger's *Hollywood Babylon* (1965): a scene of sensual corruption and cruel tyranny masquerading as moralism and the world of the 'fanzines.' The truth lies with the lynch-mob hysteria of Fritz

Lang's *Fury* (1936) and the Los Angeles riot that concludes West's *The Day of the Locust* (1939).

VI

The crux for the majority of the middle class is given by an anonymous writer in 1932: 'the ordinary peaceful citizen is in no danger to speak of – . . . he is rarely thrown into contact with the criminals, and when he is, his life is in no grave peril. They use their weapons chiefly upon each other.'[33] But, of course, he was indebted to criminals for beer, cocktails, and whisky. The ambiguous anxieties of the urban middle class are the sphere of James Thurber's fictions and cartoons. His fairy tales may manipulate solutions from good wizards, but his probes into domestic life reveal a despair within law-abiding family life no magic could dissolve. Happiness recedes before the threat of economic disaster and sexual ill-health, stoically endured, while the margins of the *New Yorker*, where so much of Thurber's work appeared, advertised escalating by expensive fantasies. But as the conclusion to one of his moral tales proclaims: 'There is no safety in numbers or in anything else.' The narrator of *A Box to Hide In* endures: 'I still have this overpowering urge to hide in a box. Maybe it will go away, maybe I'll be all right. Maybe it will get worse. It's hard to say.' The hero of *The Private Life of Mr Bidwell* is last seen 'walking along a country road with the halting, uncertain gait of a blind man: he was trying to see how many steps he could take without opening his eyes.' The protagonist of *The Remarkable Case of Mr Bruhl* gradually identifies totally with a gangster he resembles physically and is gunned down by 'silent men, wearing overcoats, and carrying what appeared to be cases for musical instruments.'[34] Lying in his hospital bed he snarls his replies to the police commissioner like any gangster; he knows his role from inside. Thurber's heroes repeatedly separate themselves from their routine life in a desperation that is neither social protest nor social adjustment.

In 'What Are the Leftists Saying?' and 'Something to Say' Thurber exposed the middle class bohemianism of the 1930s leftists, without ever understanding their profound irresponsibility towards the working class. He retained his popularity while

Edward Dahlberg, a far more complex writer and a major stylist, has never had a sizeable following – partly, at least, because his satirical targets include both bourgeois behaviour and Leftist ideological games, which are treated with a vehemence beyond Thurber's faintly comic posing. *Those Who Perish* (1934) nails the well-heeled and their carelessness for ever: their use of public events as subjects for fashionable competitive conversation; Hitler and the Nazi Youth Movement reduced to a game of Freudian analysis; Mrs Cortlandt Dinwiddie – 'related to the Astors and Bismarck' – using Jack London and his wife and World War 1 as part of her autobiography, tentatively called *I Have Only Myself to Blame*.[35] As Rexroth reports, Bohemianism was a way of evading the political in New York circles: 'People talked about communism in those days the way people talk about acid or smack . . . they didn't know anything about it. . . . People were running around talking about "the masses" and there wasn't really any contact with the masses.'[36] On the west coast, the IWW and an anarchistic tradition dominated the intellectual and Bohemian world and to some extent relieved it from that outrageous tedium of the pseudo-ideological that Dahlberg delineates in *The Flea of Sodom* (1951), his dramatized recollections of the irresponsible Left in the 1930s and the stultifying desire to live mythically that reduced so many to the grotesque. The central character, Golem, only *reads* about the hunger of West Virginia coal miners. Andromache places his sculpture of a lynched Negro share-cropper 'upon a shelf above their nuptial couch,' and dresses the part of a protest marcher in May-day parades to play out her leftist alibis:

> Everybody was living mythically and wanted to escape boiling Etna cement . . . A free-thinker, advocating contraceptives, was banished from the island by the water-front faction that was proselytizing an Irish-Catholic longshoreman. This was denied because he was already in the party; besides he had a triptych in his cellar apartment at Red Hook, the middle panel being Karl Marx, with the Virgin Mary on one side and Shirley Temple on the other.

Dahlberg's proletarian poet, Ephraim Bedlam, writes an appallingly 'Aeschylean coal miner's tragedy' and recites a poem

132

beginning: 'O pellagra, company towns, diptheria creeks, and burial funds!' Pilate Agenda is expelled from the party: 'The mother of the Passaic Falls trade union movement, and the grandmother of American communism had made a sex-complaint against him. The rank and file at once denounced him as a petty bourgeois harlot and an enemy of the people.' But although Dahlberg's satire of those who live by mythic ideology is exhilarating, his position, like that of Miller and Frost in different ways, gave no immediate direct aid to those trapped inside the shattered edifice of American capitalism.

The clearest example of a work that actually leaped out of the area of catastrophe and carried American myths with it into a euphoric future was Hart Crane's poem-sequence *The Bridge*, published in 1930. Written to counter Eliot's reactionary pessimism (a major impulse during its six-year composition) and subsidized by a friendly capitalist, the poem celebrates the mystic possibilities of American capitalism. It is an epic of Manifest Destiny, expansion, and evolutionary perfectibility.[37] Crane refuses the pastoral aristocratism of the writers in *I'll Take My Stand* and takes up 'the psychological impact of mechanization' as anything but the disaster the medievalists and agrarians believed it to be.[38] In a letter to his backer, Otto Kahn, Crane referred to his images of Brooklyn Bridge, the New York subway and the airplane as 'the encroachment of machinery on humanity, a kind of purgatory.' But machine technology is finally to be a Promethian agent ushering in an expansive and optimistic American future. The curve of the bridge is the soaring upward and outward curve of recovery, not the site of personal and national suicide.

Prophetic ecstasy of this kind, however magnificently composed, could hardly extend beyond the lyric present. The New York of Dos Passos' fictional epic *USA*, written between 1930 and 1936, is an environment of deteriorating conditions. His trilogy traces a dehumanization of city life from 1900 to the execution of Sacco and Vanzetti in 1927 and the Depression. He is the major novelist of alienation in the 1930s, and, at least at that time, took a stance that was non-ideological and secular. Malcolm Cowley recalls him shouting over to a table full of writers planning *New Masses*: 'Intellectual workers of the world

133

unite, you have nothing to lose but your brains.'[39] With capitalism on trial, Dos Passos at least articulated the economic, personal and political intersections whose catastrophic centre was 'us fellas' – J.P. Morgan, in particular. His theme is the waste and sacrifice of life that private wealth and *laissez-faire* policies necessarily imply. His characters are stereotypes with little warmth, a collective people – the readership of the funnies, the audience for *Marie Antoinette* – who demonstrate how human lives can be socially determined. Even his radicals have stony lives (though, in the case of Eugene Debs, Haywood, and John Reed, this was not true of their actual experience). His insistence on psychic numbness in 'a beaten nation' is best taken as another expression of Spenglerian cultural pessimism.[40] One major theme of the huge plot of *USA* is the survival of the fittest – the public-relations man, the arch-parasite in the soldier-worker-consumer society of coercion. Dos Passos' action is deeply related, therefore, to the dissolution of the family and community in the 1930s, since, as Christopher Lasch points out, 'the disappearance of the community destroyed that [family] authority,' and not the other way round, as it is so often reported to be.[41]

One of the most endearing aspects of the 1930s, however, is the responsibility at least some artists felt for their function in society, conceiving 'the very act of creation as one of affirmation of the value of human life' and relentlessly pursuing American experience and the truth about themselves.[42] The essential search for a mutuality without ideological rigidity, for a structure of life firmly founded in particularities of person and place, is to be found in William Carlos Williams' novel trilogy, the first volume of which, *White Horse*, appeared in 1937. The working- and middle-class lives recorded by Williams correct the mythological simplifications of the Andy Hardy film series perpetrated by W.S. 'Woody' Van Dyke II (*Andy Hardy Gets Spring Fever* dates from 1939). But in Boston, the School Committee and the Chamber of Commerce were judges in a letter competition on 'Why the Hardys should live in Boston,' and the Hardys themselves were the product of research into family norms of behaviour and consumption.[43] These whites were quite as stereotypical as Ralph Ellison's blacks and quite as manipulated. In 1923 Williams had written how 'the pure products of America go crazy.' Later he said: 'That's the trouble with us all. We're not half used up. And that unused portion drives us crazy.' Living as closed, partial and myth-driven stereotype mythicizes a man into a grotesque part of a dogmatic system. He is then by definition a mad inmate of the institution of society. Hollywood's Andy Hardy series deliberately imposed myth. Illusion infected the decade.

Actual events reduced mythicization considerably – whether through fighting in the war in Spain or by taking part in the veterans' Bonus Army, massing in Washington in 1932 to demand what Congress had promised only to be dubbed criminal Communists and dispersed with tanks, machine guns, tear-gas and bayonets by a grateful nation, led on by 'us fellas.'[44] Causes in the 1930s were repeatedly raised to the intensity of mythical appeals only to degenerate into grounds for victimization within the international power game of Left and Right. Louis Zukovsky's 'Mantis' (1934) focused the operation: 'Our world will not stand it, / the implication of a too regular form,' especially a form which does not include 'the most pertinent subject of our day – the poor.' 'The facts are not a symbol' and 'No human being wishes to become . . . An insect for the sake of a symbol.' Consequently, as Muriel Rukeyser expressed it in *A Turning Wind* (1939), for the committed writer in the 1930s each creative act seemed a 'moment of proof – that climax when the brain acknowledges the world; /all values extended into the blood awake.' From the memoirs of 1930s writers that began to appear in the 1960s there arises a heady combination of nostalgia for the euphorias of the 'moment of proof' and a sense of waste in depression. Living symbolically or mythically had its compensations, even if it was finally sacrificial. Looking back to the 1930s writers, Seymour Krim, himself an essentially 1950s man, recognizes with awe their ability to dramatize the country's myths personally. Sociology and psychology were only just beginning to encroach on the function of fiction, and films to make a panoramic diagnosis of men's lives.[45] In their sacrificial bitterness, the 1930s had a sense of scale and futurity that became impossible in the era of what Jeff Nuttall calls Bomb Culture. The full irony of the 1930s comes through in Daniel

Aaron's summary of his own study of the decade: 'During and after the war years, the thirties came to be looked upon by many men and women who had lived through them as a time of 'smelly orthodoxies' when the intellectuals took refuge in closed systems of belief. . . . With the Cold War and the crusade of Senator McCarthy, the books and issues of the thirties were considered dangerous as well as dated.'[46]

In 1934, Lewis Corey's *The Decline of American Capitalism* stated the realities: capitalism is forced against progress, the bourgeois revolution, the dream of improvement in the conditions of the masses – a set of ideals unobtainable without a new social order. But the old socialist dream of a proletariat that has 'broken the ideological fetters of the old order' and 'replaced the old faith with its own consciousness and ideals' was finally eroded by the conditions of the New Deal itself.[47]

By the 1940s, the liberal attitudes of the previous decade, generated by the shame of both capitalist and leftist catastrophes, shifted into a conservatism born under the pressures of international cold war politics. What Julien Benda in 1927 termed '*le trahison des clercs*' – their 'desire to abase the values of knowledge before the values of action' – had become a steady chronology of toadying to ideology and the security of power: Fascism in the 1920s, Stalinism and Fascism in the 1930s, Washington, the CIA and associated organizations in the 1950s and 1960s.[48] The tensions of intellectuals register equally with those of the less articulate in American society. On 1 November 1971, Americans were once again scared by a production of H.G. Wells' *The War of the Worlds*, as they had been in 1938. In fact, the Buffalo radio station put out a modified version of Orson Welles' 1938 performance (recently reissued as a gramophone record), warning citizens that the realism was only art: 'Radio stations in cities as far away as Boston, Washington and New York received enquiries from listeners asking why they had not reported the landings.'[49] As William Burroughs, the major writer of the 1960s who lived his boyhood through the 1930s, says of his work: 'None of the characters in my mythology are free. If they were free they would not still be in the mythological system, that is, the cycle of reconditioned action.'[50] To counter the fashionable mythicization of the 1930s that took place during the 1960s, we have only to recognize the institutionalized civil warfare in the United States and the increased number of outlaws and their necessity:

> the simple
> fact is, this isn/t the
> thirties anymore, either.
> the outlaws are different.
> there came a point in the
> empire when henry morgan
> stopped being pirate and
> was made the governor
> of jamaica, but you were
> born thirty years early.[51]

1972

6

Out of Sight but Never Out of Mind: Fears of Invasion in American Culture

From the founding of the American Republic in 1776 to the present day the American people have been exceptionally prone to invasion fears: of entry into the body politic and economic and into the body-mind system by forces which might impose change, as well as fears of internal disruption which might subvert the national obedience consensus. Since the British left in 1814, the national boundaries have been invaded militarily only once: by Pancho Villa and forces from the Mexican Revolution, who burned Columbus, New Mexico, in 1916.[1] (On the site of the bivouac area from which the first wholly mechanized expeditionary force launched an American drive into Mexico, there is now a Pancho Villa state park.) The fear of invasion is therefore both neurotic, shifting into the pathological, and dangerous – and it is so to an ever-increasing degree. A mixture of the religious and the political, it is the basis of American foreign policy and deep-seated: a massive interlocking of cults, sects and surveillance systems.

To separate out some of the fears by way of introduction, six over-simplified categories can be identified:

1. Fears that human beings are not the only intelligent beings in what Henry Adams called 'the multiverse'.

2. Fears of some form of underground or overground, invisible or semi-visible. These versions of the manichean vision in which the world is a battlefield of good and evil forces describe a main location for racial fears and anxieties relating to genetic engineering, secret societies, and so forth.

3. Fear of insurrection or invasion from within – by blacks, Indians, the Left, student dissenters, private armies, and so on. In the current emphasis on manic survivalism, this fear includes armageddon and the city masses invading wilderness and mountain.

4. Fears of the Mafia which have, under the guise of necessary permissions given to the FBI, CIA and other government forces, masked fears of threats to community and individual freedom.

5. Fear of invasion from without, from Russia, Cuba, UFOs, cosmic rays, communists and the rest.

6. Ambivalent fear of total surveillance by God, or some god-like authority or demonic ruler, or even of the interlocking surveillance construct maintained by the FBI, CIA, military intelligence, police and the Internal Revenue, a complex that would include the Mormon filing system, closed circuit television in public places, bugging and so on. Here the complexity of the issues becomes clear since, for many people, total surveillance fulfills a dream of freedom as security through domination, rather than a release from a totality of authority.

The American psyche is an extreme expression of a condition endemic in societies which need to believe themselves terminal and invincible, and which are therefore prone to perpetual anxiety. As the sciences continue to disclose an infinity of life possibilities, so the agencies of political economy and weaponry made possible by those sciences need to possess *the* clue, *the* key, *the* central energy, *the* wonder particle of power, *the* unhindered means of manipulation and penetration of mind and body. This condition becomes the pattern of justifications for hierarchical Control – for example, for the Army's investigations into the effects of LSD on human subjects. The explorations of science fiction and speculative psychology notoriously become political and socio-economic reality, and the required leader becomes the dream agent and executor of these powers, a figure of desire and necessity.

But underground and subversive energy also has to be used as a regenerative source. The parasite is needed to disrupt the paradigm and to place it in an outward-going continuity of social and scientific forces. New energies must prevent stagnation into too early an entropy. Tensions form, therefore, between fear of rigidity and fear of fluidity, the extremes of which constitute chaos lurching towards destruction. The Puritans' need for the Devil as energizing Enemy is still present in the writings of Norman Mailer.[2] In fact, hangovers from Christian demonology still raddle American nerves. Americans queued for miles to shiver through *The Exorcist* (William Friedkin, 1973), and television continues to show the progress of the Devil's agent from child to ambassador to Great Britain in the *Omen* series of films (1976–81). In 1976, Brian de Palma's *Carrie* offered the case of a religious maniac's daughter whose paranormal puberty experiences persisted beyond the grave. In 1974, Americans could buy a 'Resist Satan Special' personal protection kit, sold for four dollars and ninety-seven cents by C.S. Lovett's company, *Personal Christianity*. The advertisement, in heavy red and black type, was headed 'Has Satan Injured Your Family – Yet?'[3]

The narrative of films of invasion by gods, demons and things from outer and inner space (the latter recently exemplified by David Cronenberg's *They Came From Inside*) is long and repetitive. Don Siegel's classic *Invasion of the Body Snatchers* (1956) shows an American small town taken over by extraterrestrial pods whose energetic substances invade decent American bodies without resistance. The hosts subsequently have no feelings of their own and only make choices when they move against anyone who has not been occupied. They analogue precisely the inhabitants of the 'value-free' society parodied in Leonard C. Lewin's *Report From Iron Mountain* (1967).[4] Siegel intended an analogy for Americans without 'cultural aspirations.'[5] Miles, the last resister, becomes a twentieth-century Young Goodman Brown, fleeing from town and standing alone at night shouting at cars on the highway to stop and help. But alien organization wins. Siegel also admitted an analogy with the activities of Senator McCarthy in the 1950s, just as Arthur Miller's *The Crucible* (1953) injected seventeenth century Salem witchcraft trial data into the era of the House UnAmerican Activities Committee. Within the use of historical data lies a related invasory terror: the fear of takeover, or the self being invaded and its privacy ended. Cold War politics and domestic surveillance are reinforced by information obtained from inquisition, electronic brainwashing, chemical restructuring through drugs and torture, and the steady impregnation of the fact by propaganda. In fact, Siegel's film has been interpreted as both anti-fascist and McCarthyite in its exposure of conformity. In Jack Finney's novel, Miles sets fire to the pods' field; some escape to where they came from, and the hero is left with the belief that individuals and groups *can* resist in the spirit of Winston Churchill's 'we shall fight them on the beaches' speech, which is quoted.[6]

Although *Sleep No More . . .* was his original title, Siegel refuses cheap messages and simple allegory. He said that the film showed 'how a very ordinary state of mind could start out in a very quiet small town and spread to a whole country . . . the aim of fascism is that people under its rule should be like that . . . like vegetables.' (In 1972, former CIA agent Seymour Hersh reported that Alfred McCoy's findings on the American politics of heroin in Southeast Asia – which documented American complicity and worse in its production and distribution – were '90 per cent informed.')[7] W.D. Richter's script for the 1979 remake of Siegel's film shifts the location to San Francisco, more of a centre of American strength since the 1960s in Richter's opinion.[8] But, as in the *Omen* series, the invasion has already taken place – in high places. One character rejects the idea of appealing for help to the FBI because 'they're all pods anyway.' No laughter in the cinemas of America at this point. In 1964, John Frankenheimer's film of Richard Condon's *The Manchurian Candidate* proposed a top-rank political conspiracy to take over America; in his *Black Sunday* (1977), Palestinian urban guerillas attack the sacred Superbowl during America's major sports finale. By 1984, John Milius' *Red Dawn* has Russian-backed Cubans turning outdoor movie theatres into POW camps.

Films of underground forces in the United States now have an established iconography and order of conventions.[9] Horror films concentrate on vestigial life in the earth, lakes and the sea, or discover mutations resulting from freak conditions or scientific carelessness (for example, Ivan T. Sanderson's

Invisible Residents (1973) and David Cronenberg's *The Fly* (1987)), as well as from unknown centres in the galaxy.[10] Rimbaud's 'I is an other' now lies within the power of 'decades of patterns of visual imagery, of recurrent objects and figures in dynamic relationship.'[11] The huge domain of science fiction, fantasy and horror manifests popular imagination through both archetypal and historically current dreams and myths, exploring the space of earth, the heavens and the self as part of the practical investigation of earth, galaxy and the psychosomatic body. Conquest, control and resistance are dramatized as both following and creating radical changes in internal and external environments modified by technology and political needs. The results, in films and prose, contain a spectrum of imaginative skill and trite rehash, responsibility and irresponsibility. The monster can be the scientist or the inquisitorial police chief or the vestige or the mutant – or equally 'the man within,' whom William Burroughs satirizes in his *Naked Lunch* tetralogy (1959–1964), or the straight man in another version of civilization, as in Franklin J. Schaffner's *The Planet of the Apes* (1968).[12]

The original film of Frankenstein and his creation was made in 1910 by the Edison Company. The instrument of the contemporary hubristic scientist-as-monster is the invisible laser beam (*The Andromeda Strain* (Robert Wise, 1971)) or some semi-visible bacteria (*The Omega Man* (Boris Segal, 1971)). Such works articulate something of the public sense that both government and private corporation secretly investigate and create long before public demonstration. Richard Fleischer's *Fantastic Voyage* (1966) had miniaturized scientists injected into the body of a fellow scientist, a dream which radically extends the design of Hawthorne's scientist in 'The Birth Mark' (1843). As Stan Brakhage wrote in 1972, movies began with magic mysteries of conjuring and moved into the magic cave of cinema transformations.[13] When Bruno Anthony enters the Tunnel of Love after Miriam and her two lovers in Hitchcock's *Strangers on a Train* (1951) the boat is named Pluto. Greeks mysteriously descended into Hades or the Eleusian caves, and the underground has persisted with such ambiguities. As Parker Tyler observes, the police police the underground because it is the region of energies which will later become visible in society.[14]

Underground cinema challenges both sexual taboos and those technical sophistications which pose as criteria of value in art, science and religion. In 'Suburban Monastery Death Poem,' the Cleveland poet D.A. Levy – himself hounded to death by the police – sees the local connective history:

> UNDERGROUND MOVIES!
> Grade D movies on witchcraft & only three
> known covens in the country
> most of the Ohio covens supposed
> to be in Cincinatti
> TAKE THE MOVIES THERE[15]

In the 1960s an American underground movement and its press continued the European practice of subversion from below. It was soon recognized as a coven of energies whose directives helped the nation through the official disgraces of the decade – civil war and Southeast Asian war.[16] With some ancestry in socialist and populist journals at the turn of the century and in the Thirties, the alternative press spread to every major American city.[17] The underground's outlaw sense – a limitation as much as a scope – generated cultural patterns which modified clothing, styles of hair and food, musical populism, and ways of getting high or low. It also served as a laboratory to test not only social organization and style but also printing layout, journalistic methods and language, and definitions of what 'news' could be. But undergrounds function within existing structures – until they become revolutionary organizations invading the power structure, and that did not happen in the United States. Karl Fleming, a founder of the Los Angeles weekly *LA*, put it sharply: 'I think the idea of contamination by advertizing is absolute bullshit.' Or, in the words of Andrew Kopkind, founder of the muckraking magazine *Mayday* in 1968: 'Luckies outsell grass.'[18] But even the *Washington Post*, a paper with some recent investigative reputation, was excoriated as an example of 'the yellow press' when it began publication in 1877 (thirty pages for three cents).[19] Just how far muckraking substituted for revolutionary invasion is documented in Bruce Franklin's *From the Movement Towards Revolution* (1971), *Bamn* (edited by Peter Stansill and David Mairowitz in 1971), and scores of other less

143

distinguished studies investigating the latest events in the history of American nonconformity.[20] These works were published in parallel with enquiries into the official underground controls and organizations of the White House, the Pentagon, the CIA, the FBI, the Kennedy Assassination Committee and the rest.

Following the decline of the Movement and the loss of the Southeast Asia wars, America enjoyed first one public enquiry – Watergate – and then another in the same tradition – Irangate. As Kurt Vonnegut might say: so it goes. The wider context is described in the opening sentences of Peter Clecak's *Radical Paradoxes: Dilemmas of the American Left, 1945–1970* (1973):

> Americans, in the main, do not cultivate what Nietzsche called 'the sixth sense,' the sense of history. We create history for others to study, and we re-create the past to strengthen optimistic myths about the present and the future. Recently, in a national atmosphere of pessimism, many people have come to suspect that history is being made behind their backs. Yet beneath these divergent colorations of mood lies the implicit assumption that we *ought* to fashion our own personal and social destinies, if necessary, against stubborn outside forces.[21]

One of the values of Douglas T. Miller's *The Birth of Modern America, 1820–1850* (1971) lies in its analysis of technological transformations in agrarian America during the brief period of rapid transition to industrialization in the early nineteenth century, and of their consequent effects on beliefs and attitudes (John R. Stilgoe gives 1845 as the date when previous landscape constructs in the United States started to erode[22]): 'As American society changed, social cohesion was threatened. Industry, immigration, and expansion were creating a pluralistic society; yet many persons clung to a single-track vision of what the country should be. That the unfamiliar alarmed Americans is evidenced by the bitter attacks against such groups as Catholics, Masons, or Mormons.'[23]

To the latter must be added attacks on Indians and 'Asiatics' and specific laws discriminating against them, such as the California Supreme Court's 1854 ruling denying Chinese people the right to testify against whites. Chief Justice Hugh Murray argued that state law already prevented blacks, mulattoes and Indians from testifying as witnesses 'in any action or proceeding in which a white person is a party.' (Columbus had given the name 'Indians' to the North American natives, believing he was in Asia. Recent ethnology has disclosed the truth in his mistake.) Asians could not, therefore, testify against whites, even if they were an increasingly necessary cheap labour force for white capitalists.[24] In fact, industrial development augmented anxieties about increased distinctions between inherited wealth and recent wealth, and the control of labour.[25] But manifestations of such anxieties were shaped within religious and mythical traditions. Gustavus Meyers' *History of Bigotry in the United States* (1943; revised by Christman in 1960) begins with Puritan anti-Quaker repression and concludes with the Lindbergh case in 1935; Henry Christman's revision includes McCarthyism and the events that foreshadowed major struggles in the 1960s: the Montgomery bus boycott and the resistance to integration of the schools by Governor Faubus at Little Rock, Arkansas.[26] So to the terms *underground, invasion* and *subversion* has to be added *bigotry* and its historical origins in Christian settlement and the capitalist usages of labour.

The American frontier caused fear as much as exhilaration, contraction as much as expansion. The Turner dateline of 1890 is virtually meaningless since the frontier extended across the Pacific into Asia, then around the globe, and thereafter into the air and, ultimately, space. Walt Whitman, Hart Crane, and John F. Kennedy were all explicit on this fact. The related politics of conspirational fears and paranoia have been considered recently by at least two American historians. David Brion Davis' *The Fear of Conspiracy* (1971) is subtitled 'Images of un-American subversion from the Revolution to the Present,' and it includes among its massive documentation Richard Hofstadter's essay 'The Paranoid Style in American Politics,' delivered as a lecture at Oxford University in 1963.[27] The frontier these men consider is an interface between the internal space of the embattled self and the external space of terrestrial and celestial territory, the Zone of survival. Through such elements, the conflicts recorded by Douglas Miller can be pursued into the twentieth century, and at least some way into the psychopathic bases of political and religious action. The sense of invisible forces, whether underground, in the sky, within ourselves, in other races than our own, or in possible systems of Control other than the local, impregnates many accounts of experience. Davis documents 'a long succession of dark conspirational powers,' 'each subversive force . . . posing an unprecedented danger.' This 'perceived reality,' 'an intersection of private and collective fantasies,' has as one of its manifestations Hofstadter's 'paranoid style.' The issue is a proper recognition of both actual controls and the invention of control explanations for what may be suspected but hidden, in particular the belief that the human soul is a manichean battlefield for good and evil energies.

But since men made God and Devil in their own image, the 'underground' – in the form of night, blacks, the proletariat or various forms of international threat – is mobile within a hefty constellation of internal needs and external actions. As Davis puts it: 'Collective beliefs in conspiracy have usually embodied or given expression to genuine social conflict.' But his evidence also shows that if you believe in a manichean universe you will also be prone to paranoia. The 'imperial self' distrusts hierarchy *and* collective action.[28] General Midwinter, with his oil fleet, global computer, and diabolization of the Soviet Union in Ken Russell's *Billion Dollar Brain* (1967), is an example of American everyday belief. He only happens to be a Texan. Jack D. Ripper's belief that his 'precious bodily fluids' are being drained by enemy forces in Stanley Kubrick's *Dr. Strangelove* (1964) exemplifies in its black humour the paranoid fears that make up the murky foundation of politics. Beneath the dominant belief controls of Social Darwinism teem violent fantasies of invasion by hydra-headed aliens.

But extreme radical action can become coutinized action: Davis cites as an instance the abolitionist view of the Slave Power conspiracy of 1840 and the mid-twentieth century issue of Black Power. American colonists found seventeenth and eighteenth century Catholic Europe a conspiracy against liberty. By 1890 the villainous Jesuits were less feared than the atheists of the French Revolution and Illuminism. And by the mid-twentieth century Notre Dame had become a team, as had the Salem Witches. But vestigial fears remained. Once the United States began to advertise itself in the 1790s as the last modern society – terminal and Christian, at once radical and reactionary, a democracy determined to inherit empire – designs appeared to subvert it (Jesuits, Jews, Illuminists, Communists, and so on) and pundits appeared who would 'save the nation.'[29] Davis concludes that 'Americans have long been disposed to *search* for subversive enemies and to construct terrifying dangers from fragmentary and highly circumstantial evidence.'[30] Roger Daniels' *Concentration Camp USA* documents the consequences for the US Japanese community during World War II.[31]

By the 1950s, the realities of Soviet power and internal tyranny had been turned into 'international communism,' invented as a permission to curtail any system other than American-style capitalist democracy and as a warrant for vast budgeting on behalf of military-industrial interests. All protest against successive administrations became 'communist or communist-inspired,' and the FBI and CIA became autonomous (but publicly financed) agencies of intervention on behalf of anything that was defined as being in 'American interests.' An actual or supposed threat to America became a threat to law, order and various brands of Christianity and Judaism. Such transformations have a long history. Davis cites the Jeffersonian Abraham Bishop's tirade against the Hamiltonian 'power elite' in 1802, entitled *Proofs of a Conspiracy Against Christianity, and the Government of the United States*. In fact it was not only the 'depravity . . . noticeable in the Jews' that maddened Bishop but Hamilton's funding system, which he described as 'the radical cause of our evils, the political fall, which subjected us to the loss of an American Eden.'[32]

Such is Hofstadter's 'paranoid style,' defined as an 'enhanced feeling for the non-rational side of politics,' a belief in some 'single center' to be 'eliminated by some . . . final act of victory.' His examples range from a 1798 sermon to a 1951 McCarthy oration. But he does not understand that his material is more than a rhetoric of argument or style adopted by some 'perfect model of malice, a kind of amoral superman: sinister, ubiquitous, powerful, cruel, sensual, luxury-loving . . . a free, active, demonic agent.'[33] That figure is part of the history of what Eric Bentley called 'heroic vitalism' and of the nature of the sexuality of power. It is far more than a representation of eighteenth century reason and transcendental romanticism applied to political ambition or any overwhelming desire to be 'Control'.[34]

Hofstadter cites the assumed threat of the Bavarian Illuminati, founded, appropriately, in 1776 by Adam Weishaupt, professor of law at Ingolstadt University, and part of the anti-clerical rationalism of the period. The movement aimed at converting the human race to reason, and managed to convince a number of German rulers and, it is said, Herder, Goethe, and Pestalozzi.[35] That the movement drew highly ambivalent responses in New York and Philadelphia had more to do with current fascinations with the sources of power than Hofstadter cares to mention. One way of entering this part of the field – and in order to place it in context for later use – is through the writings of James Frazer. In *Totemism and Exogamy* (1910) he invents a classic statement on the conflict between law and instincts (a word which Freud – who drew on Frazer's book for *Totem and Taboo* – also used as a basis for his theories of repression): 'Civilized men have come to the conclusion that the satisfaction of these natural instincts is detrimental to the general interests of society.' For Frazer, sex ceremonies are 'indescribable,' 'obscene,' or 'secret' immoral practices. Sexuality equals savagery, and is to be curtailed. The villains are Moors, Turks, Saxons and Danes. Civilization thinly covers 'superstition' and is perpetually threatened by the underground: barbarians, savages, the body, the unconscious, the proletariat. In 'The Scope of Social Anthropology' (1908) he produces a single fantasy location for his fears, which is also a useful summary of some of the panics that lay behind invasion psychosis: 'The ground beneath our feet is thus, as it were, honeycombed by unseen forces. We appear to be standing on a volcano which may at any moment break out in smoke and fire to spread ruin and devastation among the gardens and palaces of ancient culture wrought so laboriously by the hands of many generations.'[36]

It is this kind of model that Brecht takes on in his 1935 poem 'Fragen eines lesenden Arbeiters' ('Questions from a Worker who Reads'):

Where, the evening that the Wall of China was finished

Did the masons go? Great Rome
Is full of triumphal arches. Who erected them? Over whom
Did the Caesars triumph? Had Byzantium, much praised in song
Only palaces for its inhabitants? Even in fabled Atlantis
The night the ocean engulfed it
The drowning still bawled for their slaves . . .[37]

But underground is a source for labour as well as change, and the need for a perpetual cheap labour force of immigrants and slaves was underpinned by theories of natural power held underground in the form of human energy. It is also a source of irrational as well as rational rebellion, and therefore an ambiguous agency against stasis. As Wilhelm Reich demonstrated so clearly, fascism appealed to 'the irrational, mystical and emotionally infantile elements in people . . . to reinforce their need to cling to the authority-figures who promised a "new life." '[38] Fascism promises the protection of purity at the basic level of 'blood.' For the fascist, the bad and the subversive are impure, dark and dirty, and are associated with the diabolic threats of disease and sexuality. Blacks and Jews become embodiments of the night side of life, the corruption of light, candour, and whatever the patriarchal and paternal, in its oedipal legacy, insists is permanent and good.

Chief Justice Hugh Murray of San Francisco could easily put such fantasies into legislation directed against Chinese immigrants. His 1854 ruling emphasized that 'American Indians and the Mongolian, or Asiatic, were regarded as the same type of the human species,' a common 'degraded' non-white type against whom whites had to be legally 'protected.'[39] Of course, Christians provided metaphysical bases for such corruption. In 1878 a San Francisco Baptist Minister, the Reverend Isaac Kalloch, began his Fourth of July celebration prayer: 'We pray that our rules may be righteous; that our people may be peaceable; that capital may respect the rights of labor, and that labor may honor capital; that the Chinese must go . . .'[40] The following year he became mayor. Whites in post-Gold Rush California faced limited job opportunities and looked for scapegoats. Capital could draw on a large cheap Chinese labour force, which workers took to be the tool of monopoly. Since capital could not be fundamentally attacked, the Chinese were

149

vulnerable. 'The Chinese must go,' slogan of the California Workingman's Party, rather than 'Big Business must go' entered federal law. The California constitution was re-written in 1879 to include the following: 'No native, no idiot, no insane person, or person convicted of any infamous crime . . . shall ever exercise the priviledges of any elector of this State.'

Article XIX prohibited the employment of 'any Chinese or Mongolian' in any public works below the federal level or by any corporation operating under state laws. Popular will overruled the US Constitution, and violence was again justified One female workers' organizer exploded: 'I want to see every Chinaman – white or yellow – thrown out of this state.'[41] The Chinese Exclusion Act of 1882, based on national consensus, toadied to capital by excluding labourers but not students or merchants. During the discussions leading to the Act, the official representative of San Francisco delivered the classic Christian capitalist view, complete with alibis from the Old Testament:

> The Divine Wisdom has said that He would divide this country and the world as a heritage of five great families: that to the Blacks He would give Africa; to the Red man he would give America; and Asia He would give to the Yellow races. He inspired us with the determination, not only to have prepared our own inheritance, but to have stolen from the Red Man, America; and it is now settled that the Saxon, American or European groups or families, the White Race, is to have the inheritance of Europe and America and that the Yellow races are to be confined to what the Almighty originally gave them; and as they are not a favored people, they are not to be permitted to steal from us what we have robbed the American savage of . . .[42]

One of the most popular American fantasy writers, H. P. Lovecraft, expressed the psychotic interior of such beliefs in a 1924 letter about his visit to New York's Chinatown:

> The organic things – Italio-Semitico-Mongoloid – inhabiting that awful cesspool could not by any stretch of the imagination be call'd human. They were monstrous and nebulous adumbrations of the pithecanthropoid and amoebal; vaguely moulded from

some stinking viscous slime of earth's corruption, and slithering and oozing in and on the filthy streets or in and out of windows and doorways in a fashion suggestive of nothing but infesting worms or deep-sea unamiabilities.[43]

New York provided him with further low-life thrills in 1925. The garment district yielded 'puffy rat-faced vermin hurling taunts when one does not buy and airing spleen in dialects so mercifully broken that white men can't understand them.' In his lodgings on Clinton Street he fantasized 'a *Syrian*' in the next room whose 'eldritch and whining monotones on a strange bagpipe . . . made me dream ghoulish and indescribable things of crypts under Bagdad and limitless corridors of Eblis beneath the moon-cursed ruins of Istakhar. I never *saw* this man . . . In truth, I never saw with actual sight the majority of my fellow-lodgers. I only *heard* them loathsomely – and sometimes glimpsed faces of sinister decadence in the hall.' But to Lovecraft Fritz Lang's silent film *Siegfried*, complete with Wagnerian accompaniment, 'was an ecstasy and a delight . . . the very inmost soul of the immortal and unconquerable blond Nordic . . .' He concluded that 'the stinking mongrel vermin of this chaotic metropolitan mess' resulted from 'the admission of limitless hordes of the ignorant, superstitious, and biologically inferior scum of Southern Europe and Western Asia.'[44]

As support for his belief in a two-tiered world, Lovecraft read and used Houston Chamberlain's *Grundzüge des Neunzehnten Jahrhunderts* (1899), translated into English and published in London in 1911 as *The Foundation of the Nineteenth Century*. Chamberlain wrote: 'I venerate the principle of aristocracy'; 'orientals must be kept in their native East till the fall of the white race. Sooner or later a great Japanese war will take place, during which I think the virtual destruction of Japan will have been effected in the interests of European safety. The more numerous Chinese are a menace of the still more distant future. They will probably be the exterminators of Caucasian civilization, for their numbers are amazing.'[45] The observations of Charles Manson in the 1960s and scores of science fictions, together with the sermons of preachers and the orations of politicians, re-verberate with such beliefs. Jack London has his peculiar version of Yeats's 'rought beast slouching towards Bethlehem' in his *Revolution and Other Essays* (1910): 'The menace to the Western world lies, not in the little brown man, but in the four hundred millions of yellow men should the little brown man undertake their management.'[46]

Both Lovecraft and London were and remain bestselling authors, highly sensitive to those popular fears of invasion and penetration which give life to the myths of survival and aggression in America and the West. America's penetrations into the Pacific and Japan since the early nineteenth century, through the Pacific War and thence into Southeast Asia, required myths of permission from ideologies of superiority.[47] As late as 1986, Louis Malle's film *Alamo Bay* shows the 'Nam Vets of Texas' still in need of the permissive vocabulary of 'gooks,' 'blacks,' 'Chinese,' 'Communists' and 'Catholics' to articulate enmity against Viet Nam war refugees in the Gulf. The KKK leader involved actually enlarges the target to 'the Third World.'

Lovecraft's fear of a permanent volcanic underground is the basis of his 'The Shadow Out of Time' (1936).[48] Where Frazer dubbed Australian aboriginals 'the savage in his very lowest depths,' Lovecraft takes up the cause, setting one of his stories in Western Australia, where the fate of Nathaniel Wingate Peaselee, professor of political economy at Miskatonic University, Arkham, is opened and closed. Lovecraft projects fears of the underground in history and in the psyche through 'the fabulous invaders,' whose eternal minds penetrate back and forth in time, displacing all other minds. The knowledge of this Great Race is stored in vast museum cities, the *polis* structured as a colossal retrieval system for power. These themes re-emerge in Arthur C. Clarke's *Childhood's End* (1953) and the equally popular novel by Kurt Vonnegut, *Slaughterhouse 5* (1969). Performing as benevolent dictators from outer space, Clarke's 'Overlords' are indifferent to forms of government and ideology established on Earth and carry out ruthless remedial action against the human race. Their Earthly form is the traditional horn-and-tail devil of Christian myth. American children are manipulated into support and transported elsewhere in the universe. Vonnegut's Tralfamadorians are space beings who embody fatalistic determinism.

During tests for flying saucer fuels, the universe will be blown up: 'the moment is structured that way,' Billy Pilgrim is informed by his Tralfamadorian guide. Lovecraft's Great Race has an intelligence 'enormously greater than man's' that only just kept in control an earlier race, 'half polypous, utterly alien entities' from space who sporadically erupt and who have consequently permeated the Great Race with 'a permanent fear of vengeance.' Through his experience of 'the abyss,' Professor Peaselee becomes 'the captive mind of those shambling horrors.' These themes have surfaced again in many novels of race or group power, not least in Frank Herbert's *Dune* (1965), which according to Charles Platt had by 1980 become 'the most talked-about book among anthropologists.'[49] But Herbert believes his plot turns, exceptionally, on a counter-cult, counter-overlord slogan: 'beware of heroes.'

In 1975 Illuminism emerged again in the United States in the form of volume one of Robert Shea and Robert Anton Wilson's *Illuminatus!* series, which will be considered later in this essay.[50] The fascination with this intellectual control organization began as we have seen in the 1790s in New York. Charles Brockden Brown was possessed by forms of invasion, most immediately the annual epidemic of yellow fever that struck New York and Philadelphia during the 1790s. At the time when Jedediah Morse was carrying out his crusade against the Illuminati, the great American language lexicographer, Noah Webster, wrote to William Dunlap's intellectual circle in New York – of which Brown was a member – for critical comments on *A Brief History of Epidemic Diseases*.[51] The results became sources for Brown's novels: the threat of epidemic in *Arthur Mervyn* (1799–1800) and the threat of international secret organization in *Wieland* (1798) and *Ormond* (1799). As a member of the Illuminati, Ormond is part of an international organization dedicated to the destruction of religion, government, marriage and family life. He has exceptional powers of disguise, reasoning and logic, which give him access to private thoughts and beliefs. His true purposes are masked to inflect his control towards the unknown and the infinite. Both Ormond and Ludloe, a similar character in *Wieland*, are subordinate only to an invisible Empire whose

153

object is the salvation of the world, an empire which as such is the competitor of the United States' remaining idealism.

In his diary for 14 September 1798, William Dunlap wrote: 'Read C. B. Brown's beginning for the life of Carwin; as far as he has gone, he has done well; he has taken up the schemes of the Illuminati.' Carwin is the ventriloquist instrument of the organization who traces down Wieland, a Pennsylvania aristocrat with German religious origins, to destroy him and his family. Brown's fascination with the material is clear from discussions of the Illuminati in the *Monthly Magazine* and the *American Review*, both of which he edited.[52] In the 'Jessica' fragment, later incorporated into *Jane Talbot* (1801), Henry Colden's dissenting radicalism is that of an ex-criminal who is now devoted to openness and the truth where once he had been enthralled by the Illuminati: the criminal, artist and radical figure which will be central to American literature. Adini, in a manuscript fragment, is another member, dedicated to establishing a utopia in South America, who refers to 'Socratic-land' and South Sea island communities that look forward to Melville's mid-nineteenth century preoccupations. Like Hollingsworth in Hawthorne's *The Blithedale Romance* (1852) and Frazier, the master-manager of 'cultural engineering' in B. F. Skinner's *Walden II* (1948), both of whom are obsessed with redesigning human beings through the application of superior intelligence, Brown's figures are generally concerned with rational reform. His *Arthur Mervyn* exposes a pattern of duplicity emanating from Thomas Welbeck, forger, murderer, seducer and a man of sophisticated intelligence and diabolic skills, during the Philadelphia yellow fever epidemic of 1793. The plot forms around the revelation of a concealed pattern, the discovery of how things really are, and the testing of humanitarian values against cynicism, and is the kind of plot that will have a long future in American fiction, both in the detective intelligences of Poe, Twain, and twentieth century masters Hammett, Chandler and Ross Macdonald, and in the large-scale, densely-informed structures of Pynchon, Gaddis, and others.

Brown's *Edgar Huntley* (1799) is a detective structure located in a region of concealed dangers (ravines, waterfalls, cougars in caves, Indian raiders) and night fears (tensed nerves, exaggerated response to small sounds). As in *Wieland*, key events have multiple explanations that include the possibility of supernatural power, an 'unconscious necessity' located in the hero's psyche. In 1799 Brown is already tracing paranoia to the inner spaces of human life: 'Most men are haunted by some species of terror or antipathy, which they are for the most part able to trace to some incident which befell them in their early years.'

In fact, Huntley's sleepwalking is Brown's example of how a man may enter the world of invisible forces, and how, through his unawareness, they may enter him. *Memoirs of Stephen Calvert* (1800) shows Brown's late belief in firm leadership within a plot of subterfuge and disclosure. In a structure which Poe will later use, a system of invasion and detection reveals local and universal patterns challenging confident rationality below accepted surfaces. Visiting a Shaker village at Lebanon, New Hampshire, Brown found himself absorbed by what he called their 'strange reasonings and whimsical quotations, but delivered with the utmost confidence.'[53] In 1803, during a period when America was still experiencing threats of intrusion – if not downright invasion – by European powers, he published an anonymous ninety-two page pamphlet entitled *An Address to the Government of the United States on the Cession of Louisiana to the French, and on the Late Breach of the Treaty by the Spaniards . . .* It sold out rapidly and was reprinted – partly because it was rumoured to be by Gouverneur Morris and Aaron Burr. Brown included a fictitious translation of a French politician's memorandum to Napoleon on the development of New Orleans and the need for control of the lifelines between Canada and the Gulf, on the fostering of Negro slave revolts, and on enlisting the Indians against the whites. The aim was the conquest of North America. Brown declared: 'We have a *right* to the possession,' and therefore must expel all foreigners:

To introduce a foreign nation, all on fire to extend their own power; fresh from pernicious conquests, equipped with all the engines of war and violence; measuring their own success by the ruin of their neighbors; eager to divert into channels of their own the trade and revenue which have hitherto been ours; raising an insuperable mound to our future progress; spreading among us with fatal diligence the seeds of faction and rebellion: . . . what more terrible evil can befall us? What more fatal wound to the future population, happiness, and concord of this new world?

This piece of Federalist propaganda, staged as a revelation of hostile designs against the new republic, was reprinted in the New York *Evening Post* to warn against 'the magnificent and alarming projects of a towering, ambitious foreigner.' The Jeffersonian *Aurora* of Philadelphia denounced it as a war-mongering forgery. But Brown attacked again in 1803, this time against the negotiations with Napoleon for New Orleans. His fifty-seven page pamphlet, entitled *Monroe's Embassy*, advocated war as the right method of requisition: 'Why cast millions into the coffers of strangers' when 'Fate has manifestly decreed that America must belong to the English name and race.'

The Elector of Bavaria ordered an enquiry into the Illuminati in 1787; the order was dissolved, and Wieshaupt banished. Members proceeded to France. But by this time official America was in no mood for revolutionaries (as, for instance, the treatment of Tom Paine indicates). The presence of powerful intellects and organizations continued to haunt the culture. Henry James's obsession with hidden forces generated some of his most powerful fiction. From his boyhood vision in the Louvre's Gallerie Apollon, described in *A Small Boy and Others* (1913), to his 1914 letters to Henry Adams and Howard Sturgis, that personal experience is available to us: a bottomless 'abyss,' 'the full recognition of its unmitigated blackness,' 'a huge horror of blackness . . . this abyss of blood and darkness,' and the sense of a hidden meaning within 'the treacherous years' – these are his terms for the onset of World War I, and his diagnosis reaches no further. James's sense of forces behind the visible, continually prepared to invade the visible and present, controls his vision.[54] Lincoln's assassination he considered an element of a hidden pattern of events, 'part of the lift and the swell.'[55] The Civil War seemed to him, in 1879, part of America's awakening to a consciousness 'of the world's being a more complicated place than it had hitherto seemed . . . that this is a world in which everything happens.' The Louvre experience, which he described as a 'dream-adventure,' produced an 'awful agent, creature or presence' in pursuit – on whom the small boy turns the tables since, as James so many years later can recognise, it is part of himself: '*the* sensation, for splendour and terror of interest, of that juncture to me.' His 'triumph' enabled him to peer at what lay behind, to perceive a possible Swedenborgian connection, rather than to diagnose the fuller social and historical scene.[56]

He prepared for the *Princess Casamassima* (published serially in the *Atlantic Monthly* between 1885 and 1886) by walking London's darker districts, reading newspaper reports of strikes, riots and assassinations, and studying the anarchist movement. In 'The Art of Fiction' (1884) he wrote of the artist's 'power to guess the unseen from the seen, to trace the implication of things, to judge the whole piece by the pattern, the condition of feeling life in general so completely that you are well on your way to knowing any particular corner of it.' In James's anarchist novel, Hyacinth discovers that his plebian father had murdered his English aristocratic mother. He grows up resenting society, joins an anarchist group to 'destroy society,' and pledges himself to any act of violence the group may charge him with. The American princess of the title leaves her Italian husband and, out of motives of social idealism, attempts to penetrate such subversive regions. Her instrument is Hyacinth. But he experiences the leisure of her upper class life, comes into a small legacy, and decides that the anarchists are a dangerous enemy. To the princess he is a renegade, and she turns for reassurance to Hyacinth's fellow-anarchist, Paul Muniment. When his pledge to assassinate a ruling class victim falls due, Hyacinth (Narcissus) receives a pistol. He wanders through London but, caught in a tangle of self-regard and muddled social diagnosis, turns the pistol on himself. Self-assassination is placed as a function within a society whose traditional firm structure is becoming looser, and James ambivalently provides his anarchists with a secret and effective organization. James is not as closely concerned with the rebel as Dostoevsky in *The Devils* (1871–2) or Conrad in *The Secret Agent* (1907) are. But he certainly is interested in Muniment as a man of power using the dark fluidities of society to rise. The book is in this sense nearer Turgenev's *Virgin Soil* (1876), a novel deeply located in the

Bakunin anarchist movement. In his review of that book in *The Nation* in 1877, James writes of a belief 'entertained by some people that [the] revolutionary agitation' of what he calls 'certain "secret societies,"' 'forms a sufficient embarrasment at home to keep the government of the Czar from extending his conquests abroad' – even if Turgenev's secret society does appear to be ineffectual.

What Maggie experiences in Part V of *The Golden Bowl* as 'the horror of finding evil seated all at its ease, where she had only dreamed of good; the horror of the thing hideously *behind*, behind so much trusted,' haunted James and surged in what he called his 'imagination of disaster.'[57] Imagination more than investigation: his fascination with, for instance, 'the more than "shady" underworld of militant socialism' developed into 'the suggested nearness (to all our apparently ordered life) of some sinister anarchic underworld, heaving in its pain, its power and its hate . . . just perceptible presences and general looming possibilities.' In *The Princess Casamassima*, Hyacinth's world of 'subterraneous politics and occult affiliations' is part of the drama of 'guessing and suspecting and trying to ignore, what "goes on" irreconcilably, subversively, beneath the vast smug surface.' Part of the novel's purpose is to 'catch some gust of the hot breath that I had at many an hour seemed to see escape and hover.'[58] In *English Hours* (1905) he cannot see that the apparently genial relationships between the London police and 'the mighty mob,' 'the frank good sense and the frank good humour,' had all to do with why the police patrolled Hyde Park, 'the very *salon* of the slums,' where 'the unemployed lie thick on the grass and cover the benches with a brotherhood of greasy corduroys.'[59] James shared with Frazer, Matthew Arnold, and H. P. Lovecraft a sense of underground energy in what he described (in his essay 'London' in *The Century Magazine* (1888)) as 'the murky modern Babylon.' In fact, he half expected the imminent overthrow of the British upper class.[60] He may well have met the great anarchist political writer Kropotkin, who settled in London in 1886, and at that time certainly equated 'militant democracy' with such 'radicalism.'

But he is quite as ambivalent as his older contemporary, the Republican Congressman from Minnesota, Ignatius Donnelly.

The prefatory section of the latter's *Caesar's Column* (1891) speaks of 'the many . . . plundered to enrich the few' and of 'vast combinations [which] depress the price of labor and increase the cost of the necessaries of existence.'[61] Donnelly's subtitle is 'A Story of the Twentieth Century,' but beneath the electric and glass-covered city lie the familiar American 'subterranean streets, where vast trains are drawn by smokeless and noiseless electric motors,' and an 'Under-World' of the poor and their leaders. The International Brotherhood of Destruction relies on 'the multitude [to be] like the soldiers of an army; they will obey when the time comes; but they are not taken into the councils of war' — 'the directing intelligence dwells elsewhere.' The 'domain of the poor' consists of international workers 'marching noiselessly as shades to unvoidable and everlasting misery . . . automata in the hands of some ruthless and unrelenting destiny.' (Had Fritz Lang read the novel before making *Metropolis* in 1926?) The Under-World also includes the 'criminal quarters,' the product of 'misgovernment' and 'the long ancestral line of brutality' that has become 'a new variety of the genus *homo*.' And this is where Donnelly's characteristic American fear begins: with the mutated workers, the poor and the criminals, as the source of uncontrollable energy.

The Brotherhood's arsenal of weapons, stored in abandoned Tennessee coal mines, supplies the revolt of the masses. The revolt is directed by a proletarian council and its gigantic leader, Caesar Lomellini, the exact counterpart to the directorate of the council in control of the Plutocracy above: 'Brutality above had produced brutality below. . . . High and low were alike victims – unconscious victims – of a system.' 'Unconscious' means that no one, no organization, is to blame, and Donnelly's use of natural terminology brings his plot back into Darwinian inevitabilities, where elemental forces eternally threaten invasion. When, in Chapter 33, the masses break loose, they are 'a huge flood, long dammed up, turbulent, moody, loaded with wrecks and debris, the gigantic mass . . . dark with dust and sweat, armed with the weapons of civilization, but possesing only the instincts of wild beasts.' This 'human cyclone' destroys 'civilization,' exactly in Frazer's terms, but Donnelly has not determined what civilization is, only what he excoriates as the Plutocracy. His fears are largely reserved for the mob: 'Civilization is gone, and all the devils are loose! No more courts, nor judges, nor constables, nor prisons! That which it took the world ten thousand years to create has gone in an hour.' Donnelly is reworking Puritan Christian fears and Frazer's fears of the end of the palace dwellers – but his devils have an ambivalently apocalyptic origin: the mob are 'the avengers of time – the God-sent – the righters of the world's wrongs. . . . They are omnipotent to destroy; they are powerless to create.'

Fear of mutiny penetrates nineteenth-century American writings, and especially the fictions of Herman Melville, whose Burkean opinions and rebellious lower-deck instincts plot *Billy Budd, Sailor*, a story begun in 1886 and put into fair-copy form in 1888, which is therefore contemporary with the James and Donnelly novels discussed here. Melville's attitudes towards the British naval mutinies of 1797 are suffused with his beliefs in 'Natural Depravity: a depravity according to nature' and natural authority, embodied in the State.[62] So, too, Donnelly's Brotherhood of Destruction arises both from a locally corrupt world that reduces men to 'the primal, brute instincts of the animal man' and drives them to armed revolt against both working class and racial oppression, and from the history of plutocracy from Egypt to the British Empire. Donnelly provides considerable detail concerning the structures of technology, finance and law through which oligarchy rules, but his Caesar remains a romance figure, just as Hawthorne's mutiny leader in 'My Kinsman Major Molineux' (1832) remains 'the double-faced fellow' at the head of a Miltonic rout, related to both Mars and Indian resistance. Caesar is an embodiment of the nineteenth-century American rebel enacting evolutionary theories of naturally-selected authority and leadership. Donnelly opposes 'the brute natural' to 'polished and cultured brutes.'[63]

At the conclusion of *Caesar's Column*, Gabriel Weltstein and Max Petion embark by airplane for Cythera, an African mountain. With the poison bombs falling on New York and the Commanding General of the Brotherhood erecting his column of cemented corpses, the State of Uganda, their destination, is to become the bastion of civilization against 'barbarians.'[64] Parallel to such a prospect of a liberal utopia in east Africa stands the final image of Caesar's head on a pole in the power of a bestial mob – a mask like that of Babo, still exemplary at the end of Melville's 'Benito Cereno' (1855): 'the glazed and dusty eyes; the protruding tongue; the great lower jaw hanging down in hideous fashion.' Where Babo, the enslaved Senegalese chief, continues to outstare the Spanish slaver in Melville, Donnelly's Ceasar is defeated by the subterranean. The inscription on the column commemorates 'the Death and Burial of Modern Civilization.' Donnelly has religious and Spenglerian feelings to project, a need for apocalyptic justification: Caesar's execution may be 'God's way of wiping off the blackboard,' a sort of planned Ragnarok or Decline of the West or *Götterdämmerung*. God is 'the Great Intelligence,' the God of evolution or 'the endless competitions of men in the arena of life.'[65] Like Norman Mailer and William Burroughs in the declining decades of the twentieth century, Donnelly suspects that, beyond selected 'barbarian' invaders from Earth and Space, there is 'a dark perversity . . . in the blood of the race.' In Mailer's 'The Last Night' (1962), the President of the United States arrogantly leads one hundred selected human beings to pollute another universe with the human, invading space by means of a rocket launched by exploding the Earth; in *Caesar's Column*, Max Petion's party advises Europeans amid their ruins not to seek America but to travel to 'uncivilized lands, where no men dwelt but barbarians.'[66] Uganda lies somewhere between Edward Bellamy's utopian Boston in *Looking Backward: 2000–1887* (1888) and Skinner's *Walden II*, and is a return to the hope-generating garden of the American West, 'a garden of peace and beauty.'[67] Its theory prefigures the Spenglerian reliance on some mystical 'fellahin' as a perpetual source of rejuvenation for human existence and civilization in Jack Kerouac's *On the Road* (1957) and Gary Snyder's *Earth House Hold* (1969).

In *The Iron Heel* (1907), Jack London's evolutionary garden of disaster and leadership is transferred from his Klondyke wolves in *The Call of the Wild* (1903) to a future oligarchic Chicago. He imagines a fascist dictatorship within an extreme capitalist state, liquidating the middle class and overthrowing organized labour. London's blond Nietzschean hero, Ernest Everard, is a socialist revolutionary defeated by the Iron Heel, and an Over-Man who challenges the Christian brotherhood as a substitute for working class solidarity. The underworld poor of London's 1903 book, *The People of the Abyss*, and of James's *English Hours* reappear as the Chicago mob, and, like Donnelly and Lovecraft, London wishes to penetrate the social history to reveal primitive impulses in the interior. The Californian establishment under threat become 'cave-men, in evening dress, snarling and snapping over a bone.' 'The lords of society' are Darwinian victors manipulating the workers as 'phrase slaves'; 'the pack' who hold 'the lordship of the world' become 'growling savages in evening clothes.' Where Donnelly's spokesmen stress Cunning over Muscle and Intellect, so London observes: 'Not God, not Mammon, but Power. Pour it over your tongue till it tingles with it.' The society of the Iron Heel is a divisive dystopia of oligarchs, secret service men, mercenary armies, counter-revolutionaries, and ghettoes of labour slaves who provide energy for productivity before they fall back into the semi-bestiality of the Abyss – an organized chaos only too familiar in the dreams and ordinances of the extreme Right and Left in the twentieth century and in the fictions of Joseph Heller and Thomas Pynchon that will follow. In Heller's *Catch 22* (1961), Yossarian will try to drop out of 'a world boiling in chaos in which everything was in its proper order.' Pynchon's *Gravity's Rainbow* (1973) will be built from propositions of irreversible entropy: 'the persistence of structures favouring death,' the 'paranoid structure' of a mega-cartel, reality as a barely visible system of signatures and interlocking meanings, 'the stone determinacy of everything,' 'the Listening Enemy,' and Von Göll's re-enactment of Ormond and Ludloe: 'I can take down your fences and labyrinth walls, I can lead you back to the Garden you hardly remember. . . . Elite and preterite, we move through a cosmic design of darkness and light, and in all humility, I am one of the very few who can comprehend it *in toto*.' Tchitcherine's belief within that totality – 'But survival with creative dignity? – Forget it!' – is a characteristic twentienth century response to the locked paranoia on which Pynchon's plot is maintained.

By 1940, London's totalitarian vision had become commonplace reality. His trained elite 'looked upon themselves as wild-animal trainers, rulers of beasts.' His ambivalent system resembles Brown's secret international order's dream of what Lewin parodied: the value-free state, freed from reward and punishment laws and motivated by 'love of the right' – except that it is no longer secret: 'The great driving force of the oligarchs is the belief that they are doing right. Never mind the oppression and injustice in which the Iron Heel was conceived. All is granted.' It is exactly the state of mind of the FBI man in Tom Robbins' *Another Roadside Attraction* (1971): authority is always right, and therefore justified. His basis is: 'Ever since we crawled out of caves, retribution has followed wrongdoing as night the day. . . . You can't possibly question authority. . . . Who are you to question it . . . the authorities of this nation saved it as a free and decent place for you to live in.'[68] Therefore, 'all is granted.' The tribal regroupings that follow chaos in London's novel have, for the mid-twentieth century, appropriate historical alibi-names: The Wrath of God, the Bleeding Hearts, the Morning Stars, the Comanches. (They resemble only too closely the names of rock groups in volume three of *Illuminatus!*: the Wrathful Visions, Key to the Scriptures, the Crew of the Flying Saucer, the Druids of Stonehenge, Civilization and its Discontents, the Slaves of Satan, the Second Law of Thermodynamics, Armageddon, the Call of the Wild, Mere Noise, and so forth).[69]

In London's unfinished novel, *The Assassination Bureau*, the undergound is a self-righteous oligarchy employing not only the style later to be identified with 1920s gangsterdom, the mafia, Murder Inc., the CIA and paramilitary private armies and police forces, but also the depthless sense of multiple conspiracy later exemplified by the belief in an underground plot to kill President Kennedy.[70] Ivan Dragomiloff, chief executive of the organization, states its principles: 'Operating as we do outside the law, anything less than the strictest honesty would be fatal to us.' Slow reform towards socialism has to be displaced by murder. These forerunners of the official and extra-official international terrorists of the 1980s call themselves executioners and operate within a secret order: 'We have to be right with one another, with our patrons, with everybody and everything. . . .

We have the sanction of right in all that we do. . . . We have our own code of right, and our own law. . . . The organization is as near perfect as the mind of man can make it . . . from emperor and king down to the humblest peasant – we accept them all, if – and it is a big *if* – if their execution is decided to be socially justifiable.' To any consideration that this is an 'ethical monstrosity,' the reply is that society can no longer manage itself (it is the reply of every vigilante individual and group, and of their novels and films, in American history). Winter Hall puts the case against such outlaw action, much as Washington Irving offered the case of Ichabod Crane's ultimate victory over Brom Van Brunt and the legend of the headless Hessian horseman in 'The Legend of Sleepy Hollow' (1820): 'The time had come in the evolution of society when society, as a whole, must work out its own salvation. The time was past, he contended, for the man on horseback . . . to manage the destinies of society.'

But finally both Hall and Dragomiloff agree that 'social expediency' is the determining measure; the chief executive even agrees that the murders may have been individually right but socially wrong, and they certainly include major bullies and exploiters of society and individuals. In his last letter to Hall and his daughter Grunya, Dragomiloff admits that 'in essence we *were* wrong. The world must come to recognize the joint responsibility for justice; it can no longer remain the aim of a select – and self-selected – few.' But he still maintains that 'no man died whose death did not benefit mankind.' Those executed were 'removed . . . from the social organism on the same principle that surgeons remove cancers.' Dragomiloff decides to leave the 'web' which his 'master mind' has created, the 'perfect machine': 'Never has it failed to destroy the man appointed. I am now the man appointed. The question is: *is it greater than I, its creator?* Will it destroy its creator, or will its creator outwit it?

To Hall the executioners are 'ethical lunatics,' but, such is the madness of those who desire to belong to theocracy and its political and religious variants, he becomes their Temporary Secretary in order to execute the master mind. London probes the nature of political morality: '[These were] learned lunatics who had made a fetish of ethics and who took the lives of fellow humans with the same coolness and directness of purpose with which they solved problems in mathematics, made translations of hieroglyphics, or carried through chemical analyses in the test-tubes of their laboratories.' Sacrifice is the essense of religion and politics and of the sciences that inaugurate or sustain them. Such expressions of 'practical sociology' in the hands of 'high priests at the altar of right conduct,' of fearless 'philosopher assassins,' loveless in their 'mental processes,' are the very types of paranoid fear of invasion by any alternative, especially by love and mutuality. The executioners believe themselves terminal, and must terminate the rest: 'All they knew was love of thought.' Such 'slavery to thought' is the analogue of all self-righteous power organizaitons. But for Dragomiloff the members are 'right-rulers and king-thinkers', . . . the touch and the promise of God-head come true!' London finally matured beyond the responses that had resulted from reading those crucial books he took in his bed-roll to the Klondyke in 1897 (at the age of twenty-one): *The Origin of the Species by Means of Natural Selection, or The Preservation of Favoured Races in the Struggle for Life*, Haeckel's *Riddle of the Universe*, and *Paradise Lost*. As William Burroughs condenses the issues in 'The Four Horsemen of the Apocalypse': Most of the trouble on this planet is caused by people who must be *right* . . .'[71]

One of the Assassination Bureau's main instruments is 'the voice of Nakatodaka.' The voice, which 'enunciates the final word,' is, in late twentieth century terminology, an explosive device that is irrevocable once set in operation – the predecessor of the crazed dreams and achievements of political physics and chemistry parodied in Stanley Kubrick's *Dr. Strangelove; or How I Learned to Stop Worrying and Love the Bomb* (1963). London defines madness and logic within governmental systems by asking whether it is ever sane 'to allow those to live whose course of action leads to the taking of innocent lives.' In the notes London used in completing the book, Dragomiloff is wrecked in the Marquesas Islands and takes poison in the valley of the Typees, where Melville's Tommo experienced the enslaving benevolence of an enclosed, self-righteous, and possibly cannibalistic culture. Escape through violence was his only solution.

The web of overground power and the underground sources of energy to be tapped are parts of a system which extends into space and back into time. The space is both external and internal, psychological and celestial, compounded of endless exchanges between fact and illusion. Organizations become entropic through their mania for control and fear of invasion; they authorize counter-invasion. The underground is a source of fearful alternatives to their paranoia, but it is also – for example, in the Greek Cave of Trophonius or the *kiva* of the Taos Pueblo Indians – a place of descent in pursuit of necessary fertilizing energy, either for the hero or for any member of a society. The Eleusian Mysteries and their counter-parts in other cultures had their social necessity in the social benefit derived from them. Charles Manson's belief in the Hopi 'hole' was a perversion of the Native American custom. In his epic of connections and simulacra, *The Recognitions* (1955), William Gaddis writes of another 'Indian' rite: 'Their death pursuing its descent, the Piute Indians followed the sun to that hole where it crawled in at the end of the earth, creeping constricted to earth's center, there to sleep out the night, and to waken and creep on to the eastern portal. The sun emerges, eating the stars its children as it rises, its only nourishment; and those on earth at the dawn see only its brilliant belly, distended with stars.'[72] The Hopi version of such origins of continuity refers to an underground world from which the nation will emerge to dwell on the earth's surface. In 1968 Charles Manson, manic leader of one more in the long history of utopian and dystopian bands within the United States, found a hole in the desert where he and his 'family' could wait out armageddon in paradise: the Devil's Hole. Manson relied on myths of a city-sized cave under Death Valley National Monument and on key passages in *Revelations*, including the bottomless pit in chapter nine.[73]

No mysteries of race or the barbarian below haunted the Underground Railway which functioned in the nineteenth century as an escape route into Canada for black slaves fleeing what Mrs. Beecher Stowe in *Uncle Tom's Cabin* (1852) called that 'one great market for bodies and souls' and its 'Christian

Legislature.'[74] A century later, the underground movement of
the 1960s and its press and music helped many young
Americans gain insights into alternative ways of living and into
their country's strong history of nonconformism and civil rights.
In fact, it is necessary to evaluate the Movement, from 'beat' to
'hippie' and 'yippie' and the Chicago Seven, as a rejuvenation of
health in American culture, in detailed contradiction to those
journalists, reactionary evangelists and academics who emphasized
the hard drugs rather than expanded consciousness, and
'commie' subversion rather than the major protests against the
inhumanities of official national policy between 1950 and 1970.

Those decades also saw the re-publication of the writings of
an extraordinary outsider who challenged all righteous lunacies:
Charles Fort. Following efforts by Theodore Dreiser, who had
been attracted to the book's epic scope, Fort's *The Book of the
Damned* was published in 1919.[75] Through Dreiser, Buckminster
Fuller came to know Fort's work and, after the publication of his
own *Nine Chains to the Moon* in 1938, was invited by Tiffany
Thayer to join the Fortean Society. Fuller speaks of Fort as a
man who 'tried to show the irreversible evoluting scenario of the
universe and [to] suggest that the next installment is always a
surprise, the grand theme eternally elusive.' Fort became the
arch-enemy of certainty and completion, those weapons of over-
lord rule, of Burroughs' 'people who must be right,' while at the
same time acknowledging (as does Fuller) the overall completeness of Nature and Law. When the Fortean Society was formed
in 1931 its members included Dreiser and Ben Hecht, who had
written an important review of *The Book of the Damned* in the
literary section of the Chicago *Daily News* (then edited by Henry
Blackman Sell).[76] Hecht spoke of Fort's 'onslaught upon the
accumulated lunacy of fifty centuries.' Fort wrote to the *Daily
News* about his book's monism or 'the oneness of allness': 'We
and all other appearances of phantasms in a superdream are
expressions of one cosmic flow or graduation between [two
classifications]; one called disorder, unreality, inequilibrium,
ugliness, discord, inconsistency; the other called order, realness,
equilibrium, beauty, harmony, justice, truth . . .' Near the
beginning of *The Book of the Damned* he writes: 'I conceive of one

167

inter-continuous nexus, which expresses itself in astronomic phenomena, and chemic, biologic, psychic, sociologic. . . . All attempted organizations and systems and consistencies, some approximating far higher than others, but all only intermediate to Order and Disorder, fail eventually because of their relations with outside forces. All are attempted completenesses.' But then Fort shifts into a familiar science–fiction assumptive mode: 'we are property,' objects of study for an alien people. His vision passes through naturalism into epic and, ultimately, the paranoias of Gaddis, Pynchon and others.

Monism is obsessed with the detection of oneness, and some of its origins lay in the detective novel itself, from Brockden Brown through Poe and into Hammett, Chandler and Macdonald. As Louis Pauwels and Jacques Bergier write in *The Morning of the Magicians*:

> Before the first manifestations of Dadaism and Surrealism, Charles Fort introduced into science what Tzara, Breton and their disciples were to introduce into art and literature: a defiant refusal to play at a game where everybody cheats, a furious insistence that there is 'something else.' A huge effort, not so much, perhaps, to grasp reality in its entirety, as to prevent reality being conceived in a falsely coherent way.[77]

(Paul Feyerabend's *Against Method* (1975), an anarchist assault on the desire for dominant theory, which can only be achieved by omitting facts, is a more recent exposition of the importance of the Dada method in science.)[78] Fort spent a lifetime collecting facts that had been omitted from schemes of completeness in order to dominate or rule. His basis was that oneness in the study of the universe does not require dominant theory – just an inventory of facts. Secrecy is unnecessary conspiracy. Secret intelligence is an instrument of power. Detectives are an analogue of these desires for penetration to origin. To the detective, everything reveals. In Poe's 'The Murders in the Rue Morgue' (1841), analytical reason is 'that moral activity that disentangles' and, like chess, 'a comprehension of *all* sources of information whose legitimate advantage may be derived. These are not only manifold but multiform, and lie frequently among recesses of thought altogether inaccessible to the ordinary understanding.' Mark Twain's *Pudd'nhead Wilson* (1894) engages in exactly Poe's 'retracing' in field analysis, and, like the Chevalier Dupin, is an aristocratic intelligence entering multiple spatial logic. In his essay 'Morals of Chess' (1779), Benjamin Franklin recommends the game as a form of training in power skills. Twain parodies detective skills in 'A Double-Barrelled Detective Story' (1902), by providing his detective with one supreme advantage: his violent birth gives him a psychic 'birthmark' – 'the gift of the blood-hound is in him!' 'a grand natural talent . . . but no intellect in it.'[79]

McLuhan recognized Poe's detective sense of spatial inventory for the discovery of some interior set of clues to completeness – the basis of Korsybski's non-Aristotelian logic, which was a process in turn learned by William Burroughs at the University of Chicago.[80] Pudd'nhead Wilson's study of hand prints reveals invisible identity – the inner truth exposed as external design. In Twain's case, hidden pattern exposes identity behind the apparent surfaces of black and white, the clues to race and racism. Tom Chambers is indeed an 'invisible man,' and raises the deep American fear which plots, for example, Robert Penn Warren's *Band of Angels* (1955): that 'black blood' may be concealed behind surface whiteness. Twain's 'destiny-analysis' is a crucial step between Poe and what Ross Macdonald in *The Underground Man* (1971) calls 'a winding symmetry in the case.'[81] Books on psychoanalysis, the underworld of crime, and detective novels enjoy a bestselling popularity by coordinating a sense of the hidden and a need for revelations, for monism. (Freud was fascinated with detective fiction). If, to use Fort's phrase, we are property, then any person who *owns* (orders, controls, dominates, has the clues) holds power. This force increases in the later twentieth century, decades of total surveillance and endless probing into manipulation and the structure of energy. The huge bulk of fiction and film on detectives, cops and spies is the bible of the age of UFOs, socio-biological determination by genetics, electronic surveillance, and what James Schlesinger, former Defence Secretary and Energy Advisor to President Carter, termed in 1975 'a nuclear

169

war environment.'[82] The detective may well be replaced by the pseudo-religious connectiveness of computerized information. In 1967, Frank J. Donner contributed 'The Case of the Private "I" ' to *The Nation*, which summarized the large amount of investigative work (including six Congressional investigations carried out between 1960 and 1967) into electronic surveillance, computerized dossiers, long-range photography, closed-circuit television, psychological testing, and other means of invading privacy 'on a vast and unprecedented scale.'[83]

Gaddis's *The Recognitions* is an organized inventory of anxieties and obsessions with detection, forgery, fake and copy throughout the history of religion and art; a fiction that dramatizes what Benjamin's 'The Work of Art in the Age of Mechanical Reproduction' is supposed to have defined in 1936. His novel is an epic recognition that, as Michel Foucault demonstrated in *The Order of Things: Archaeology of the Human Sciences* (1966), the detective hunt for origins below is a form of recessive archaeology. How far back in time and down in space is 'original' to be located? The concern is rather like Harold Bloom's anxiety about the backward abysm of influence, a useless obsession that intends to reduce imagination to detection. We recognize similarities and connections and then begin to worry about the invasion of the thing that proposes itself as 'genuine' or 'the thing itself.' Reproduction means both creation and copy; the forger is an artificer, as Joyce has it at the end of *Portrait of the Artist as a Young Man*; in Watt Gwyon's terms: 'How far back do you go, anyhow?' Gaddis plays on Nietzsche's aphorism, 'what can be thought must certainly be a fiction': 'By seeking origins, one becomes a crab. The historian looks backwards; eventually he also believes backwards.' You may make an archaeology of the palimpsest, but absolute singularity you will not find. For Gaddis, damnation is the winkling out of purity, single identity, the single source of a religion, the dream of one authority or one opponent or one god, the belief in a grip on totality or the futile *ouroboros*. It is being haunted by a universal loom of basic laws. (Umberto Eco's popular novel *The Name of the Rose* combines voyeurism for the closed religious order with private-eye detection to produce, once again, the ancient plot of the devil's mocking laugh, believed to be undermining rather than secular, necessary and intelligent. A reductive film was inevitable). In Gaddis' terms: 'To recognize, not to *establish* but to *intervene*. A remarkable illusion?'[84]

His plot is necessarily spatial and multiple and invites paranoid reading: all that linking exegesis, scholarship, criticism and connoisseurship deconstructs itself. *The Recognitions* is, in this sense, as much of a trap-plot as Pynchon's *The Crying of Lot 49* (1966). In Pynchon's second novel, Oedipa Maas inherits a dual legacy: of hidden meanings and of a need to be involved in detection, the twentieth century craze and justification. Pynchon makes her into a Lady of Shalott heroine, caught in mirror and web enclosures from which she must escape. As she gazes on it from above, she identifies the town of San Narciso as the paradigm of her existence: '. . . a hieroglyphic sense of concealed meaning, of an intent to communicate. There'd seemed no limit to what the printed circuit could have told her (if she had tried to find out).'[85] This 'religious instant' confirms her entrance into a world of imagined and actual systems. The Illuminati are now the Tristero system, an ancient, ubiquitous and self-reliant conspiracy engaged in the counter-control of communications. Oedipa's notebook entry – 'shall I project a world?' – invites a web of projections which lock all decisions into a system. As Gertrude Stein once remarked: 'The trouble with organization is it's just like perfection, the more you have the more you want.' Oedipa ends up with four symmetrically placed alternatives for her researches – either:

> a secret richness and concealed destiny of dream . . . a network by which X number of Americans are truly communicating whilst reserving their lies, recitations of routine, arid betrayals of spiritual poverty, for the official government delivery system . . . a real alternative to the exitlessness, to the absence of surprise to life, that harrows the head of everybody American you know, and you too, sweetie.

or: 'you are hallucinating'; or: 'a plot has been mounted against you . . . so labyrinthine that it must have meaning beyond just a practical joke'; or: 'you are fantasizing some such plot, in which case you are a nut, Oedipa, out of your skull.' But she wishes to be the worst addict of all, a detective prophet of revelation: 'Beyond the hieroglyphic streets there would either be a transcendental meaning, or only the earth.' Oedipa is the type who must see symbols and metaphors everywhere in what is taken to be a meaning-laden totality:

> Another mode of meaning behind the obvious, or none. Either Oedipa in the orbiting ecstasy of a true paranoia, or a real Tristero. For there either was some Tristero behind the appearance of the legacy of American, or there was just America and if there was just America then it seemed the only way she could continue, and manage to be at all relevant to it, was as an alien, unfurrowed, assumed full circle into some paranoia.

The final enclosure dramatizes a reality at last: that change and revolution cannot result from joining an entropically repetitive system, inheriting a legacy of utterly connective Control. Pynchon's theme is wasted sacrifice. Oedipa replicates, becomes a system object, a Bureau thing – becomes, in fact, typical. She is an example of Bataille's master-slave interaction:

> . . . the decisive moment in the history of the consciousness-of-self, and, one must say, to the extent we must distinguish each thing that touches us one from another – no one knows anything of himself, if he has not grasped this movement that limits and determines the successive possibilities of mankind . . .[86]

As Michele Richman adds:

> Sovereignty is located within the moment of sacrifice and sacred horror as they constitute the 'entire' movement of death . . .[87]

Bataille further identifies 'the servile consciousness' with Inca cultures: 'Everything was planned ahead in airless existence,' the culture of fear and invasiveness, the organization of the religious sense and sacrifice to mad unity.

In his *Essays on Science*, Einstein observes that the 'unified field theory' was in fact a way out of alternatives which might not fit:

The idea that there were two structures of space independent of each other, the metric-gravitational and the electromagnetic, was intolerable to the theoretical spirit. We are forced to the belief that both sorts of the field must correspond to verified structure of space.

The 'unified field theory,' which represents itself as a mathematically independent extension of the general theory of relativity, attempts to fulfil this last postulate of field theory.[88]

('Theory' seems to be derived from both *theos* – god – and *theoria* – a sight or spectacle). Pynchon's *Gravity's Rainbow* (1973) reads like a nervous collection of interlocking obsessions and parodies of Einstein's beliefs, an epic plot of the all-enclosing Spenglerian curve – that systemic device which haunts General Cummings' dream of orgasmic power and American military dominance in Norman Mailer's *The Naked and the Dead* (1948) – drawn from Herbert Stencil's meeting with a Peenemunde V-rocket engineer in Pynchon's first novel, *V.*, (1963). Pynchon's encyclopaedism produces a demonic network of inheritance, every bit as paranoid as Oedipa Maas's legacy: information, puns, acronyms and paronyms, an inventory of dazzled skills which are intended to delineate chaos. The fiction itself is entropic, a closed system within which a chance factor – Benny Profane in *V.*, and now Tyrone Slothrop in *Gravity's Rainbow* – may roam and be extinguished. For the rest: 'They must have guessed, once or twice – guessed and refused to believe – that everything, always, collectively, had been moving toward that purified shape latent in the sky, that shape of no surprise, no second chances, no return. Yet they do move forever under it, reserved for its own black-and-white bad news certainly as if it were the Rainbow and they its children. . . .'

In *Gravity's Rainbow*, God's covenant to Noah has become the human inheritance's covenant to itself: cannibalistic self-sacrifice. And to Pynchon that is inevitable. The word 'paranoia' and its derivatives appear many times in the book, indicating the limits of any vocabulary of alternatives and of naturalistic fiction, theory and practice, as well as the parameters of international rocket cartel control: '. . . *everything is connected*, everything in the Creation . . . not yet blindingly One, but at least connected.'

173

The aim of the Blicero type of Control is to fuse human and inanimate energy and forms into a blinding One, a rocket immolation for the transvestite sacrifice victim, Gottfried, swathed in secret plastic, Imipolex G, and for the human race under its apocalyptic blast. In a parody of Joyce's *Finnegan's Wake*, the novel concludes 'Now everybody . . .' But there is no funeral wake chorus for Here Comes Everybody. Rocket Man explodes. Rocket City is the end of Man. The only question left hovering in the debris dust is: how do you experience total connection except by total explosion into the atmosphere? How do you confront Blicero, the Ormond or Adam Weishaupt, or the machine of the master-mind that Dragomiloff believes in, in the twentieth century? 'The terrible politics of the grail' has come to this sacrificial waste again and again. It is 'the goat-god's city,' a response to Dionysian panic and what Pynchon calls 'images of the Uncertainty.' The would-be rebel, Byron the Bulb, has little to do, and Slothrop is left 'to thin, to scatter' his personal identity within the futile expediting of the dream of Friedrich August Kekulé von Stardonitz, which revolutionized chemistry and led to the foundation of IG Farbenindustrie in 1865:

> So that the right material may find its way to the right dreamer, everyone, everything involved must be exactly in place in the pattern. It was nice of Jung to give us the idea of an ancestral pool in which everybody shares the same dream material. But how is it we are each visited as individuals, each by exactly and only what he needs? Doesn't this imply a switching-path of some kind? A bureaucracy? Why shouldn't the IG go to séances? They ought to be quite at home with the bureaucracies of the other side.

So Kekulé dreams of 'arcs through the silence,' part of 'the solemn binary decisions' of agents whose structure is, once again, the *Ouroboros* or cosmic Serpent biting its own tail. Counterforces are not counter since they too exist within the system, a design of priorities, whose 'last phase' is America, Blicero's 'edge of the World.'[89]

The four volumes of Shea and Wilson's *Illuminatus!*, along with Wilson's *Right Where You Are Sitting Now* (1982), extend

Pynchon's fatalist encyclopaedism into huge mythical areas of the underground, drawing invisible agencies and monism to dreams of power into a parodistic inclusiveness that is both farcical and totalitarian. Wilson's note on the back of *Right Where You Are Sitting Now* – 'this book [is] a machine to disconnect the user from all maps and models whatsoever' – combines in exorcism with part of his 'Credo' chapter: 'The illumination is a discharge of compressed energy and information.' Wilson's purpose is to illuminate the meaning of total authority without entirely eliminating the need for some concept of 'god'; to confront conspiratorial invasion and the fears of a huge universe of order, parasitically using human lives, by placing massive quantities of information and interpretation at the disposal of a vulnerable reader. Weishaupt's Bavarian order of 1776 is part of this universe of interlocking and interpretative systems and controls, too extensive ever to know. Encyclopaedism cannot become knowledge, merely information. The first three volumes of Wilson's book draw materials and quotations from most of the writers mentioned in this essay – and many more – into an uneasy amalgam of beliefs and anxieties, facts and fictions. Robert Shea and Robert Anton Wilson are both exhilarated and overwhelmed by connection, and perhaps, from time to time, appalled by it. The state of demonic sensibility and the covert and manic work of politicians, the military-industrial complex, the mafia, and all such sacrificial organizations edge into a world where uncertainty tends to eliminate the distinctions between fact and fiction inside a huge mythical poetics.

The result is a system not unlike that recorded by Thomas Pynchon in his May 1966 description of black Los Angeles, 'A Journey into the Mind of Watts':

. . . that creepy world full of pre-cardiac Mustang drivers who scream insults at one another only when the windows are up; of large corporations where Niceguymanship is the standing order regardless of whose executive back one may be endeavoring to stab; of an enormous priest caste of shrinks who counsel moderation and compromise as the answer to all forms of hassle; among so much well-behaved unreality, it is next to impossible to understand how Watts may truly feel about violence. . . . Far from sickness, violence may be an attempt to communicate, or to be who you really are.[90]

Shea and Wilson operate as devils for that 'library angel' invented by Arthur Koestler as a guardian of endless, coincidental research. Their politics are not revolutionary but right-wing libertarian (Wilson is, or was, a leading member of the Immortalist movement, believers in cryogenic suspension). *Illuminatus!* probably achieved its brief popularity because it combines sceptical exuberance about systems, ideologies and hidden powers with a complete fascination for the possibilities of terrestrial-celestial communications which rivals any Renaissance theory of universal signs and connections. Shea told his *Guardian* interviewer in 1977:

> We set out to write a fairly simple espionage thriller with science fiction overtones but it didn't quite work out like that. . . . Any intelligent person who looks at it will immediately realize that it's a put on. But then there's another level beyond that where I think the fantasy blends in with the reality to the point where it's not easy to determine whether you're being put on or not. . . . Since 1972 things have happened that seem to make it more fact than we'd imagined: the discovery of the link between the Mafia and the CIA and their attempts to assassinate Castro, the revelations of the informal international organization of financiers called the Bilderbergers, who meet once a year and seem to determine the financial fate of the earth.
>
> Then there's the somewhat similar Trilateral Commission headed by David Rockefeller [whose symbol] is a triangle and the symbol of the Illuminati is an eye in a triangle. So as soon as I heard that I couldn't help but wonder if it wasn't the Illuminati at work again.[91]

Illuminatus! brings together the methods of spy and detective fictions, the documentary history of secret societies, and many techniques from science fiction. It combines belief in the implications of power in shamans, brujos, witches and psychiatrists with those of the intersecting rings of the Mafia, the Collective Unconscious, the underground, the narcotic underworld, and those studies that treat the earth as a secret and sacred ecology. It both celebrates and mocks power and powerlessness, and enjoys elaborate initiation rites. For Shea and Wilson, privacy has been dissolved in drugs and electronic controls, and the universal unconscious has become an organization of powers operating through the theory and practice of synchronicity. That much of their text is hilarious is partly a matter of recognizing so many sources which are not at all funny being exploited for sheer entertainment.

In the two centuries between the founding of both the Illuminati and the Republic of the United States in 1776, and the cult of *Illuminatus!* in 1976, we have accumulated sufficient information to understand those American responses to control and authority that are the particularities of invasion. It has to be continuously asked who stood, and who now stands, against the lineage of Ludloe and Blicero, and why they do so. What is it that Control fears in the chthonic energies of nature and human nature? The immediate political issue in 1973 was expressed by Senator Wayne L. Morse of Oregon. Americans, he said, should now awaken 'to the reality that their government is being rapidly undermined by police-state techniques and procedures. . . . Presidents have been leading us for some years towards a government of unchecked Executive will through usurpation of power not granted them by the Constitution.'[92] His examples are Eisenhower's enunciation of the military containment policy and the founding within the Nixon White House of 'a special investigation unit,' later known as the Plumbers. To quote Andrew Kopkind again: 'Those who hold steadfastly to the old values are true conservatives; those who only sense the new are worried liberals; those who see the whole pattern very clearly are radicals, and they don't know what to do about it.'

In the popular press, paranoia is treated superficially – for instance, in *Harper's Magazine* in 1974:

Paranoia is a recent cultural disorder. It follows the adoption of rationalism as the quasi-official religion of Western man and the collapse of certain communitarian bonds (the extended family, belief in God, the harmony of the spheres) which once made sense of the universe in all its parts. Paranoia substitutes a rigorous (though false) order for chaos, and at the same time dispels the sense of individual insignificance by making the paranoid the focus of all he sees going on around him – a natural response to the confusion of modern life.[93]

Burroughs is more intelligent with his paranoid defined as the man in possession of all the facts. To use Wilson's statement in *The Guardian* in 1977:

> Nowadays scientists admit they don't know everything, that there's more than one model for what's going on, at the sub-atomic or cosmological level. . . . What we've done in *Illuminatus!* is to give several versions of reality and let the reader choose for himself or herself which one is the more believable. People ask us which is the real explanation. Our answer is we don't know any better than anybody else. Everybody should think for themselves.

But while we think for ourselves, decisions are being made with far-reaching consequences over which international decision-makers themselves do not have total control.

During the 1960s, as a result of the confusions caused by fears of infiltration, it became impossible to know who was an FBI or CIA agent and who was a figure from the so-called underground, a term loosely applied to anyone protesting against the draft, the Southeast Asia wars, government financing of university involvement in weaponry experiments, or the condition of black Americans. In its May 1978 issue, *The Washington Monthly* printed a 1968 memorandum from FBI director J. Edgar Hoover on the 'Counterintelligence Program, Internal Security, Disruption of the New Left' which included instructions on infiltration of agents into protest and New left groups, and on 'the creation of impressions that certain New Left leaders were informants for the Bureau and other law enforcement agencies.' Some of these leaders, as well as chief activists in the Black Nationalist movement, were indeed later found to be law agents. Geoffrey Ripps's *The Campaign Against the Underground Press* (1981) contains considerable evidence of invasion of dissident groups in the United States during the 1960s by government and Army agents and by private business systems.[94] The Federal Privacy Act and the Freedom of

Information Act of 1974 enabled limited public access to government surveillance documents, but not to private company files. For decades Hoover had denied the existence of organized crime and its connections with big business, but he organized surveillance of Martin Luther King's bedrooms, put Allen Ginsberg on the Dangerous Subversives Internal Security list in 1965, and issued fake letters from 'the Black Panther Party' attacking Leroi Jones/Amiri Baraka.

Hoover's Bureau could, however, only be heavily financed for decades by the American people as an instrument of the panics and manicheanism this essay has slightly indicated; as an agency of, for example, those dogmatic anxieties Ezra Pound broadcast over Rome Radio during World War II; beliefs that led him to be arrested for treason and imprisoned in an open cell in Pisa, but which he held in common with millions of Americans: 'The Bolshevik anti-morale comes out of the Talmud, which is the dirtiest teaching of *that* race ever codified . . . [The civilization of North Africa] has Mediterranean origin. . . . Barbarian tribes beat against its margins; corrupters infiltrate into it, just as they had infiltrated into the United States for the past 100 or 160 years.'[95] Pound is like Lovecraft in the 1920s – 'Meet a few mongoloids or tartar communists' – but he goes further: The Kike is all out for power. 'The Kike and the unmitigated evil that has centred in London since the British Government set the Red Indians to murder the American frontier settlers, and hurled the Mongols, the Tartar openly against Germany and Poland and Finland and secretly against all that is decent in America. Against the total American heritage.'

But Dean Rusk, when Secretary of State, was only slightly calmer: 'While two-thirds of the world is sleeping, one third of the world is awake and probably up to some mischief.' Emerson might have been unpleasantly surprised at the future of his well-known belief that 'society is a conspiracy against the manhood of every one of its members.' The same paranoia affects the world today. In 1986, the assistant to the Director of the Strategic Defence Initiative proclaimed: 'We aspire to a complete defence against strategic forces for the US and all our Allies . . . [a] transition to total defence. . . . We hope to catalyze an evolution towards a more secure world.' A current American Air Force manual quotes some general claiming America's total right to 'dominate in space and on earth.'[96] Star Wars is part of a long history of American cultural belief and conduct. But – to state it again – America is an extreme case of a certain endemic condition. As Montaigne wrote some time ago, during French religious wars:

> Between ourselves, there are two things I have always observed to be in singular accord: super celestial thoughts and subterranean conduct.

1987

7

Dionysus in America

During the 1950s and the 1960s in the United States, a number of works were performed which transgressed the traditional boundaries of Western genre in the arts of music, theatre and dance. But the field of happenings, rock festivals, street theatre and intermedia events has its historical roots in American cultural aspirations. Writing on contemporary performance, Richard Schickel recalls Poe's early nineteenth century premonition: 'The next step may be the electrification of all mankind by the representation of a play that may be neither tragedy, comedy, farce, opera, pantomime, melodrama or spectacle, as we now comprehend these terms, but which may retain some portion of the idiosyncratic excellence of each, while it introduces a new class of excellence as yet unnamed because as yet undreamed of in the world.'[1]

A new society, it is assumed, introduces a new morphology of culture. America's emancipation had, sooner or later, to take cultural as well as economic and political shape. Melville anticipated an American Shakespeare on the Ohio river, but by the mid twentieth century the requirement that cultural form should challenge the European had become insistent. John Cage, Abstract Expressionism, and the rock festival finally made it as *American* art, and in each case traditional form is challenged by a boundary-crossing and ecstatic programme which immediately takes on both a social and a political implication.

How the release from limitation is both Dionysian and anarchic can be focused through a now celebrated passage in

Norman O. Brown's *Love's Body*, a work which appeared as American city culture moved towards the climax of the civil conflicts of the 1960s: 'Dionysus, the mad god, breaks down the boundaries; releases the prisoners; abolishes repression; and abolishes the *principium individuationis*, substituting for it the unity of man and the unity of man with nature. In this age of schizophrenia, with the atom, the individual self, the boundaries disintegrating, there is, for those who would save our souls, the ego-psychologists, 'the problem of identity.' But the breakdown is to be made into a breakthrough'.[2]

Brown, the classical scholar, had absorbed the implication of Freud's exposure of infantile sexuality and in his previous work, *Life Against Death*, had begun to investigate the fracturing of continuity in our vision of the human body.[3] One main instance of this breakdown is the demonic power of Dionysus as he appears in Euripedes' *The Bacchae*: a force challenging the boundaries of authority and self-possessive identity through erotic, transgressive ecstasy. When Robert Jay Lifton cites Brown's work in *Boundaries: Psychological Man in Revolution* (1970), it is to criticize what he takes to be an escalation of 'spiritual warfare with ourselves' and to emphasize the need for 'images of limit and restraint, if only to help us grasp what we are transcending.' Lifton translates Thomas Kuhn's idea of the changing paradigm of scientific revolutions as a necessary 'breakdown and re-creation of the boundaries of our existence,' without recourse to permanent walls but still maintaining 'directions and possibilities.'[4]

But the social effects of accelerated frontier-crossing have been widespread. American men escaped from the Earth's gravitational field soon after the destruction of Hiroshima and Nagasaki. The results of both events have no boundary. In fact, Lifton introduces the concept of 'Protean Man' – a figure lacking fixed shape or conceptual identity, and nearer than Lifton imagines to Brown's polymorphous erotic and creative figure – to indicate the change. Released from national-social delineation, terms such as 'character' and 'personality' gain an evolving definition. 'Self-process' or, again using Lifton's terms, 'the continuous psychic re-creation' of self as 'the person's symbol of his own organism,' takes place in 'social constellation.'

182

A man is now not restricted to a singular, nor is his culture strictly centred. He is versatile within the world, a virtuoso of the multiverse of cultures, accepting John Cage's principle of 'omniattention' without necessarily becoming 'unhinged' as he refuses the life that Marcuse calls 'one-dimensional.'[5]

Rock music is essentially an electronic synthesis of various forms of popular American music, with the addition of blues and jazz elements. The bulk of the sounds have been studio produced, or imitated from such production in live performance. The electro-visual aspects of performance – wires, microphones and speakers – gear the human body into the energy of circuitry as much as an astronaut becomes the cyborg of his capsule. One performer has developed a plasticized silver space-suit into whose front pouch he inserts his guitar, which is then immediately connected to concealed circuits, the result being no wires and no visible generation. But in the hands of a major musician the use of electronics can be genuinely creative. In his essay on 'Musical Technique' Pierre Boulez speaks of new divisions and subdivisions of sound and silence in music, to be determined by 'the invention of electro-mechanical procedures' in the performance of the interpreter, the indeterminate factor of art.[6] One outstanding inventor who became a major focus of the rock synthesis, the black American guitarist Jimi Hendrix, developed an extraordinary degree of guitar electronics, from 'Hey Joe,' his first record success, to his early death in 1970. In *The Aesthetics of Rock* (1970), Richard Meltzer describes part of the experience: 'Jump from speaker to speaker, alternate sounds and silences, you're finally conscious of all the implications of musical spatio-temporality . . . Hendrix's spatial relationship to his guitar transcends any standard finite batch of propositions. It even requires a few new sexual position-process metaphors.'[7] So that when, in one famous number, he asks *Are you experienced?* the question is multilevelled, part of what Meltzer calls rock's 'Dionysian dimension': 'Relationship = intersection in two places, at least, sometimes, or anything else'.[8]

The intersections could include electronic feedback from the circuitry which had become his performing field, partly determined and partly indeterminate. He worked in an interface between initiation and accident which transcended both; the old

183

boundaries of *either* intention or accident became irrelevant. As Wittgenstein once wrote: 'it is the field of force of a word which is decisive' – and for *word* we may read any term in the language men have invented to articulate process and the generative. Rock is the music of *bricolage*, to use Lévi-Strauss's celebrated term: a picked-up mosaic of styles and metamorphoses combined in a celebration essentially public rather than private; the electronic projection of sound by disc and speaker system to thousands of listeners in open space. The performer's authorial sounds are amplified into technological universality. The music moves towards the condition described in Samuel Delany's story, 'Corona,' in which the new release of Bryan Faust, a rock singer from Ganymede, is distributed throughout space, from planet to planet, penetrating the nervous system of everyone: a cosmic amplification equivalent to the God of *Paradise Lost*, or indeed to the prologue to Goethe's *Faust*.[9] How near this is to reality can be sensed in Charlie Gillett's *The Sound of the City*: '[D]uring the mid-fifties, in virtually every urban civilization in the world, adolescents staked out their freedom in the cities, inspired and reassured by the rock and roll beat.'[10]

Gillett's 'freedom' is a permission to follow style. It is not the freedom of 'free jazz' and does not have the political implications of improvised black musical performance, as proposed, for example, in Alfred Willener's *The Action-Image of Society*: 'Whether collective or individual, improvisation presupposed the dialectical synthesis created by a group or an individual, redefining known elements, elements that have just been played and experienced, while inventing new elements in the course of the activity itself. . . . There has appeared a variety of jazz . . . *free jazz* – which claims to be revolutionary, both politically and artistically.'

Free jazz, free poetic forms, and the Free Speech Movement at Berkeley and other American campuses in the 1960s, are related in complex ways but, as Alfred Willener points out, they do have elements in common: 'the expression of a revolutionary desire for social emancipation . . . the emancipation of the non-formal . . . the desire to avoid being confined within a particular school, within existing rhythmic patterns.'[11] The new jazz has not therefore been governed, as rock music to a large extent has, by the same pattern as other popular arts in capitalist democracy: market industrial dynamics, the search for market-able trends, and the requirements of the Golden Disc. Rock is an art pre-eminently reliant on performance and reproduction technology. Its equipment is highly expensive and its distribution costs inflationary. In Jean-Luc Godard's *One Plus One* (1968), the Rolling Stones' studio performance is intersected with a Black Panther-type resistance movement based on a used car lot in London – a confrontation of controlled rebellious style in the precious world of rock and the improvisatory world of race resistance. The film's alternative title is *Sympathy for the Devil*, since Mick Jagger's group originally offered a vulgar and noisy threat to bourgeois life, and by this time were playing with a certain loose diabolism in their songs; and since the black man has always been, within white Christian ideology and especially in America, the analogic figure of the Devil. Dionysus is a major source for the Devil in Christian mythology and is deeply associated with ecstatic rituals of change. Clearly, Godard's film is profoundly suspicious of rebellion rooted in anarchistic power of any kind, and is perhaps as ambivalent as Richard Brooks' *The Blackboard Jungle* (1955), in which the city kids reject their well-meaning liberal teacher's jazz and swing tastes, and smash his records, while the soundtrack emphasizes the nature of social change through Bill Haley's 'Rock Around the Clock.' By the following year, 'rock'n'roll' had become firmly associated with youth rebellion.

1956 was also the year of Allen Ginsberg's *Howl and Other Poems*. At the time, Ginsberg's orientation lay towards classical music; in a famous photo by Fred McDarrah he is seen in his apartment with Peter Orlovsky and one of Orlovsky's brothers, and the sleeve of a record of Heifetz playing Bach. In the 1960s, however, his tastes moved towards Bob Dylan, a prominent counter-culture figure in Ginsberg's 'Wichita Vortex Sutra' (1966), and the Beatles, the focus of 'Portland Colosseum' (1965). 'Big Beat' celebrates a Prague pop group, and 'From Bratislava to San Francisco' projects youth responding to 'ancient body rhythm beat out thru airwaves in electric mantric rock,' an action which is part of the necessary recovery of liberatory archetypes.[12] In these poems, collected for the most part in *Planet News*, rock has become an international action cutting across traditional nationalist boundaries, attacked by media controllers and by conservative and leftist politicians alike. White Citizens Council groups linked it with sin and communism while the Soviet Union linked it with sin and capitalism. Certainly, the god had begun his descent. By 1962 the Stones had started up in a London pub called the Bricklayers Arms. Three years later they were creating their own synthetic form in 'Satisfaction.'

By this time, Phil Spector, a leader in multitrack electronic mixing in the trade, had become the *auteur* of electric rock: the engineer in sole command of the sound of production: 'I felt it had to be dynamic enough to overcome any bad material so people would respond to the sound rather than to the song.' In 1959 Berry Gordy founded Motown and by the early 1960s its characteristic sound had been discovered: in David Morse's words, the listener 'immerses himself in an all-embracing polyphonic immediacy that seeks to cancel time. There is an emphasis on synchronic rather than diachronic complexity.'[13] Immediately we are in the mid-twentieth century and what Walter J. Ong calls the 'synchronic present,' a release from linear into space-time relationships: 'The purely linear sense of time, what we have called the purely diachronic sense, the sense that events are strung through time and no more, fails to do justice to the present situation because one of the characteristics of the present is the way in which it appears to have caught up into itself the entire past. Our mid-twentieth century sense of time is synchronic.'[14]

Motown musically synthesized a number of black styles into 'a musical territory without frontiers,' resisting boundary and cultural edge. The equivalent in musical theatre opened as the Electric Circus in downtown New York. This 'total environment discotheque,' synthesizing music, light shows, films and dancing, operated as a container in which boundaries were eliminated: Alan Freed's 1954 radio 'Rock'n'Roll Party,' the Negro Church, the Revivalist meeting and the disco fused into an continuous intermedia happening.[15] The political implications were similar to those of the Revivalist sessions in eighteenth and nineteenth century America, so carefully delineated by Perry Miller in *The*

Life of the Mind in America: the awakening of emotions in forms contrary to established modes of assumed rationality, and the promotion of an expanding experience from ecstasy to new community. The Electric Circus ousted intellect and edged into fanaticism and orgy; Miller quotes the revivalist Charles Grandison Finney: 'Don't wait for feeling, DO IT.'[16]

But as Richard Schechner observes, the twentieth century context is less dialectically a matter of reason invaded by rationality:

> Over the past century the physical sciences have steadily expanded the premises of Newtonian mechanics until today physics, mathematics, and astronomy can deal with indeterminancy. And much current theater – happenings, environmental theater, places like the Electric Circus – reflect a general dissatisfaction with the tradition. . . . The discotheques – the Palm Gardens, the Fillmore, the Electric Circus – are places of public assembly and direct political action. A new way of living is being demonstrated.[17]

Like Robert Lifton, however, Schechner is wary of the forces released; like Lifton he recalls the action of the Red Guards in China: 'This same ecstasy, we know, can be unleashed in the Red Guards or horrifically channelled toward the Nuremberg rallies or Auschwitz. There, too, at the vast extermination camps, an ecstasy was acted out. The hidden fear I have about the new expression is that its forms come perilously close to ecstatic fascism.'[18]

Certainly there were elements of fascism in the contempt for ordinary people expressed by Marlon Brando and Lee Marvin's bikers in *The Wild One* (1955) and in the attitude towards audiences projected by the Living Theatre. The term 'soul' could express, both in rock music and in other pop forms, the mixture of musical *bricolage* generated by 1965. But it also meant unleashed sound ecstasy and the sense of permission it activated.

Motown under Berry Gordy marketed 'super-soul' at 'the General Motors of rock' in Detroit (David Morse's terms), seeking big business in the black city ghettos, through a revival of resources broadly focused against white tyranny and broadly emphasizing black achievement and black potentiality. It undermined the Beatles' white rock just as Aretha Franklin's 'Satisfaction' exposed the gap between black style and the 'synthesized Negritude' packaged for manufacture and sales anywhere in the world.[19] The rock mix became capitalist business. Its electronics combined art and engineering. Its so-called underground press serviced enthusiasts with information and hagiography, as well as promoting clothing fashions, the fan-cult scene, and a certain degree of political radicalism. Rock synchronicity achieved ecstasy through drugs: marijuana to create community nonresistance, and acid to heighten and loosen consciousness towards psychedelic simultaneity and the inter-transference of the senses. Rock became the most powerful cultural synthetic force of the decade. Marketing insistence on accelerated invention of novelty undermined its quality almost immediately. Rock yielded to consumerism and competitiveness.

At the height of the rock achievement in Los Angeles and San Francisco, with mainly white groups such as The Grateful Dead, Moby Grape, Jefferson Airplane, Big Brother and the Holding Company (Janis Joplin's first starring group), Country Joe and the Fish, and The Doors, the fusion generated unique powers. Musical idioms, experiments in electronic presentation, drug experience and a subculture of beach boys, hippies and Hell's Angels constituted a world. Its politics were overt – from ecological anarchism to The Doors' self-styled performance as 'erotic politicians.' The words of many rock numbers mattered politically, a new element in a popular music, generated mainly by the initial impetus of Bob Dylan, who himself inherited folk-protest lyricism from Woody Guthrie and later incorporated the symbolist and surrealist linguistics of Ginsberg and others. This kind of example moved groups like The Doors and especially their writer and lead singer, Jim Morrison: 'The world we suggest should be a new Wild West. A sensuous evil world, strange and haunting, the path of the sun . . . We're all centered around the end of the zodiac, the Pacific.'

Everywhere in Dylan and The Doors the message is: this is The End. American resources have been exhausted. A prophetic sense that the function of the rock synthesis is to celebrate the apocalyptic and even holocaustic collapse of a culture impregnates the sounds and the words: Dylan's 'Subterranean Homesick Blues' in 1965, Buffalo Springfield's 'For What It's Worth' (with its criticism of the inner passivity of youth disturbance in Los Angeles) in 1966, the Byrds' 'Eight Miles High' (1966). Janis Joplin's 'New Christ Cardiac Hero' in 1967 (with its criticism of the deterioration of the Jesus freaks as they fall back into anarchism), and The Doors' song:

> Got the world
> Locked up
> Inside a plastic box:
> She's a twentieth century fox

Jim Morrison performed the beautiful street poet, the charismatic rebellious leader looking like a mad angel in some Renaissance Italian painting. In what he called 'a goodbye song,' 'The End' (1967), he sang:

> No safety or surprise,
> The end . . .
> . . . Wierd scenes inside the gold mine . . .
> It hurts to set you free
> But you'll never follow me
> The end of laughter and soft lies
> The end of night we tried to die

The music is ritual, the performers shamans inviting the soul-voyager to a trip – the romantic voyage of changed consciousness, drugs and visionary scenes, a twentieth century version of the mix of Beddoes and Rimbaud, deathly, suicidal. This is a journey into a place where myths are re-enacted to regain the power of priests and acolytes:

> When the music's over turn out the lights
>   turn out the lights, turn out the lights
> For the music is your special friend
> Dance on fire as it intends

Morrison said explicitly that his aim was a new and wild synthesis of American, Indian, African and electronic music. He dreamt of a new genius of popular art, the democratic creator. He preferred the intimacy of club performances to the 'mass hysteria' of the concert, and believed that '[n]othing else can survive the holocaust, but poetry and songs.' The danger was self-consciousness which converted energy into an 'involuted' and 'incestuous' art.[20]

In 1969 he told *Rolling Stone* that the origin of rock lay in the need for 'psychic purge' after the Korean War: 'There seemed to be a need for an underground explosion, like an eruption. So maybe after the Vietnam War is over . . . it's possible that the deaths will end in a couple of years, and there will again be a need for a life force to express itself, to assert itself.'[21]

'The End' was The Doors' basic position – the Dionysian is experienced through music and it is the death of the dying self. Ecstacy, the experience of music, sex and intoxicants or drugs bring the self to the doors of perception and possibly to revolt. (The group were named after Huxley's *The Doors of Perception*, which was first published in 1954 – the title is itself a phrase from Blake.) The gist of the rebellion is given in 'Five to One':

> *The old get old and*
> *The young get stronger*
> *It may take a week and*
> *It may take longer*
> *They got the guns but*
> *We got the numbers*
> *Gonna win, yeah*
> *We're takin' over . . .*

The core is revolution through change in the soul, through mind-blowing sounds and words: 'Break on through to the other side.' So 'The End' cries 'Father, I want to kill you.' In 'The Celebration of the Lizard,' which provided material for a number of songs later recorded on *Waiting for the Sun*, Morrison sings:

> *I am the Lizard King,*
> *I can do anything.*

Part of his shamanistic aim derived from Nietzsche, part from Artaud's 'theatre of cruelty,' and part from the performance in sound and dance of the shaman in Indian rites. Part of 'The End' was suggested by Andreas Lommel's *Shamanism: The Beginning of Art*, where he discusses the myth of the shaman descending into the lake to gain medicine from the Great Snake: 'The two shamans ride on the snake in the water . . . the snake scatters crystals around it. After a while it disappears into the depths again. But the two shamans distribute the crystals to all those present.'[22]

The key passage in 'The End' goes: 'Ride the snake. To the ancient lake, baby . . .' Morrison also spoke of his reading in *The Birth of Tragedy from the Spirit of Music*, where Nietzsche writes of the primal Dionysian art as the spirit of music. As his understanding of its interior impulses became clear to him, so Morrison moved his performance towards shamanistic theatre. 'The Lizard' took nearly half an hour to perform in concert as a 'theatre composition' – it is an act of descent:

> *Not to touch the earth*
> *Not to see the sun*
> *Nothing left to do but*
> *Run, run, run . . .*
> *Let's run . . .*

But watching a film of The Doors' concerts, *Feast of Friends*, Morrison realized the limits of his control over the frenzied arena and found himself shocked by a sense of being a manipulated theatrical puppet. The spectacle both energized and controlled him. Performance 'test[ed] the bounds of reality' and 'push[ed] a situation as far as it'll go' until music, the rushing audience and the cops worked together in what he called 'degrees of fever': 'the only incentive to charge the stage is because there's a barrier.' The cops, 'secure [in] their position of power,' were 'a chance to test authority,' itself a uniformed, armed boundary. Like John Cage, Morrison was drawn to chaos and liberation, an intersection of *acte gratuite* and the Lord of Misrule's carnival:

I'm interested in anything about revolt, disorder, chaos, [and] especially activity that appears to have no meaning . . . Play. Activity that has nothing in it except just what it is. No repercussions. No motivation. Free . . . activity. . . . There should be a week of national hilarity . . . a cessation of all work, all business, all discrimination, all authority. A week of total freedom. . . . People would have to be real for a week.[23]

This 'human sculpture' in ritual form would, however, have no ideology and no immediate political revolutionary aim. Somehow rite would invade malign energy or politics. Morrison's audience participated in an amalgam of demonism, fear, authoritarian games – and on one occasion the transference of a skirmish with the police in New Haven to a simulation-stage. But as Richard Schechner observes: 'Liberty can be swiftly transformed into its opposite, and not only by those who have a stake in reactionary government. Ritualized experience without the built-in control of a strong social system . . . can pump itself up to destructive fury. . . . Can we cope with Dionysus' dance and not end up – as Agave did – with our sons' heads on our dancing sticks?[24]

By 1972 the Dionysian rock scene had a number of more or less talented agents. The Alice Cooper group, allegedly straight males acting as transvestites, claimed to purge evil in the souls of their fans. Alice, their leader, threw live chickens into the audience, axed dolls to death, used a snake between his legs, wore a strait-jacket, and in mock penance had himself electrocuted in an electric chair or hung beneath a gallows. During a performance in Muskegon, Michigan, the fans ripped off his clothes and jewelry and cut his back – 'They're like piranha fish. I like an audience that's alive.' Three of the group's LPs – *Love it to Death, Killer* and *School's Out* – cashed a million dollars for Warner Brothers. At the concert which produced his tremendous American success at Carnegie Hall in Manhattan, David Bowie's Dionysian elements were equally clear: his bisexuality, orange-tinted hair, feline gestures and walk, his parody of Andy Warhol and his use of science fiction magic. *Ziggy Stardust* (1972) records the rise and assassination of a rock 'n'roller who fuses Dylan, Jagger, Alice Cooper and others

– Bowie said 'I know that one day a big artist is going to get killed on stage, and I keep thinking it's bound to be me.' But he has survived through the very energies he generates, through their ancient tradition of conquest, and through his own highly selective self-transformations and ritualized decors.

The Dionysian breakthrough – breakdown needs the social context of viable revolution if it is not to diminish into mere rebelliousness, licenced orgy or ritual which re-energizes the reactionary and lethal status quo. In New York between June 1968 and July 1969, Schechner produced the Performance Group's *Dionysus in 69*. The published text is the score of the performances, based on a translation of *The Bacchae* transformed by the actors and transcribed from tapes.[25] The location was an environment of levels, towers, ladders and objects in a large disused garage. The performers exercise and warm up in silence; the opening chorus begins before the audience are welcomed in one by one and told 'this is a rite of initiation.' They sit where they wish – exposed or tucked away. No stage line divides the acting area from the audience. Different actors play different roles throughout the run of performances, interchanging male and female roles. The text is controlled according to need rather than imposed as a static masterpiece. Early on the question is put: Would you like to go through our ordeal with us? Have you come to join the revels of the god or just to watch? The god is the Orphic Dionysus who is the process of destruction and creation – in the words of the poet Robin Blaser: 'The god who is both joyous and terrible, who is bringer of wine, who can be defeated, thrown into the sea by a mortal, locked in a chest, torn to pieces by giants, and who dies. That he holds within himself all the contradictions, the change and the process of the world as it is known, and the terror that goes with that process.'[26]

In his 1957 essay, 'The White Negro,' Norman Mailer had understood some of the implications of the latest American manifestation of the contradictory force: 'Hip, which would return us to ourselves, at no matter what price in individual violence, is the affirmation of the barbarian, for it requires a primitive passion about human nature to believe that individual acts of violence are always to be preferred to the collective violence of the State; it takes literal faith in the creative possibilities of the human being to envisage acts of violence as the catharsis which prepares growth.'[27]

In a time of war in South East Asia, Black Protest, student revolt, and the ecological analysis of the excessive conquest of natural resources for consumption in America, the invitation of *Dionysus in 69* is to a transformation which might break the conforming social self, radically challenge the Security State through the insecurity of creativity, and even challenge the presumed fixed boundary of male and female. The minimal clothing and nakedness of the performers is the costume of chosen vulnerability rather than erotic suggestiveness. An actor comes naked to tell the audience 'I am a god,' but then states the time and place, his age and his parentage, as he plays Dionysus or Pentheus or Cadmus. The performers learned how to move words, mime, dance and music into a spiral involving the audience, who are in turn moved and invited to dance. They do or do not move and dance. When Tiresias warns Pentheus, the arrogant monarch who refuses Dionysus,

> Do not be sure that power
> is what matters in the life of man; do not mistake
> for wisdom the fantasies of your sick mind . . .

the action enters the politics and counter-culture of the 1960s. As one of the actors, Patrick McDermott, records: 'When I spoke these words I enacted [Julian] Beck, Chomsky, Arden, Laing, Brown, even Faulkner – and all the modern prophets who have seen that slave revolts are rational acts but wars of nationhood are not, who have called for new definitions of madness and sanity, and who have not been afraid to diagnose the insanity of those most rational of men, the managerial warmakers.'

But the original was a Greek play and this is 1969. Euripides could not imagine a people successfully resisting gods and kings in order to regenerate their lives, nor could he imagine a radical change of course. Today, by contrast, the god has become selfserving and is not allowed his 'true form.' The audience is encouraged to perform his rite, with the aid of folk and popular songs, and to sacrifice Pentheus for the ecstatic god with long hair, sexual beauty and demonic power. Pentheus wants silence and stasis; the ecstacized people want dance, and deride him until he exhausts himself under their challenge. His patience, authority, dignity and stamina are dismantled – at least in some performances. In others, however, the actor of Pentheus might triumph over Dionysus: man over god, realizing his own restrictions and forming a positive relationship with the celebration of ecstatic energy. In one performance, some of the audience drag Pentheus from the environment and a volunteer improvises his role. In McDermott's words: 'Participation is a challenge to the ability of both actors and audience to create symbols. . . . Ritual assembles; it dispels the illusions of routinization and privacy. It does not pretend to the public performance of private acts.'

The centre of the action is the erotic, political and religious confrontation of two sources of power: Dionysus and Pentheus. In performance, this *agon* of the sexuality of power shifted according to whether men or women played the roles: the scene could be heterosexual or homosexual; the kiss and the caress a scene of possibilities of ecstasy and possession. The audience found themselves engaged in physical encounters with the performers and the results could be both beautiful and unpleasant. As one Messenger actor says:

Who knows the beat of liberation? Who knows the pulse of his own life? What happens is that Dionysus, according to his convenience and popular demand, becomes another Pentheus. Most of us have a pretty cheap fantasy of self-liberation. And if Dionysus, or someone else, could lead us into the Promised Land, then Dionysus, or someone else, could lead us right out again. Don't bother to get The Man unless you plan to close his office down, permanently. The first rule of the revolution is: Dig yourself. Dig yourself. So don't understand too much too quick . . .

Let the play become the war in the heart of every man. Let the play be revolution in the heart of William Blake. . . . The inciting incident is divinity. Can god be in us, do we have it in us . . . if so, there is no need for political powers. If so, the concept of political control is called into question. Divinity will set you free. The man in god does not need the President and patriotism. Let only servants rule; let all be servants. No man can serve two masters.

The day of the Lord of Misrule, the return of the repressed enacted as the reign of the Proletariat, and the euhemeristic analysis of gods as science fiction projections of human needs for eternal patterns of domination and submission are fused in this strictly contemporary and American cry in 1969. Another actor of the Messenger says: 'A man like Pentheus has everything set up to protect his comfortable position. We all know his rules. So along comes Dionysus, living by impulse, a tempter who points out the planned obsolescence of our lives. He promises a trade-in. Our rigid structure for his expanding one. But he doesn't say where he stops. Just the promise of freedom.'

The promise includes any protest against the Pentheus world, however violent, from bombing Chicago to putting acid in the city water supply: the familiar threats of anarchism in the 1960s. Pentheus learns to dance naked, in one performance, and his ecstacy itself moves him towards sacrifice: to be killed by and for Dionysus and his agents, a ritual assassination such as became familiar in the 1960s. Pentheus is torn apart by his mother, Agave, and her Bacchantes, female ecstatics under her leadership. The erotic caresses turn to erotic dismemberment. Revels turn to the ultimate transgression of boundary. In the words of Georges Bataille:

> It is the common business of sacrifice to bring life and death into harmony, to give death the upsurge of life, life the momentousness and vertigo of death opening on to the unknown. Here life is mingled with death, but simultaneously death is a sign of life, a way into the infinite. Nowadays sacrifice is outside the field of our experience and imagination must do duty for the real thing. . . . Underlying eroticism is the feeling of something bursting, of the violence accompanying an explosion.[28]

The erotic political assassinations carried out by Charles Manson's self-justificatory *band à parte* – and certainly Manson was originally part of the West Coast late rock scene – take place within permissions given for the descent of Dionysus into the human. In Schechner's work, the acting area is at least one point alive with naked people splashed with blood. Dionysus, as Lifton fears, has been accepted in a society otherwise unchanged. Too much has been understood too quickly. A god has complete power and that power is both a-moral and a-social. 'Dionysus has destroyed us all,' an actress of Agave says.

Denial of the god leads to the enaction of his destructive permission. The actors clean away the blood with water, sponges and brushes, but Dionysus curses the company with the guilt of their transgression of his dance. In one version he appeals in familiar language to his fellow Americans to arm, explode the slums, and shoot to wound authority: 'explode your feelings' beyond mere fantasy. In another form his curse is that the performers will be absorbed into the contemporary system, in another that the play will be performed endlessly, and in another, since 'only a god knows the will of the people well enough to make it work,' that he will run for Mayor of New York. His platform will be solely 'power is power' and his slogan 'Power Power' – a parody of Black Power, Red Power, and the rest. But he is now alone. The actors have gone and the audience is down to a handful. Still he speaks on and on, trying to induce the people into a painless, value-free state, the kind of totalitarian democracy beloved by the political behaviorists of America, but a condition in which no one involved in the previous action could possibly be interested. Dionysus, in this version, is an outsider.

Dionysus in 69 proposes serious contemporary versions of the nature of social and personal boundary. But the outlaw in American society embodies an historical ambivalence of energy in a culture whose development has long been impregnated with an accelerated inflow of technology and access to personal power. The barbarian in Whitman's and Melville's writings – and particularly the knowledge of cannibalism in the latter – works for a *self*-fulfilment which preaches *laissez-faire* and then attempts to pressurize the agent of enterprise into the conformities of the genteel, the legalistic, and those nuclear forces of family, state, and labour, all of which limit a man's freedom to be reborn.

Youth in America traditionally carries this double burden of investment for the future, with an expectation of innovation, plus the imposition of inheritance. The abandonment of the parent therefore haunts American culture. Increasingly in this century 'youth' has come to mean anyone prepared to sustain rebellion in music, poetry, drugs, civil rights and anti-war campaigning, and hair and clothing styles. 'Beat' styles became hippie styles, which became national styles and thoroughly impregnated the middle classes. A language of social behaviour was established. Underground man surfaced and obtained power because he did not ideologically plan a new society but simply hoped that a life-style would somehow become sufficiently political and radical. Capitalism shifted ground. The warfare state continued its programme. As *Dionysus in 69* infers, there are no ideological answers within the Greek scheme of ecstasy and revolt. The Greeks reached little further beyond a sense of powerlessness and destiny under forces which were largely inexplicable and therefore dubbed *divine*. Dionysus is a barbarian god who destroys and energizes but leaves men to organize themselves after a vision of ecstasy and liberation. And it becomes clear that in the rock field, too, the Spenglerian barbarian who haunted the generation of Yeats, Eliot, and Shaw would make his Second Coming in the form of a god turned devil.

Back in 1959, Lawrence Lipton observed in *The Holy Barbarians*, the Beat poets reintroduced 'the nonrational' into the forefront of American culture 'as a way of knowing and a therapy to overcome squareness.'[29] Like Walter J. Ong in *The Barbarian Within*, Lipton uses E.R. Dodds' influential work of 1951, *The Greeks and the Irrational*, to relate American cultural movement to the cult of Dionysus. Dodds writes that the social function of the Dionysian ritual was 'essentially cathartic, in the psychological sense: it purged the individual of those irrational impulses which, when dammed up, give rise, as they have done in other cultures, to outbreaks of dancing mania and similar manifestations of collective hysteria; it relieved them by providing them with a ritual outlet.'[30]

But, of course, if the Dionysian experience is to be a rite of passage to a social democracy, there must be more than a group

198

ego-trip. The god manifested as 'Beat' may have initiated nothing more than a pre-revolutionary beginning. In Ong's words: 'A professional outsider, he becomes of paramount interest to philosophers themselves precisely because of his declared intransigence. He is a kind of barbarian in reverse, for he insists that he, the outsider as outsider, is the real Greek who has the integrity which the insiders or squares have sacrificed to cheap security. . . . He knows that the squares have an interest in him, which is even an academic interest.'[31] In fact, Ong, as a Jesuit, believes that the Beat is negative, self-delusory, and futile. He sees the Greek and the Barbarian as a permanent tension whose only solution is refuge in the god turned into the Christian God, the ultimate Greek in whom 'tensions do not die but come to fruition' and 'active conciliation.'[32] Ong has no concept that his God is the figure of external authority from which all examples of authority derive and in which they are summarized, one which therefore has to be erased from human conceptualizations if the social democratic is to be truly invented. This is the central vision of the work of William Burroughs, whose novel *The Wild Boys*, written in 1969 and published in 1972, concerns the victorious revolt of the young barbarians against the authoritarian god, Bradly Martin, and his international agencies.

One particular step towards the invention of democracy might have been made in America in the 1960s – at least, that is how it was felt by many of the young in a spirit of hope. By 1969, it has been estimated there were ten thousand music festivals of every kind in America.[33] The first American music festival occured in Worcester, Massachusetts, in 1858. Thereafter, improved transportation, a shorter working week, and longer vacations gradually improved working conditions. By the mid 1940s, hundreds of festivals were being held annually. By 1969, festival was a major summer activity, taking people thousands of miles in search, especially, of folk and rock music. A festival rallied energies already spread through radio and record electronics, but the brief centre included the association of folk and rock with civil rights and anti-war protest, with sit-ins, with Bob Dylan's 'Blowin' in the Wind' and the words of other folk and rock musicians, and with Timothy Leary's slogan – 'turn on, tune in, drop out.'[34] The styles of the 'hippie,' born out of 'beat' and 'hip,' were less wary and alienated than the parental sources, more visible and audible, less cautious, more aggressive, and linked, at least tentatively, to a political group, the Yippie Party, who claimed as a founding father no less a figure of American anarchism and critical intelligence in liberatory thinking than Paul Goodman. Through the media of TV, radio, and press – both underground and traditional – hippie styles eventually turned fashionable across age and income brackets. Style became boundary and uniform; attitudes congealed into an aggressive conformity which could be assumed and purchased like any other consumer-spectator product. Hippie capitalist and rock millionaires inevitably moved into control. But in 1965, San Francisco's Haight-Ashbury district for a time focused the liberation possible through folk and rock music, through a style of love-making, clothing and drugs which made for a politics of freedom associated with a small effort by the Diggers to demonstrate that food and clothing could be free in an abundance society.

In 1965, San Francisco could still contain the San Francisco Mime troupe, whose performances of radical plays were supported at a benefit by Lawrence Ferlinghetti, Allen Ginsberg, Jefferson Airplane, John Handy's jazz group, and the Fugs, a radical rock group led by Ed Sanders and Tuli Kupferberg.[35] A second benefit, at the Fillmore Auditorium, featured the Grateful Dead, the Great Society, and the Mystery Trend. In January 1966, the Oregon novelist Ken Kesey, author of *One Flew Over the Cuckoo's Nest* (1962) and *Sometimes a Great Notion* (1964), asked the business manager of the Troupe, Bill Graham, to produce a three-day mixed media festival that would, by means of rock music, lights, dancing and costumes, recreate the acid experience without acid.[36] As at the Electric Circus, media boundaries were melted; the Trips Festival simply used psychedelic designs, a popular derivation of *art nouveau* biomorphic styles, and alleged to be the natural style of vision under LSD. The acid trip, under the influence of Leary, Richard Alpert and others, had become a religious experience to encourage consciousness-expansion and liberation – one neatly focused in the festival sign which read: ANYBODY WHO

KNOWS HE IS A GOD, GO UP ON STAGE. The new Kafka 'Nature Theatre of Oklahoma' manifested as the Trips Festival: 'Everyone is welcome! If you want to be an artist, join our company! Our Theatre can find employment for everyone, a place for everyone! . . . At twelve o'clock the doors will be shut and never opened again! Down with all those who do not believe in us![37] In San Francisco it became a festival of musical, sexual and drug changes within a revivalist programme of possession by the God.

In 1967, the San Francisco Be-In, a 'Gathering of Tribes,' substantiated the revivalist elements. Forty thousand people assembled at the Polo Ground of the Golden Gate Park in a demonstration for peace against imperial warfare. The Diggers provided a free food table whilst Ginsberg and Gary Snyder chanted mantras for a new age. The Hell's Angels and Timothy Leary were on hand and rock groups included the Grateful Dead and the Quicksilver Messenger Service. The political proclamation was: 'The police, like the soldiers in Vietnam, are victims and agents!'

That same year the first pop music festival was held on Mount Tamalpais, northwest of San Francisco. Two weeks later came the Monterey International Pop Festival, the first to involve high finance, massive organization, and police fears (that is, a force of forty-six, a local population of thirty thousand, and an incoming population of possibly ninety thousand). In the event, the participants and police did not clash. Plenty of marijuana was smoked and not prosecuted. The music was heard – Moby Grape, Jefferson Airplane, Big Brother and the Holding Company, Otis Redding, Jimi Hendrix, The Who, and Ravi Shankar, the Indian classical sitarist who had been encouraged to appear by George Harrison of the Beatles. (Shankar's reception demonstrated how certain Hindu ritualist sources were found usable in the 1960s, in this case partly because the vibrational quality of the sitar sounds constituted a counterpart to the highs of drug ecstasy).

Monterey set a pattern – a scenario that included any element required to encourage a generation to consolidate its separation from mainstream American culture. But in Denver, bikers, gate-crashers and police armed with clubs, tear-gas and

Mace turned the event into civil war; violence and bad organization let down several festivals. But the general mood was peaceful. Aggression came either from adults who feared the style, the noise and the numbers, or from bikers and Hell's Angels whose fascism used any meeting for their erotic-punishment ends. Damage costs and the fees of the rock groups did, however, turn festivals into financial problems. City organizations began to legislate against potential festivals, and vandalism had certainly been a fact in Californian events. At the 1969 Palm Springs Easter Festival, thousands of cars, overflowing toilets, an inadequate sound-system, a police helicopter constantly circling overhead, a poor stage which made the acts invisible for many of the crowd, destruction by bonfire and dismantling, and acres of broken wine bottles which wrecked people's feet – all contributed to disaster. Some who believed the festival should be free, gate-crashed violently. When the Don Ellis orchestra was stoned, the lead saxophonist had to be taken to hospital.

In the later 1960s attendance at festivals grew enormous. Their Dionysian energy polarized finally between two distinct events: the positive of Woodstock in the summer of 1969 in the East, and the negative of Altamont in the winter in the West. Woodstock, originally advertized as 'three days of peace and music,' became a social and political event of such major significance that even the *New York Times* had to admit that it was 'essentially a phenomenon of innocence . . . a life style that is its own declaration of independence.' The Yippie leader Abbie Hoffman called his book of the event *Woodstock Nation* (1969), recognizing that this was beyond a rock and pop festival, and placing it in the context of the Chicago 1968 trial. *Polis* in America – the art of the city – became Woodstock: its population was larger than that of Phoenix, Louisville, Portland, Nashville, Birmingham, Oklahoma City, or Albuquerque. It was the largest spontaneous gathering in the history of the Western world and it included the main artists of the rock peak. Local citizens organizations tried to kill it, but excellent organization triumphed. The festival had been designed as a participatory event. It achieved peace. Automobiles nearly caused an initial disaster, until they were abandoned in the countryside. Bad weather, too, had to be turned into part of the grand design.

Woodstock Ventures' vice-president, Artie Kornfeld, was a twenty-six year old singer, song-writer, talent scout, and Artists and Repertoire man for Capitol Records. The producer, twenty-four year old Mike Lang, owned a Florida psychedelics shop, was a business administration student at New York University, and possessed a white Porsche and a BSA bike. These two organized the event – and later fought a court battle for the control of Woodstock Ventures. The money came from John Roberts, son of a cosmetics millionaire and a millionairess mother. These men wanted to make money out of a repeat of the Monterey success.

In the event, their private police security and food supply organizations broke down. Local water wells proved to be impure. Glass injuries, sun stroke and drug collapses invaded the design. Survival became the central action of Woodstock, making the festival into a *polis* or a nation. The staging and electronics were excellent, the pre-festival sales of tickets rose to a million dollars, and by a stroke of luck Chip Monck, the electronics expert from the Monterey festival, not only organized the Woodstock system but acted as a master of ceremonies, immediately setting the right tone. He said to the participants: 'We're turning a little of the responsibility back onto you. We have the ability to gather this many people here and now – it's also our responsibility to take care of ourselves in the midst of a phenomenon. And it's a responsibility no one ever had.'

The drugs probably helped, as well as causing some personal disasters. By 1966 at least, 'pot' and 'psychedelic' had become national terms and part of an accepted alternative to the parent generation's alcohol and pill culture. Drug experience penetrated rock group names and their songs. 'Head music' and 'head shops' entered American society. Those under twenty-five in college learned the truth or falsity of official propaganda about drugs – that they were or were not expensive and liberatory. The Dionysian possession had to be experienced. The god was not necessarily supportive, but his descent had to take place in the years of the Movement. The prospect of the draft and a future of tightening conformity contributed to experiment with a life-style of rock, drugs, nakedness, political resistance and a more open sense of sexuality. In the later stages of the Movement, too, there developed a mediational and religious phase. Rebellious-ness edged continually into confrontation with the law in so far as narcotics prohibitions and political oppression could be enacted by police and soldiers under an official political direction which included the CIA. Kent State and Chicago were the peaks of a general confrontation. 'Hippie' and 'student' became target terms for a parent generation and its local and national government. But Woodstock caused Joe Kimble, a California police chief present as an observer, to report: 'It proves something I've believed for a long time – that people are capable of policing themselves if they want to.' The Digger contribution of earlier festivals was taken over by the Hog Farm, a commune group largely focused on Hugh Romney, Beat poet and cafe comedian, who became one of Kesey's Merry Pranksters. Its members were dedicated to protecting and forwarding the social, political and chemical changes of the 1960s. They provided the pig nominated as President in Chicago in 1968. At Woodstock they offered drug consultation, prepared and delivered food supplies, and assisted with medical help.

Woodstock developed a huge family responsibility, a sense of peaceful community which the adult community had failed to sustain. But it did have a certain political enclosure, exemplified when Abbie Hoffman leaped on stage during The Who's performance and shouted into a microphone that the festival was meaningless while the manager of the MC5 rock band was imprisoned on a pot charge. The Who's leader, Pete Townshend, chased him off stage with his guitar, without losing a beat. Festival meant music and survival in an immediacy of response and responsibility which precluded, for the time being, the surrounding national scene. It held together as a large-scale community design. Three people died from an overdose, but there were no fights, rapes, assaults or robberies, unlike the American *polis* beyond the festival. Woodstock participants followed their own code of order: the gap between training for community and belief in imagination and ecstasy closed. In *Wolf Net*, Michael McClure writes of the contemporary American students' pleasure in concerted revolt – the so-called riots of the period taken, not as a necessary assertion against official totality, but as a complex theatre: 'a challenge that allows new openings for glandular, organic, hormonic, intellective energies,' a surge against 'biological ignominy,' and the beginning not only of 'the long march through the institutions' – in Rudi Dutschke's phrase – but of 'a new relation with nature.' Here was a social relationship which proposed a future.[38]

The Isle of Wight festival, in Britain, the next significant rock festival, centered on Bob Dylan and drew in European as well as British people. The focus proved to be Tom Paxton, one of whose songs, 'Talking Vietnam Pot Luck Blues,' told of a GI, turned on to marijuana by his fellow soldiers, encountering a Viet Cong soldier who turns him on to some better grass. But again this festival involved big money. Dylan received 84,000 dollars.

In America rock was under attack from another political direction: the women's liberation movement attacked its blatant sexism. In *Rat* magazine an article appeared entitled 'Cock Rock: Men Always Seem to End up on Top': 'for the female 51% of Woodstock Nation . . . there isn't any place to be in any creative kind of way.'[39] Women had to be like Janis Joplin or Aretha Franklin – completely outstanding and tough – to get anywhere. The Beatles sang 'rather see you dead little girl than see you with another man,' and 'to catalogue the anti-women songs alone would make up almost a complete history of rock.' Rock was based on stars – the Rolling Stones 'kept thousands waiting several hours till nightfall before they would come on stage at Altamont.' Janis Joplin was hounded about who she was alleged to be sleeping with; her death was in the terrible precedent set by Billie Holliday and Marilyn Monroe. Rock and its commercial subsidiaries had become a major part of the male-dominated capitalist entertainment system. *Rolling Stone*, in particular, was the organ of rock big business, rock star gossip, and the politics of the so-called post-ideological society, indulging in muck-raking journalism without attacking the military-industrial complex at source. In Craig Pyes's words:

> In Revolution there are no spectators, but in *Rolling Stone* nearly everyone is a spectator surrounding a few rock stars who arise electronically above a nation of groupies. A fitting advertisement to attract business!

> But the ruling class remains the same. Rock has not changed
> the way money-changers change money, it has only changed the
> money-changers; the money still goes to the same people and is
> deposited in the same banks.[40]

Pyes supplies sufficient examples to substantiate his attack. *Rolling Stone* appealed to its readers not to demonstrate against the Democratic Convention in Chicago in 1968 (even *Esquire* sent in Genet, Burroughs, and Southern to report it), and its editor, Jann Wenner, attacked the Fugs, Leary, Phil Ochs and anyone who was politically committed towards the liberal-left. His explicit enemy was 'the New Left,' and when Jerry Rubin, the organizer of the Yippie demo at Chicago, tried to encourage rock groups to participate, Wenner wrote an editorial criticizing him for relating music to politics: 'Rock and roll is the *only* way in which the vast but formless power of youth is structured, the only way in which it can be defined or inspected. The style and meaning of it has caught the imagination, the financial power and the spiritual interest of millions of young people. It is indeed so powerful and full of potential as all that, and more. It has its own unique morality.'

In 1969 *Rolling Stone* increased its political articles, making copy out of political coverage without, however, disturbing the Hip Capitalist position taken by the editor and his *Rolling Stone – Straight Arrow Books* empire. Once, the magazine was saved from bankruptcy by a coffee millionaire; then a financial backer of McGovern and former executive at the Xerox Corporation became a partner. Clearly, 'the financial power and the spiritual interests of millions of young people' were deeply involved.

On 6 December 1969, Woodstock West, a promotion organization, produced a free all-day concert at Altamont racetrack, given by the Rolling Stones and others. One casualty list gave four people dead at the end of it. One Black eighteen-year-old youth 'was killed in a ritual stabbing by several ageing Hell's Angels twenty five feet from the stage as Mick Jagger sang "Sympathy for the Devil." Two others were run over by cars driven by unknown people.' In addition, 'some one hundred people had their heads bloodied or ribs cracked or were otherwise pummeled and violated by the Hell's Angels, semi-official border guards of the concert.'[41] Several hundred or more were damaged by acid. Two musicians were wounded on stage.

> The whole evolution from Trickster to Devil and on into the pseudosecular demonic of capitalism shows the progressive triumph of the death instinct. . . . The withdrawal of Eros hands over culture to the death instinct; and the inhuman, abstract, impersonal world which the death instinct creates progressively eliminates all possibility of the life of sublimated Eros, which we nostalgically so admire in the ancient Greeks. . . . 'This problem is bound up with the larger one of power – and of possession.'[42]

When Dionysus sheds Eros his energy turns negative. He becomes the Devil, and the Devil, as Norman O. Brown emphasizes in *Life Against Death*, is the form of excrement, waste, and 'filthy lucre.' The true Dionysus offers an opportunity to affirm the dialectical unity of male and female, destruction and creativity, men and the Earth. Dionysus deteriorated, as Nietzsche understood, gives us a 'mixture of sensuality and cruelty,' the sexuality of sado-masochistic power. Capitalism and any form of enforced control under ideology therefore gives sympathy to the Devil, where sympathy derives from *sun pathos*, feeling together, a source of revival or of malign ecstasy.

Altamont shook the famous rock groups into silence and withdrawal. The Hippie movement remained stunned and has not revived. Notwithstanding his performance of 'Street Fighting Man,' Mick Jagger refused to give any money for the Chicago Eight. The 1960s ended in confusion in America, in this field as elsewhere. The Dionysian rock festival promised regeneration: Jagger, like Dylan, was to be a magic man, the star and god to lead the populace to rebirth. But shamanistic ecstasy never guaranteed regeneration.

In a closely-written article based on personal witness, 'Altamont: Pearl Harbor to Woodstock Nation,' Sol Stern, a former *Ramparts* magazine editor, has described the end of the 1960s festivals.[43] Thousands of young people poured into Altamont, mainly working class rather than the middle class participants at Woodstock. The latter cost twenty dollars or more; Altamont was free and attracted kids from the Bay Area industrial centres. These children of the silent majority were still only then turning on to what the media had reported of Woodstock and the Sixties changes. As far as they were concerned, therefore, overt politics was out. When the Panthers tried to collect money for the legal defence fund for Fred Hampton, who had been murdered by the Chicago police a few days earlier, the crowd was indifferent or hostile – and probably had little money in any case. The Committee on Public Safety, or COPS, a fourteen-member group attempting to connect cultural to political changes, tried to organize free food along earlier Digger or Hog Farm lines, but the organizers of the festival refused them. Vendors sold bad food and drink at inflated prices. COPS, believing this was to be truly a free concert, began to harass the vendors, many of whom were obviously working class. Sol Stern reports that COPS were among the first to see their mistakes – after the event.

The essential electronics were well organized. Santana opened and the tensions temporarily cleared in their sound. But this was violent urban music – the Sound of the City – and the group's style included looking like a street gang. Pills were swallowed in handfuls by kids who were already freaking out (Timothy Leary was present as observer). Then a fat naked man began to dance and stumble towards the low stage (only four feet high). A fight began around him. Three Hell's Angels with five-foot pool cues dived into the crowd, some of whom were vainly trying to reinaugurate the old be-ins by chanting 'peace.' One man who tried to help the fat man was stomped on by the Angels as they thrashed and kicked the fat dancer. This kind of scene recurred throughout the Santana set. A freaked-out kid tried to get on stage. A photographer tried to take pictures. A bystander simply stood in the way. The Angels moved in. The crowd stood impotent, packed so tight they could only stand. (At Woodstock there was space for everyone to sit and move). Jefferson Airplane repeatedly stopped in mid-number until finally the Angels took over. The group's lead guitarist, Marty Balin, tried to reassert musical power, but as a black man was being stomped at the back of the stage and Balin tried to pull the Angels off, he himself was beaten down. Crosby, Stills, Nash, and Young played badly in late afternoon. It was Crosby who had said of the Chicago Eight appeal: 'we don't need any politicians, politics is bullshit.' Now he stood impotently while the Angels beat his audience. The group left by helicopter, leaving the nearly half a million spectators and consumers.

While the Rolling Stones waited for darkness, the Angels taunted the crowd with contempt.. Then they parodied the rituals of religious cults. In Stern's words: 'One of them, wearing a wolf's head, took the microphone and played the flute for us – a screeching, terrible performance; no one dared to protest or shut off the microphone.' The Mediterranean wolf cults and the flute music of Dionysus, the wild music of the *joujouka* – the vestigial music of the God which had entranced Brian Jones, Brion Gysin, William Burroughs, Paul Bowles and Ornette Coleman – had come to this, a preparation for a star.

Timothy Leary, who had himself experienced the Bou Jeloud dancers of Morocco, wrote in his *Jail Notes* that 'Brian Jones had been there and danced all night.' The moment of panic for Jones, who was also in Morocco to investigate the ritual music of Pan, Bou Jeloud, the Father of Skins, came when the sound of music and the whirling of the dancers fused: '. . . the one beautiful boy-girl, and the other man-animal and with drumming hooves and rush of wind Pan Dionysus swept down from the mountains and tongues of firelight and the energy of God struck . . . Bou Jeloud horned God of herd pasture and wine and root and seed whirled and leaped into the fire and disappeared.'[44]

The product of rock and publicity ultimately aped the god who had become the Devil of the West. Jones had been with the Rolling Stones since 1962 and was still part of the band when they recorded *Their Satanic Majesties Request* in 1967. The coroner reported his death in 1969 as a result of 'drowning by immersion in fresh water associated with severe liver disfunction and ingestion of alcohol and drugs.[45] In tribute, at the Hyde Park free concert two days after the death, Jagger quoted Shelley's *Adonais*:

'Tis we who, lost in stormy visions,
Keep with phantoms an unprofitable strife,
And in mad trance strike with our spirit's knife
Invulnerable nothings.

Jones had played out the emotional centre of the Stones, translating his skill as a musician into the generation of magic control by rock group life in the 1960s. Greil Marcus wrote on 3 July 1969 that perhaps the Stones understood something of their life through 'Sympathy for the Devil':

> *I lay traps for troubadours*
> *who get killed before they reach Bombay.*
> *Pleased to meet you, hope you guess my name.*
> *But what's confusing you*
> *is just the nature of my game.*

Marcus quotes Lovecraft's *The Case of Charles Dexter Ward*: 'I say to you, do not call up Any that you cannot put downe; by the which I meane, Any that can in turn call up somewhat against you, whereby your powerfullest devices may not be of use.'[46]

Into the darkness of Altamont, through the protective circle of the Angels on the blood-splashed stage, came the Stones, led by Mick Jagger in a black and orange cape and tall hat. They played well but their music spoke out of the interface between savagery and erotics, between the controls of art and the controls of magic, between Apollo and Dionysus. Jagger began 'Sympathy for the Devil' – 'They call me Lucifer and I'm in need of some restraint.' The earlier Angels' attacks now climaxed. In the spotlights, while Jagger went on singing this number, they stabbed to death a black youth from Berkeley named Meredith Hunter. Panic-stricken, Jagger tried to cool the screaming people, but the death ritual operated as part of his own performance. In Stern's words:

> Jagger danced around the stage, weaving through the snarling Angels, propelled by some inner, powerful motor which caused him to lash out at the violence around him with his most popular songs. After a long hour of hard singing he ended with 'Street Fighting Man':
>
> > *But what can a poor boy do*
> > *'Cept sing in a rock'n'roll band?*
> > *In sleepy London town*
> > *There's just no place for*
> > *A street fighting man . . .*[47]

Jagger had come a long way from the Bricklayers Arms, but the song accurately expressed that element of anarchism which the violence of stars, angels, and gods necessarily generates. They are centres around which we are intended to orbit in half helpless gravitation, nourishing them with adulation and money (which is our own stored energy), and to receive in turn the chance of hypnotic ecstasy. The main demand of their centre is sacrificial death. The recognition of this fact and the imaginative analysis thereof can come from David Bowie and William Burroughs respectively:

> For the West, Jagger is most certainly a mother figure . . . more like a brothel keeper or a madam. . . . The rock business is a pale shadow of what the kids' lives are usually like. The admiration comes from the other side. It's all a reversal, especially in recent years . . .[48]
>
> The Rolling Bones killed ten thousand fans in their seats with a rousing rendition of 'Good Little Bad Little You' alternating sweet and vicious 24 times per second.[49]

The Grateful Dead did not play at Altamount, but their belief in the ecstasy of large festivals was shattered by it. *Rolling Stone* magazine characteristically failed to do more than report what it called 'perhaps rock and roll's alltime worst day.' In spite of the 1960s record of the police and the law in America, and the Movement's accurate diagnosis of 'pig,' it was in fact the county sheriffs who cared for Meredith Hunter's body, informed his parents, and tried to bring the assassins to justice. American kids were too used to assassination and official slaughter to care, and too terrified of the boots and cues of the Angels. The distance between people and stage had grown as large as the distance between the incomes of the rock capitalists and their spectator-consumers.

The dream of a counter-culture community, as alternative to the official America of the 1960s, ended. It had begun as the culture of communal living, free food, the Mime Troupe, the Airplane, the Dead, free Sundays in the parks, a non-violent scene in which, in the words of the rock journalist Michael Lyndon, 'everyone looked like a rock star and rock stars began

211

to look like people, not gods on the make.' By 1968, rock had become a commercial success and its energy accepted: it had to radiate from the *stage* as a magic centre, and not from the crowds. Bill Graham moved from managing the Mime Troupe benefit to being the first major big business rock entrepreneur. The first major rock magazine, *Crawdaddy*, begun in 1966, had a circulation of 25,000. It missed issues, did not hunt for record company advertisements, and described the whole scene rather than the rock stars alone. When the founder-editor, Paul Williams, left for a rural commune and his own writing, *Rolling Stone* took over and became the rock industry's trade paper, pushing the star system and rock imperialism. The Electric Circus, and dancing in the space before the bands and groups, turned into concerts. The sense of 'message' in the music became only too clear. The Hell's Angels were always there, exemplifying the fascist underground of American power. At Altamont, the Stones, Rock Scully of the Grateful Dead, and ex-Digger Emmett Grogan had hired them as a security force in the fashion of private hired armies throughout the capitalist world. Music was supposed to be the supreme power to counter the mercenaries, and had been built up to absurd heights of political capacity.

The Angels had themselves been falsely mythicized by a number of writers. Hunter S. Thompson's *Hell's Angels: The Strange and Terrible Saga of the Outlaw Motorcycle Gang* (1966) produced them as traditional all-American outlaws, barbarians of American energy – although he concludes with his own beating-up by 'four or five Angels who seemed to feel I was taking advantage of them.' When he lay on the floor spitting teeth and blood, his reaction was simple: 'Exterminate all the brutes!'[50] Michael McClure wrote up the memoirs of Frank Reynolds, secretary of the San Francisco chapter of the Hell's Angels, in *Freewheelin' Frank* (1967), an extension of his own critical fascination with stars, including Billy the Kid and Jean Harlow.[51] In *Freewheelin' Frank*, Reynolds is a star of hatred who believes in leaders as gods. He turns one of the earliest great universal symbols of energy into his own version of fascist insignia: 'We feel that we are a superior race. The swastika signifies a superior race . . . it helps us generate togetherness.'

The world is a game of chess in which the Angels are horsemen, 'knights of brotherhood' using acid, guns and bikes as a triple technology of angelic revenge and impositional power. Guns, like acid, are in Reynolds's words 'a trip,' a mythic 'trip' of religious permission: 'But who in the hell do you get in an argument with when the kill trip is on the table? I love this gun. It gives me confidence. . . . When I wear my gun and think about it, I feel as though it is a rendition of the sling in this era. In other words, when approaching any Goliath large or small – and there are so many of them around – I'm ready to make that Bible trip clear of how David brought down Goliath'.[52]

In 1965 Allen Ginsberg attempted to deflect the Angels from disrupting peace demonstrations in California, providing a set of instructions on 'How to Make a March/Spectacle' which also became, of necessity, an address of advice to the Angels:

> The parade can be made into an exemplary spectacle on how
>   to handle situations of anxiety and fear/threat
>   (such as Spectre of Hells Angels or Spectre of Communism)
> To manifest by concrete example, namely the parade itself,
>   how to change war-psychology and surpass, go over, the
>   habit-image-reaction of fear/violence.[53]

Ginsberg's appeal worked temporarily but the Angels were not dedicated to love and peace. Ginsberg has always been attracted to group ecstasy and is well aware of its potential for good and evil. The following year in *Underdog 8* he published 'First Party at Ken Kesey's with Hell's Angels.' On the record of the Spoleto reading, he prefaces his performance with a reference to the Angels as 'an American fascist group' – but the poem itself includes them, rock music, marijuana and the Merry Pranksters in a single focus to mock the attendant police.[54]

Tom Wolfe's fascination with the Pranksters and Angels falls short of the ambivalent excitements of McClure and Ginsberg in 1966. But *The Electric Kool-Aid Acid Test* (1968) achieves its own kind of accuracy on the ecstasy of acid, rebelliousness, and bike and automobile technology, fusing 'the unholy alliance, the Merry Pranksters and the Hell's Angels,' with one root going back to the 1950s and the Beat Generation heroes. Neal

Cassidy, the model for Dean Moriarty, feverish mobility star of Jack Kerouac's *On the Road* (1957) and a man who features in Alan Harrington's *Psychopaths* (1972), joined the San Francisco acid publicist Ken Kesey, and their electronics-and-acid group joined the Angels. The chain analogues a characteristic double charged energy in American culture: on the one hand, the fine creativity of Kerouac's and Kesey's novels; on the other the perversion of energy into control power, from the creative and the democratic to the rebellious and the hallucinatory inside the star system.

Electronic sound and acid psychedelics were supposed to create a community of ecstasy, revolt and potential social change. Electronic coordination was to be an analogue of community. These two forms of engineering 'synch,' or synchronization, which was the goal of Kesey's leadership and sense of mission, would take Leary's slogan into social action, the hope being that practical joking (and the slightly medieval tone of 'Merry Pranksters' suggesting the Lord of Misrule once again) would work toward mobility and lightness rather than rest and reactionary stability. The Pranksters were to be 'immune' – the very term used by Richard Fariña's Gnossos Papadopoulos, the brilliant drop-out graduate astronomer hero of *Been Down So Long It Looks Like Up To Me* (1966). Kesey dreamed of being Martian superman Valentine Smith, the god-like star who had descended from Earth parents following their space migration in Robert A. Heinlein's *Stranger in a Strange Land* (1961). This science fiction novel eventually became one of the most popular books among the young in America during the 1960s, and Kesey kept a copy on his own shelf as a reminder that the 'synch' had to be under god-like command. The Beat Generation turned into Kesey's Beautiful People.

Kesey met the Angels through Hunter Thompson, and on 7 August 1965 the Pranksters and Angels had the party which Ginsberg wrote up in his poem. Bike Man met Acid Man in the presence of the chief Beat poet and the San Francisco police. McClure's Freewheelin' Frank took his first acid: 'By nightfall he had climbed a redwood and was nestled up against a loudspeaker in a tree grooving off the sounds and vibrations of

Bob Dylan singing 'The Subterranean Homesick Blues.'[55]
But Tom Wolfe recognises other aspects of the scene:

> The only bad moment at Kesey's came one day when an Angel
> went berserk during the first rush of the drug and tried to
> strangle his old lady on Kesey's front steps. But he was too
> wasted at that point to really do much.
>   So it was wonderful and marvellous, an unholy alliance, the
> Merry Pranksters and the Hell's Angels . . . the people of La
> Honda felt like the plague had come, and wasn't there anything
> that could be done. More than one of the Pranksters had his
> reservations too. The Angels were like a time bomb . . . they
> were capable of bursting loose into carnage at any moment. It
> brought the adrenalin into your throat. . . . Kesey was the magnet
> and the strength, the man in both worlds.[56]

But that scene was forgotten four years later at Altamont, and
it is doubtful if any of the crowd had even heard of Ken Kesey or
Tom Wolfe. When Ronnie Davis, a member of the Mime
Troupe, questioned the Altamont producers – why had a free
festival charged admission? why weren't groups from the
ghettoes invited? – Ralph Gleason, an editor of *Rolling Stone*,
denounced him as a political fool who did not represent the rock
masses or the rock industry. Eventually, the Altamont festival
and the murder of Meredith Hunter became part of a popular
money-making film. The energy of the searching young in
America remained depoliticized and exploited. Dionysus remained
rampant in forms of violent anarchy. Already the 1960s is
becoming a decade for nostalgia.

One of the finest reporters of the counter-culture in which he
took part was Don McNeil. At the age of twenty-three, he
drowned accidentally in a New York lake. But he left one of the
most necessary documents of the period – *Moving Through Here*
(1970). The introduction is by Ginsberg and the epilogue is by
Paul Williams (of *Crawdaddy*). McNeil grasped the rapid
transience of the scene, its opportunity for descent with the
traditional hope of regenerative ascent, and its real danger
within the invitation to live mythically:

The transient rut is not a creative one. It is a fertilizing, pre-creative experience for a few. It is an interim for a few. For more, it is a long road down, laced with drugs . . . Many dig the descent . . . There is a fascination in being strung out for days on amphetamine, a fascination in Rolling Stones echoes, a fascination in the communal chaos of the Lower East Side, as far removed from Westchester as is India. If you wade in too deep, you may learn that the East Side undertow is no myth.[57]

The god exists and may recruit his angels at any time, especially when the paradigm of a culture begins to lose its boundaries, and experience and knowledge start to challenge the frontier. The Greek concept of games united body and psyche into a praxis celebrated by Pindar and enacted by Pythagorus, who wrestled in the Olympic games. Separation of body and psyche is a fall the Renaissance repeatedly exposed. In Blake's *Jerusalem* it is a primary curse. George Leonard's *The Ultimate Athlete* (1975) repudiates the cult of winning in modern competitiveness, or sport as therapy for work conditions. Professional sport degrades the dance of athletics into technique and money. If Huizinga's idea of *Homo Ludens* is correct, play must include pain of ordeal, risks of boundary-breaking, and even 'death in ecstasy' – in Leonard's terms a Dionysian dance of 'liberating disorder.'[58]

The classic case of entropic Dionysian enfeeblement is Kenneth Anger's film *Scorpio Rising* (1962–4), a celebration of sexual sterility and death played out through motorcycle technology and the rebel Angels of entropy. According to Mick Brown, writing in *Crawdaddy* in 1976, Anger was first introduced to Aleister Crowley's teachings at High School in Beverly Hills by Jack Parsons, a physicist who contributed to the development of the fuels used in the Apollo space shots. Anger became Crowley's 'magical son,' appointed to carry on his work after his death.[59] Apparently L. Ron Hubbard, the inventor of scientology, was sent by Naval Intelligence in 1945 to investigate him and disperse the magical group he worked with. But according to Anger they in fact worked together as student magicians until Hubbard betrayed Parsons, stealing his bank account, yacht and wife. Parsons allegedly conjured up a storm, wrecked the boat off Florida, and Hubbard crept back. Parsons may have been murdered by Howard Hughes, who wanted Parsons to work for him. Hughes had him kidnapped but Parsons refused to work, and shortly afterwards his house blew up. After that episode Anger lived for a time with Parsons' wife, a witch, while studying Crowley's work intensely. Later he lived in Crowley's old home at Boleskine House in Loch Ness. In 1955 he went to the Abbey of Thelema, a deserted farmhouse in Cefalu, Sicily, to restore the ritualistic erotic wall-paintings which had been whitewashed over by Mussolini's police after Crowley's expulsion. Local people were angry enough for Anger to leave after only three months there. But he still retreats twice a year to practice Crowley's system of 'magical retirement,' once in spring and once in autumn. His left arm is tatooed with the Seal of Crowley, his right arm with the Seal of Lucifer.

Anger asked Jagger to be Lucifer Three in *Lucifer* (*Invocation of My Demon Brother*, a 'magical' short, has a Moog synthesizer soundtrack by Jagger). He agreed, but broke off before filming began – 'at a time,' Mick Brown quotes Anger as saying, when 'he wrote "Sympathy for the Devil" . . . a song I guess I must have influenced in some way, he really *meant* it, but he's lost that charisma. After Altamont he got scared of becoming too closely identified with that whole *Their Satanic Majesties* thing; it was all becoming too literally true in a way that was destroying the group.'

One of the latest intellectual prophets of the Anger-Crowley energies is the American poet and editor of one of the finest contemporary journals, *Io*, Richard Grossinger. His *Book of the Earth and Sky, Book 2* (1971) shows the extent of his seduction. He quotes Anger: 'rock'n'roll is a genetic thing you can fit them all under. What *Scorpio* represents is me cluing in to popular American culture.' Power through machinery and patterns of intimidation and submission are to be a way out of the mundane – in Grossinger's terms: 'learning is: being changed, is being torn apart and rebuilt of the other, is making stodgy knowledge go mad.' Anger therefore identifies Christ and Hitler as energy resources of violent change: 'they are working miracles. . . . Christ is the ideal cyclist; he's high all the time . . . he doesn't have to get high; he's made it without speed . . . it means the same thing in America: Christ, Hitler, the devil, commies, religion, politics. The breakthrough itself, right wing or left wing, is more important than even life. Is the greater magic. Life can come later.'[60]

The dominant slogan is: ecstasy *now* – pay later, what Burroughs calls the biologic price. *Scorpio Rising* makes 'opposite meanings simultaneously possible: rebel, saint, murderer, saviour, ecstasy, torture, piss, gold, wipeout, rebirth. . . . The body is seized by a drama, with a power, not beyond reason, but beyond understanding, is the body naked, falling in love with the sheer process of growth . . . the will to die and be reborn, to yield finally, as we all must, to metabolic death.'[61] The film is a death ritual enacted by 'the angels who established Earth, and lie upon the deep structure of all life.' Love may surpass death but the film concentrates on those stars which obsess McClure and others – 'the rampaging stars are turned from their lesser fears, that they will be extinguished and their personalities blended imperceptibly back into the universe, to their greater possibilities.' And the latter are subsumed in the phrase that fascinates many contemporary American intellectuals who deeply fear democracy: Aleister Crowley's 'EVERY MAN AND EVERY WOMAN IS A STAR.' For Grossinger 'every intentional act is a magical act; the spaceman – motor-cyclist, the ecstatic saint, is falling into his own power of the universe, into himself.' This is indeed a statement of that anarchic streak of 'the imperial self' which penetrates and wrecks American culture from the early nineteenth century to the present day.[62]

In *Closing Time* (1973), Norman O. Brown is still using the Spenglerian version of change through the barbarian radical:

> Indeed, only barbarians are capable of rejuvenating a world
> labouring under the death throes of unnerved civilization
>
> . . .
>
> Man is maniac
> the Dionysian origin of civilization
> enthusiasm
>
> . . .
>
> the fortunate fall[63]

In *Caesar's Gate* (1972), Robert Duncan acknowledges the dialectic of Dionysus and his counter-god, Apollo, as a post-Nietzschean presence in his poetry: 'My music not Apollo's but that of Mercury the Thief, the Dissembler, Lord of the Musical Comedy turn. But name me there, and I shall be offended Apollo. The two musics belong to one myth and mystery of the god of rapture and disease and of the other, his counterpart and instructor, magician-master of the lyre, the trickster god of what is too easy to believe.'[64]

Duncan's 'Passages 30/Stage Directions' returns to the theatre of violence. Out of Macbeth, and its assassination parallels in 1960s America, he moves towards the ambivalent god of authoritarian power:

> . . . in the assassin's mind
> the world is filled with enemies,   the truth
> itself is enemy and quickens   action to override
> subversive thought.
>   . . .
> Dionysus, Zeus's Second Self,
>   Director of the Drama
>   needed.[65]

Allen Ginsberg's sense of that need is just as ambivalent: 'I think orgies should be institutionalized: impersonal meat orgies, with no question of personality or character or relating to people as people. Anyone who insults Dionysus had better watch out! The leopards come and get them, or else they get turned to vine leaves, in Ezra Pound [Canto 2], when they practice god-slight, the insult to Dionysus.'[66]

Any definition of the triple action of Dionysus, Apollo and Eros – the three orderers – is entangled in excitement. We have to go further than any of these writers and artists, and this essay, into how the Greek Dionysus and the sixteenth century Renaissance Faust dramatize both the intimacies of destruction and creation and our profound ambivalences towards power. In *The Two and the One* (1965), Mircia Eliade shows the bond through Goethe's life-work. It is Eros we must choose beyond Dionysus. The Devil is death if you let him stop you:

What Mephistopheles asks of Faust . . . is *to stop*. 'Verweile doch!' . . . the moment Faust stops he will have lost his soul. But a stop is not a negation of the Creator; it is a negation of Life. . . . In place of movement and Life, [Mephistopheles] tries to impose rest, immobility, death. For what ceases to change and transform itself decays and perishes. This 'death in Life' can be translated as spiritual sterility . . . damnation . . . the negating Spirit. The crime against Life, Goethe gives one to understand, is a crime against salvation. . . . However, though Mephistopheles uses every means to oppose the flux of Life, he stimulates Life.[67]

1975

8

'Laws Scribbled by Law-Breakers': Law, Confidence and Disobedience in American Culture

National confidence is generated in a people's behaviour within law and in outlawry, and especially at the edges where disobedience and obedience exemplify belief and conscience in action. Law is intended to control and elucidate values – even to invent them – with masks of reason and security where the nation is new and on the frontier of civilization, as America was until well after the Declaration of Independence. In the seventeenth century New England tribunals, witches, the archetypal dissenters, were convicted for their own good as much as for the self-constituted legal State. Public ambivalence towards law results from attempts to impose an order of discipline and punishment on human existence, when the latter is mobile in differing degrees between self and community. The fit is never complete. As Denis Diderot understood in the late eighteenth century: 'there are two attorneys-general – the one at your beck and call, who prosecutes offenders against society. The other is nature. It takes cognizance of all the vices that escape the law.'[1] In 1940, the great American geographer, Carl Sauer, put the issue for America in terms of a discipline under the aegis of Social Darwinism: 'The design of science that Montesquieu, Herder and Buckle forecast failed because we know that natural law does not apply to social groups, as eighteenth-century rationalism or nineteenth-century environmentalism thought. We have come to know that environment is a term of cultural appraisal, which is itself a "value" in cultural history.'[2] In terms of cultural history, therefore, law stands judicially between the past (or precedent) and the future (or change), and tends to restrict both to contemporary usage and belief. Explanations of liberty are caught in the net of various evaluations of what order might be. As James Fenimore Cooper's frontiersman, Leatherstocking, proposed in *The Prarie* in 1827: 'the law – 'Tis bad to have it, but, I sometimes think, it is worse to be entirely without it.'[3]

But law moves to that popular self-righteousness satirized in a song on Bob Dylan's *The Times They Are A-Changin'* in 1963: 'If fire them we're forced to/ Then fire them we must/ One push of the button/ And a shot the world wide/ And you never ask questions/ When God's on your side.'[4] Or, turning the volume down a little, we might cite Gerald Stanley Lee's *Crowds* of 1913: 'Turning the other cheek is a kind of moral jiu-jitsu.'[5] Law intervenes in the very action of survival, especially in a tight spot. When a few survivors cling to the only lifeboat in Alfred Hitchcock's 1944 film, *Lifeboat*, John Hodiak offers the challenge: 'Whose law? We're on our own here. We can make our own law.' Henry Fonda, playing the lawyer president in John Ford's *Young Mister Lincoln* (1939), gives the last word on the archetypal and extreme expression of American frontier law, lynching: 'If those boys had more than one life, I'd say "Go ahead. Maybe a little hanging mightn't do 'em any harm." But the sort of hanging you boys'd give 'em would be so – so permanent . . . Then, the next thing you know, they're hanging one another just for fun till it gets to a place a man can't pass a tree or look at a rope without feeling uneasy.' And since so many Americans relate to immigrant ancestry, we can recall that when a snobbish woman boasted to Miss Mae West 'My ancestors came over with the *Mayflower*,' that redoubtable comedienne replied: 'You're lucky. Now they have immigration laws.'[6]

Law penetrates every part of society and its histories. That fine film director, Sam Peckinpah, grew up in a family of lawyers and judges, and we may measure the extreme nature of justice in his films when he reports that 'sitting around a dining table talking about law and order, truth and justice, on a Bible which was very big in our family, I suppose I felt like an outsider, and I started to question them. I guess I'm still questioning.'[7] In his 1855 poem, 'Great Are the Myths,' Walt Whitman tried to locate justice and law cosmically by making them mobile between the European past and the American present, the archetype and the practicality, the controllers and the majority – and in a state still questioning its bases:

Justice is not settled by legislators and laws – it is in the Soul,
It cannot be varied by statutes, any more than love,
    pride, the attraction of gravity can,
It is immutable – it does not depend on majorities – majorities or what
    not come at last before the same passionless and exact tribune.

For justice are the grand lawyers and perfect
    judges – it is their Souls,
It is well assorted – they have studies for noth
    -ing – the great includes the less,
They rule on the highest grounds – they oversee all
    eras, states, administrations.[8]

But then, in a poem of 1860, he has to add:

    To me, any judge, or any juror, is equally criminal – and
any reputable person is also – and the President is also.

And in a poem using the experience of the union's collapse into Civil War in the 1860s:

States!   .
Were you looking to be held together by lawyers?
By an agreement on a paper? Or by arms?
Away!
I arrive bringing these, beyond all the forces of courts and arms,
These! to hold you together as firmly as the earth itself is held together
  . . .

Whitman speaks not of the Constitution but of his faith in the spirit of love and friendship, in what he called 'adhesiveness,' in his country's idealism and mutual aid, through which conflict might still be overcome.[9] William Kapp's *The Social Costs of Private Enterprise* (1971) deteriorates into liberal platitudes, but it does at least point to the ineffectuality of Whitman's position as a programme. In view of 'the abandonment of the belief in a beneficial natural order in social affairs and in the basic rationality of man, long abandoned by modern philosophy and psychology,' Kapp holds, there should be a 'recognition of strong and cumulative tendencies toward disorder and dis-equilibrium under conditions of competition.' He says nothing further on the effects such a recognition would have on the functions of law, which is itself a competitive function. (This fact provides the entire plot for the television law-soap series *LA Law*).[10] All that Edward T. Hall can offer in *The Silent Language* (1959) is a certain nervousness Americans have concerning practical law and the myths of rules: 'Americans . . . have comparatively few technical and formal restrictions placed upon them but are loaded with informal ones. This means that Americans are apt to be quite inhibited, because they cannot state explicitly what the rules are. They can only point to them when they are violated.'[11]

Nor has America ever been able to stabilize a sense of being a class system within classic European definitions. For example, commenting on the Civil Rights movement of the 1960s in *Counter Revolution and Revolt* (1972), Herbert Marcuse, now settled in California, checks his training: 'Not the working class but the universities and the ghetto presented the first real threat to the system from within.'[12] Presumably he is only referring to that decade. The Thirties certainly could not confirm his diagnosis. Anyone working in the United States in the 1960s would recognize the truth of a different attitude in Anthony Scaduto's biography of Bob Dylan: that changes of belief and action might well result from 'understanding that laws are not written out of scruples of human instinct . . . if anything they are dim reflections of the realities of power. By the sixties Dylan and the Movement and everybody just knew the world is run by these criminals in power, knew how powerful these criminals are. The lamentable deaths, the losing of hope – it comes as no surprise.'[13] But part of the termination of legal disobedience, well within Kapp's 'social costs,' is explained by Marcuse in his earlier book, *One Dimensional Man* (1964): 'Under the conditions of a rising standard of living, non-conformity with the system itself appears to be socially useless, and the more so when it entails tangible economic and political disadvantages.'[14]

In the Fifties, Norman Mailer tried to place American anticipations of liberal law in the figure of John F. Kennedy by getting him into the gunslinger tradition as 'the outlaw sheriff.'[16] By 1975, William Eastlake had set out the whole American frontier law myth – its violations and bourgeois sense of territory endlessly to be defended by the strongest. The activator of his novel, *Dancers in the Scalp House*, tries hard: 'Mary Forge came to live with the Indian nation because on the big white reservation the strong were eating the weak. This is called competition. All the walking wounded were piled in a city ghetto and told to behave themselves. This is called law and order. When a rescue party arrived it was too late. The Indians are placed in outdoor ghettoes and told to behave themselves. This is called honouring our treaties.'[16]

The legal bases extend back to the New England theocratic state and its exclusions from priviledge. A certain purity of legal belief among Puritans is present whenever a statement is made about 'the Law.' As the mid-twentieth century novelist Brion Gysin puts it: 'The idea of law is that everyone remains pure within the law . . . and everyone who is not pure within the Law is an outsider . . . a criminal.'[17] But Oedipal paternalism in practice is impure. A major part of Melville's *Pierre* (1852) proceeds from a young American's demolition of a father-saint whose white marbilization assured certainty and confidence through inheritance. The resultant loss for the next generation's identity turns law into an accumulation of ambiguities, or relativism. Murderous revolt can only be punished from the Oedipal remains. In 1831, De Toqueville – always anxious when confronted by the primal horde stealing the father's thunder – noted in his Olympian manner:

In visiting the Americans and studying their laws, we perceive that the authority they have entrusted to members of the legal profession, and the influence that these individuals exercise in the government, are the most powerful existing security against the excesses of democracy. . . . In America there are no nobles or literary men, and the people are apt to mistrust the wealthy; lawyers consequently form the highest political class . . . they have therefore nothing to gain by innovation. . . . The courts of justice are the visible organs by which the legal profession is enabled to control the democracy. . . . Armed with the power of declaring the laws to be unconstitutional, the American magistrate perpetually interferes in political affairs.[18]

In 1978, Victor H. Li, professor of international legal studies at Stanford University, begins his *Law Without Lawyers: A Comparative View of Law in China and the United States* thus: 'In 1974 a benchmark in the American legal system was passed: The number of lawyers in this country reached 400,000. . . . approximately one person out of every 500 in our population is a lawyer. Since most law school graduates are at least 24 years old, and if we arbitrarily define an adult as a person over the age of 24, then approximately one out of every 250 adults is a lawyer.' Since until recently very few women were in the profession, he adds that the ratio should be restated as 'one in 125 adult males is a lawyer.' However, most American citizens know very little about the law, and it is not taught as a regular subject in schools. But 'the law assumes that all of us know and are responsible for a considerable portion of the contents of our local law libraries.' Furthermore, 'legal officials at all levels [have] some discretion regarding how to apply or even whether to apply the rules of law.' But little is known about how 'discretionary power takes place' or how 'plea bargaining' exists as a set of procedures. 'The cost of legal services in practice limits public access to the law,' Li continues, and 'to a considerable degree, the legal system is something detached from the public, existing in a world of its own. . . . [Lawyers] speak primarily to each other, using their own language and symbols.' Professor Li concludes: 'One of the benefits of this separate existence is that law is placed above individuals and especially above manipulation by individuals. The price that we pay is that the general public does not have full and immediate control over this fundamental social institution.'[19] And this condition is spreading all the time. Ross MacDonald moves in on one kind of result in his 1954 novel from the Lew Archer series, *Find a Victim*. The veteran private eye tells the sheriff, Brand Church: 'I understand this. I'm trying to solve two homicides, and something is trying to stop me. Something that looks like law and talks like law but doesn't

226

smell like law. Not in my nostrils. It smells like zombie meat. A zombie that takes the public's money and sits behind a courthouse desk pretending to be an officer.'[20]

An extreme case is recorded in Eldridge Cleaver's memoirs of Black dissidence, *Soul on Ice* (1968), in which he claims that the rape of white women is a necessary 'trampling upon the white man's law, upon his system of values.'[21] (The necessary context is *Sex and Racism in America* (1965) by the Black sociologist Calvin Hernton, still a standard work on the pathology that necessarily exists within law: 'the racism of sex creates derangements within the races as well as between the races.')[22] Cultural studies reveals what the law resists – that law arbitrates at the frontiers of dominance and submission in their most pathological states, however much they masquerade as rational patterns of control. William S. Burroughs necessarily has his comic villain, Doctor Benway, operating at the intersections of medicine, psychiatry, and law in *The Naked Lunch* (1959), saying 'As one judge said to another, "Be just and if you can't be just be arbitrary." '[23] This dark joke carries within it a fundamental truth summarized by Barbrook and Bolt in their *Power and Protest in American Life* (1980): 'If the Constitution had established a system of federal courts and a government of laws shaped by representatives of the people, many Americans in rural or frontier areas long retained a hostility to the law and its practitioners, regarding them as imposing cynical constraints upon their natural intelligence and freedom.'[24]

Laws certainly contain injustice. The Smith Act of 1940 made it a crime to 'knowingly or willingly advocate, abet, advise, or teach the duty, necessity, desirability or propriety of overthrowing or destroying any government in the United States of America by force or violence.' Through its vague terminology the act aided the authoritarian and reactionary. It was reinforced by the Internal Security Act of 1950 which in turn created the Subversive Activities Control Board. The activities of the Board, which could and did withhold passports and restrict travel and movement, were directed ostensibly against Communists but in practice against critical nonconformists of many kinds. In 1952, the Immigration and Nationality Act was applied to 2.5 million so-called 'aliens' who 'could be arrested without warrant, held without trial and deported for an action that was legal when committed' – for example, membership of any organization said to be subversive by the Internal Security Act. Anonymous information could be given at deportation hearings, but those liable to deportation did not have to be given a hearing if considered a threat to 'national security.'[25] Throughout the 1950s and 1960s, when people refused questioning by the House UnAmerican Activities Committee by citing the Fifth Amendment – on freedom of speech – that in itself could be taken as inference they had something to hide and were presumably guilty.

As Charles Brockden Brown enables one of his characters in *Wieland* (1798) to believe: 'Ideas exist in our minds, that can be accounted for by no established laws.'[26] Further, men's ideas of what is permitted and not permitted, of what is to be placed as law and as out of control, differ within one society. In Hawthorne's story, 'Earth's Holocaust' (1844), an executioner who tries to stop wild reformers from burning his gallows is supported by 'men of a far different sphere – even of that consecrated class in whose guardianship the world is apt to trust its benevolence.' One of these advises: 'You are misled by a false philanthropy! . . . The gallows is a heaven-oriented instrument! Bear it back, then, reverently, and set it up in its old place, else the world will fall to speedy ruin and desolation!'[27] A reform leader shouts: 'Into the flames with the accursed instrument of man's bloody policy! How can human law inculcate benevolence and love while it persists in setting up the gallows as its chief symbol?'

Then the people throw their marriage certificates into the bonfire. With his usual wry duplicity, Hawthorne writes that they 'declared themselves candidates for a higher, holier and more comprehensive union than that which has subsisted from the birth of time.' Then other expressions of law are thrown in – money, title deeds, and ledgers – so that 'the whole soil of the earth revert to the public, from whom it had been wrongfully abstracted and most unequally distributed.' Hawthorne's narrative shares the field with Thoreau and, a century later, William Faulkner. But his urge to nihilism now emerges. It is suggested that 'all written constitutions, set forms of government, legislative acts, statute books, and everything else on which human invention had endeavoured to stamp its arbitrary laws' should be thrown into the fire as well. Hawthorne withdraws from stating whether this part of the destruction actually took place, but he does assert that the apparatus of the Christian churches was burned. Now he moves towards his central proposition, an issue that permeates a culture founded on the frontier between, on the one hand, a Manichean belief that good and evil are engaged in a continual battle for the human soul, and, on the other hand, an Enlightenment belief that good can overcome evil in a benevolent, egalitarian, competitive republic: that human laws can direct human life towards utopia. But 'higher laws,' as Thoreau called them, may be frustrated by the chance that no law, no social foundation in enlightenment philosophy and the laws of property, can avoid human evil. The story continues: 'a dark-complexioned personage [whose] eyes glowed with a redder light than the bonfire' suggests that the people should burn 'the human heart itself . . . unless they hit upon some method of purifying that foul cavern' and its legacy and future 'wrong and misery.' This is 'the Evil Principle . . . the fatal circumstance of error at the very root of the matter!'

And democratic legislation for the future? Hawthorne ends: how is 'the Heart' to be rectified? The desire for 'perfection' may be wrecked 'if we go no deeper than the Intellect, and strive, with merely that feeble instrument, to discern and rectify what is wrong.' What if the young and innocent heart challenges the Oedipal fathers? From *Billy Budd, Sailor* (*An Inside Narrative*) in 1891 to the trial, multiple sentencing (of both the defendants and their lawyers), and eventual aquittal of the Chicago Eight for their alleged conspiracies in 1968, the treason of the young is a constant American anxiety. An act of mutiny or critical subversion becomes, in time of war or potential war, an act of betrayal. The debate between law and natural innocence or natural depravity, between paternal leadership under law and the people's rights, tightens, and the semantics once again begin to drift alarmingly. In *Billy Budd*, Melville plots the terms *allegiance, law, order, duty, leader* and *free* into a fiction exposing the ambivalences of command under law in a democracy, and the ambiguities of single leadership – the choice of one man to rule under the disguises of republicanism. Ezra Pound opted, as many people did in the 1930s, for what he believed could be benevolent totalitarian rule, and in *Hugh Selwyn Mauberley* (*Life and Contacts*), his poem sequence of 1920, prefigured the key American issues of the next six decades. Citing the ancient Greek city state's commissioner of legal and religious drama, Pound wrote, 'All men, in law, are equals./ Free of Pisistratus,/ We choose a knave or an eunuch/To rule over us.'[28] Pound was indicted for treason in 1945 and awarded the major Bollingen Prize for poetry in 1949. The advisory board included ten of America's senior writers.

Laws of daily order, and their unstable compatibility with 'the Law' and even 'Justice,' also need to be geared into that set of alibis for permission and proscription known as 'natural laws' or even 'natural law' – especially since Darwinism became Spencer's Social Darwinism and was then translated into American naturalism at the turn of the nineteenth century. The resultant triumphs of conservatism are notorious. John Steinbeck's massively popular novels exemplify an American obsession with allegedly universal doctrines of order – visible and invisible – to which all life is legally subject. We are sentenced to the 'ferocious survival quotient' of the tide-pool which 'excites us and makes us feel good' and exhibits natural selection as a 'perfect and God-set balance.' Converted into an ontological law of permissive capitalism, this plot provides an excuse for any violation of any man or woman by any man or woman in the name of survival. For Steinbeck, writing from his Californian experience of the Depression, this law infers that there can be no blame for unemployment since that too is part of 'natural conditions' which cover 'all life in this benevolently hostile planet.' Steinbeck plots semantics of 'choice' and 'law,' and his teleological explanation governs all self-reliance in ways which Emerson might have been surprised to discover.[29] In his 1936 novel, *In Dubious Battle*, as the title borrowed from Milton's *Paradise Lost* suggests, the organization of agricultural workers in California fails because it is a disobedient, not to say illegal, intervention into natural law. Satan's disobedience against God is naturalized: 'man has engaged in a blind and fearful struggle out of a past he can't remember, into a future he can't foresee or understand.' Steinbeck, issuing *The Grapes of Wrath* in 1939, wrote that 'every bomb is proof that the spirit has not died . . . [and] every little beaten strike is proof that the step is being taken' – a step within the natural law of Social Darwinism. This world is summarized in *Cannery Row* (1945) by Doc, the marine biologist, as the 'system': 'The things we admire in men, kindness and generosity, openness, honesty, understanding, and feeling are the concomitants of failure in our system. And those traits we detest, sharpness, greed, acquisitiveness, meanness, egotism, and self-interest are the traits of success. And while men admire the quality of the first they love the produce of the second'.[30] From tide-pool survivalist law to the success ethic is a natural step in the mystification of the term 'law.' The next step, as President Reagan and millions of his fellow Americans believe, is Armageddon.

The odour of the supernatural penetrates 'law' and elevates it into an absolute, complete with priests and acolytes whose intonation of Social Darwinist language – *market forces, the law of supply and demand, fitness,* and so forth – makes them advocates of what T.H. Huxley dubbed, in his Romanes Lecture of 1893, 'Evolution and Ethics,' 'the gladiatorial theory of existence.'[31] As a study of, for example, the huge mass of American films incorporating western, gangster, courtroom, police, and private eye themes will show, the nation is obsessed with the frontier of desire and law, where 'the naked opening of Desire' meets the attempt to regulate, 'the authorities of delimitation.'[32] Richard Slotkin's *Regeneration Through Violence* (1973) documents the confrontation between Puritan and Indian, the wilderness and the backwoodsman, and their textual apologetics. Most recently, analysts have investigated the activities of the House UnAmerican Activities Committee in the 1950s and the manichean dimensions of contemporary US foreign policy, backed as it is by a mass voting populace of reactionary Christians.[33] Only in recent years has the history of obedience and disobedience, of discipline, punishment and law been investigated carefully. Thomas S. Szasz pioneered the work in America in the 1960s, investigating how the state needs to contain and punish, and how law is thereby immediately involved in psychology and psychiatry, in his *Law, Liberty and Psychiatry* (1963) and *Ideology and Sanity* (1970).

In *The Life of the Mind in America* (1965), Perry Miller began to document the instability of the bases of law, the struggle between the codifying of law and its opening toward desire, and the meaning of words like *right* and *liberty* which had remained so axiomatically fluid in legal terms from 1776 onwards.[34] As mediators of this instability, lawyers became a powerful and wealthy category. At the end of the eighteenth century, Jesse Root is already an exemplary Americanist, arguing that Common Law – that is, English Common Law, taken as starting point – was the law of 'a people grown old in the habits of vice' and therefore suspect. Any Newtonian and Enlightenment symmetries of law were resisted by pleas on behalf of frontier individualism. Courts became theatres for rhetorical pleading and attack – still familiar from countless films and television performances, and projected throughout the world as the essence of America. Perry Miller dates to the administrations of Andrew Jackson the conflict between 'cultivated reason' and 'automatic functioning,' from which there emerged the judge as the day-to-day coder of law and the Supreme Court as a constant arbitration centre. In Miller's terms, law moved from 'a system of jurisprudence' to a source of power. Included in a continued American allegiance to Sir William Blackstone's *Commentaries* of 1765–69 – the bible of Common Law – had also to be the English belief that law was 'the proper accomplishment of every gentleman and scholar . . . part of a liberal and polite education.' Such beliefs laid foundations for the fears raised by future lawyer-President Abraham Lincoln as early as 1838, when he was twenty-nine, that an ambitious leader could take advantage of American chaos for his own ends: 'it will require the people to be united with each other, attached to the government and laws, and generally intelligent, to successfully frustrate his designs.' For such Americans, law was intended to check genius and Caesarism, and the people's inclination to follow a charismatic man. Lincoln shares such lucidity with Hawthorne and Melville.

But in 1851 *The United States Monthly Law Magazine* declared that law should be like 'other sciences' – 'never modified' in its 'immovable basis.' Natural law, under Blackstone's God-dictated initiatives, had to be secularized into a binding ukase or edict. Nevertheless, in a competitive society, law had problems with equity. George Robertson stated in 1837 that equity *was* justice and was invariable, but this took little account of unequal distribution of income, opportunity and power, let alone of those economic and racial issues that would contribute to Civil War fifty-three years later. Part of the profession's self-absorption is exposed in Theodore Sedgewick's comment of 1857: 'Arbitrary formulae, metaphysical subtleties, fanciful hypotheses, aid us but little in our work.' Gradually, fear of the jury as 'the infallible mob' became endemic, especially when the jury challenged what *The Western Law Journal* of 1849 termed the 'great code of Divine Law.' When Jeremy Bentham offered to codify American law for President Madison, lawyers grew angry. 'God preserve us from the extreme remedy of general codification!' the historian George Bancroft had cried back in 1827. The dispute between stability and evolution in law is not a simple matter. Murray Bookchin, in his 1982 book *The Ecology of Freedom*, points to the characteristic and historical problems:

> It is not the ethical calculus that comprises the most vulnerable features of utilitarian ethics but the fact that liberalism has denatured reason itself into a mere methodology for calculating sentiments – with the same operational techniques that bankers and industrialists use to administer their enterprises. . . . Anarchism and revolutionary socialism profess to be concerned with freedom. Fascism is concerned neither with justice nor with freedom but merely with the instrumentalities of naked domination; its various ideologies are purely opportunistic. Hence the fate of justice reposes with the fate of the ideas of such serious thinkers as John Stuart Mill and his followers. Their failure to elicit an ethics from justice that could rest on its rule of equivalence leaves only Bentham's utilitarian ethics – a crude, quantitative theory of pains and pleasures – as justice's denouement.

Bookchin shows how utilitarian ethics motivates American justice through a terminology of benefits and risks, gains and losses, and 'the lifeboat ethic.' He concludes: 'The inequality of

233

equals still prevails over the equality of unequals' and freedom so quickly becomes 'cynical opportunism' in the ditherings of well-meaning liberals.[35] It is said that when Vice-President Lyndon Johnson spoke about President Kennedy's assembly of a brains-trust, the Speaker of the House, Sam Rayburn, said: 'Well, Lyndon, they may be as intelligent as you say, but I'd feel a helluva lot better if just one of them had ever run for sheriff.'

During the Civil Rights years in the 1960s, Henry David Thoreau's ambivalent 1848–49 text, 'Resistance to Civil Government,' which challenged both the rule of power and the rule of majority, became as axiomatic for American resistance as it had been for Mahatma Gandhi in East Africa: 'Can there not be a government in which majorities do not virtually decide right and wrong, but conscience? . . . We should be men first and subjects afterward. It is not desirable to cultivate respect for law, so much as for the right. . . . Law never made men a whit more just; and, by means of their respect for it, even the well-disposed are daily made the agents of injustice.' His two 'conscience' issues of the day were the war against Mexico and the Fugitive Slave Law – and again, on the latter, Thoreau juggles the semantics of his key terms, scarcely hiding his despair as he reaches into the recesses of how law is made and maintained: 'When the majority shall at length vote for the abolition of slavery, it will be because they are indifferent to slavery, or because there is but little slavery left to be abolished by their vote. *They* will then be the only slaves. . . . Unjust laws exist. . . . Men generally, under such a government as this, think that they ought to wait until they have persuaded the majority to alter them. . . . Why does [government] always crucify Christ, excommunicate Copernicus and Luther, and pronounce Washington and Franklin rebels?'

Control systems have to fight off criticism. Thoreau's advice was repeated during the Sixties in the United States, when the issues of conscience were again black Americans and war: 'If [the official remedy] is of such a nature that it requires you to be the agent of injustice to another, then, I say, break the law. Let your life be a counter-friction to stop the machine. . . . Under a government which imprisons any unjustly, the true place for a just man is also a prison.' Thoreau did not mean: become an

impotently imprisoned martyr. His basis was wild Nature –
'absolute freedom and wilderness,' the old frontier stuff, as
distinct from 'a freedom and culture merely civil.' The west, he
says, is 'but another name for the Wild' – 'Give me wilderness
whose glance no civilization can endure. . . . The most alive is
the wildest.' But he did not 'light out for the Territory' or
imitate the American farmer and Leatherstocking and live
among the Indians.[36] Richard Slotkin shows how moving West
included 'the destructive career of [Davy] Crockett and his
heirs, who treated the woods as "raw material" for their own and
socio-economic development,' and the urgencies of Ishmael
Bush, the patriarchal axer of forests who leads his clan west
from settlement in James Fenimore Cooper's *The Pioneers*
(1827), the man for whom Indians and *their* laws of tribe and
ecology are simply interference.[37] Cooper provides him with Old
Testament 'rules of punishment' as 'the laws of God,' for whom
he acts as sheriff-executioner. At least he has a clan. For many
Americans, ideal law is symbolized by figures such as the Lone
Ranger (with his Indian friend and subordinate, Tonto), a
masked Robin Hood able to rectify in justice and the limitations
of daily law and daily power from a mythical position at once self-
righteous and pastoral. As Humphrey Bogart says between his
teeth in William Faulkner's script for Howard Hawks' *The Big
Sleep*: 'Such a lot of guns around town and so few brains.' The
Lone Ranger, and Philip Marlowe in 1939, operate outside
police law but are liable to be its agents. Their clients are those
for whom official law is inadequate. They are part of the
unofficial law whose centre is lynching and the vigilante – and
the latter is having a powerful comeback in the 1980s.

But such positions are not restricted to one nation. In *Clarel*
(1876), Melville could formulate law in generally sceptical terms
– his immediate reference is to Frederick II of Prussia, read
through Carlyle, and the scene is what Christians used to call
The Holy Land. The plot of *Clarel* is in fact a young and
disaffiliated American's interminable search for the origins of an
absolute faith:

> There is an Unforeseen.
> Fate never gives a guarantee

235

> That she'll abstain from aught. And men
> Get tired at last of being free –
> Whether in states – in states or creeds.
> For what's the sequel? Verily,
> Laws scribbled by law-breakers, creeds
> Scrawled by the freethinkers, and deeds
> Shameful and shameless. Men get sick
> Under that curse of Frederic
> The cynical: For punishment
> This rebel province I present
> To the philosophers . . .[38]

In 1974, Robert Nozick, professor of philosophy at Harvard, published *Anarchy, State and Utopia*, a study of rights composed after at least a decade of the violations and violence of the Civil Rights movement, government legislation and martial confrontation, and the failure to secure the full demands of either black Americans or of those Americans who did not wish to fight America's official wars. Nozick's analysis is strikingly similar to that of the mid-nineteenth century anarchist-transcendentalist Thoreau:

> How much room do individual rights leave for the state? . . . Our main conclusions about the state are that a minimal state, limited to the narrow functions of protection against force, theft, fraud, enforcement of contracts, and so on, is justified; that any more extensive state will violate persons' rights not to be forced to do certain things, and is unjustified; and that the minimal state is inspiring as well as right. Two noteworthy implications are that the state may not use its coercive apparatus for the purpose of getting some citizens to aid others, or in order to prohibit activities to people for their *own* good or protection.

Thoreau sharpened the issue: 'That government is best which governs not at all' – and: 'Any man more right than his neighbours constitutes a majority of one.' Nozick reduces the issue of rights to another kind of chaos: 'No one has a right to something whose realization requires certain uses of things and activities that other people have rights and entitlements over.'[39] This conceivably freezes Mill on liberty into that abstract absurdity that the United States initially took as its inheritance from John Locke in the late seventeenth century: 'Man being born . . . with the title to perfect freedom and uncontrolled enjoyment of all the rights and priviledges of the law of nature.'[40]

By 1900, 'the law of nature' signified the survival of the strongest and the most usefully armed. Ronald Dworkin's *Taking Rights Seriously* (1977) is still proposing such positions without stating clearly how an individual is to *claim* and *maintain* his rights and entitlements, especially if he cannot afford law, perhaps does not even know law, or is part of what a high official in the US Embassy in London recently referred to as a bottom class of 'untouchables,' who 'don't get their motor started,' who 'haven't got the giroscope in them,' and who 'are outside the dream': 'Individual rights are political trumps held by individuals. Individuals have rights when, for some reason, a collective goal is not a sufficient justification for denying them what they wish, as individuals, to have or to do, or not a sufficient justification for imposing some loss or injury upon them.'[41] After asserting that 'the language of rights now dominates political debate in the United States,' Dworkin points to a source of confusion about 'rights against the government,' in a divided society, in the Constitution itself. Although it does provide *legal* rights through 'due process, equal protection, and similar clauses,' and although the Supreme Court can declare state legislation void if it offends these provisions, the structure is less than protective because 'the Constitution fuses legal and moral issues by making the validity of a law depend on the answer to complex moral problems,' particularly on the bases of equality. This takes us back to Theodore Sedgewick's 'metaphysical subtleties' of 1857.

It appears, then, that Americans live mythically in an unstable equilibrium between concepts of control and liberty established by a written Constitution, with floating dreams of lone anarchists and private eyes, Superman, Batman, and Snoopy, and such recent dreamers of individual rights as Paul Goodman. As Dworkin observes: 'Judges stand for different positions on controversial issues of law and morals, and . . . a President is entitled to appoint judges of his own persuasion, provided that they are honest and capable.' Dworkin also adds that the Walker

Report, or the President's Commission on Violence, found that, during the events in Chicago associated with the Democratic National Convention in 1968, the police were too busy contributing to violence to contain it. But it was not the police who were on trial in Judge Julius Hoffman's lunatic court hearings.[42]

Another study from the post-Civil Rights period also emerged from Harvard: John Rawls's *A Theory of Justice* (1972). He immediately confronts the politics of 'rights and entitlements,' but in a peculiar way: 'Compensating steps must . . . be taken to preserve the fair value for all of the equal political liberties. . . . In a society allowing private ownership of the means of production, property and wealth must be kept widely distributed and government monies provided on a regular basis to encourage free public discussion.'[43] The issue of 'free public discussion' became chronic once again during the Freedom of Speech movement's clashes with the controllers of the University of California at Berkeley in 1964. Sit-ins and other peaceful demonstrations were met with arrests and authoritarian abuse. But once again the clear issues turned into a crude, inconclusive exchange: judges versus anarchists. The following year, the great San Francisco poet Robert Duncan, then aged forty-seven, read his poem 'The Multiversity' at Berkeley. His text is partly directed against President Clark Kerr, and is enlivened by citation from the great British dissident, William Blake:

> not men   but heads of the hydra
>
> his false faces in which
> authority lies
>
> hired minds of private interests
>
> over us
>
> here: Kerr (behind him, heads of the Bank of America
> the Tribune,
> heads of usury, heads of war) . . .

Then he speaks of the lies in the official university statement:

that the Free Speech Movement has no wide support, only
an irresponsible minority   going on strike

Duncan's criticism of the controllers is that of the Transcenden-
talists and Robert Nozick:

                              conscience
                no longer alive in them,

                the inner law silenced,   now
                they call out their cops, police law,
                the club, the gun, the strong arm,
                gang-law of the state,
                hired sadists of installd mediocrities

Duncan's analysis can be placed with the substance of the
Amherst College scholar, Alexander Meiklejohn, whose *Political
Freedom: The Constitutional Powers of the People* was published in
1966:

                simulacra of law that wld over-rule
                    the Law man's inner nature seeks,
                coils about them,   not men but

                heads and armors of the worm   office is

                There being no common good, no commune,
                no communion, outside the freedom of

                        individual volition[44]

   Duncan's lineage is clear in an essay entitled 'The Lasting
Contribution of Ezra Pound,' in which he places Pound's use of
Confucian principle with the notorious trial and execution in
1927 of anarchist Bartolomeo Vanzetti, which created another
martyr: 'My concern with the nature of Law was inspired and
continues to be inspired by the poet of the *Cantos* who brought
Kung into our studies, tho I derive from the concept that all
order proceeds from and depends upon its root in man's inner
order, the politics of a lawful anarchism, Vanzetti's voluntarism,
opposed to the politics of coercion, be it the 'democracy' of
majority rule or the 'fascism' of Mussolini's dictatorship.'[45]

In the 1970s, American scholars of law made useful statements evoked by the events of the previous fifteen years. For example: the preface by Thomas Emerson, Emeritus Professor from Yale Law School, to Tiger and Levy's *Law and the Rise of Capitalism* in 1977, itself a major text; Richard Harris's *Justice: The Crisis of Law, Order and Freedom in America* (1970), which concludes with a warning that the message of the Sixties is that American freedom may have been eroded by people 'turning their common fate over to their leaders in a way that would have been inconceivable five years ago'[46]; *The Culture of Inequality* (1979) by Michael Lewis, professor of sociology at the University of Massachusetts, which is sceptical of the chances of combining 'an economics of individual acquisitiveness' and one of 'collective welfare,' 'given the limits imposed on the American imagination by the individual-as-central sensibility.'

Lewis voices a growing American sense of inherent design against equality since the culture of inequality requires failure, disinheritance of 'the poor, the racially stigmatized, the uneducated, and those presumed criminally deviant.' These and the dissident will be termed lawless and policed accordingly. Lewis shares Victor Li's apprehensiveness the year before: the culture of inequality will 'increasingly make the individual and *only* the individual accountable for his or her social destiny, and in so doing it will victimize most of us.'[47] This is partly to do with the continuous sense of America being at war, causing a monstrous growth in 'the sanctity of the State.' The phrase is that of Randolph Bourne, writing as World War I ended. The nation, Bourne believed, moved towards the 'peacefulness of being at war': ' "minority opinion," which in times of peace was only irritating and could not be dealt with by law unless it was conjoined with actual crime, becomes, with the threat of war, a case of outlawry. . . . "Loyalty," or rather war orthodoxy, becomes the sole test of all professions, techniques, occupations.'[48] How this condition affected the Chinese, leading up to the 1882 Chinese Exclusion Act, is carefully documented in Cheng-Tsu Wu's *Chink! A Documentary History of Anti-Chinese Prejudice in America* (1972), a measure inaugurated by the California Supreme Court's 1854 ruling denying Chinese people the right to testify against white people.

But the necessity and courage of black resistance, war resistance, and various other kinds of disaffiliation in the Sixties and Seventies can also be studied as a continuation of a strong tradition of civil disobedience and its anarchist programmes. In 1973, Norman O. Brown – scholar of Hesiod turned social analyst, author of *Love's Body* (1966) and *Life Against Death* (1959), then working at the University of California – summarized the battle in *Closing Time*, citing one of the radical leaders who were on trial in Chicago in 1968:

> Force is the theater of impotence.
> In a situation of general social paralysis
> stasis, sterility, stereotypification
> the aim is not the seizure of power, but the dissolu-
> tion of power.
> Karl Marx in *The Eighteenth Brumaire*
> demolishing the cult of the leader
> bringing Napoleon's statue down.
> Abbie Hoffman: 'we are outlaws, not organizers.'[49]

But that theatre is the theatre of violence. In 1970, one instance of campus murder by national guardsmen – the killing of dissenters protesting the extension of the South East Asia war into Cambodia, an act initially denied by the government – became notorious. The Department of Justice's report saying that the guardsmen had lied about student demonstrations at Kent State University was held back from the grand jury investigation by the Governor of Ohio. When official manipulation of law prevented justice, those outside the systems of law and law enforcement had to enter the theatre. It was, for example, Noam Chomsky, the analyst of psycholinguistics and the 'deep structure of linguistic universals,' and Paul Goodman, Gestalt psychologist and distinguished fiction writer, as well as philosophers and poets and one or two rock musicians and folk singers, who investigated the deeper situation. In fact, during the Sixties the history of nonconformism was written up for the first time in studies like Edward H. Madden's *Civil Disobedience and Moral Law in Nineteenth Century American Philosophy* (1968), Lillian Schlissel's *Conscience in America: A Documentary History of*

Conscientious Objection in America, 1757–1867 (1968), and Staughton Lynd's *Nonviolence in America: A Documentary History* (1966). Such works were needed to challenge the official propaganda that dissidence was unAmerican. It was the *New York Times* of 1 October 1968 that reported: 'A reasonable man can hold the view today that the war in Vietnam is illegal, the Government said in Federal Court today on the third day of the trial of nine war protesters accused of burning draft files in a Baltimore suburb last spring.' The First Assistant United States Attorney, prosecuting, said that this was 'the first time the Government had made such a statement in court,' and then quickly played down what he had admitted. *The Times* added its own significant typographical error (substituting 'we' for 'he'): 'All we said was that the Government does not contest that the defendants' view that the war was illegal is an unreasonable view.'[49]

These were also years in which substantial reflections on violence in American history, probing the myths and assumptions behind the terms 'law' and 'State' from the Puritans to the present, became part of day-to-day analysis of the nation's condition. In 1968, for example, Arthur Schlesinger Jr., John F. Kennedy's Special Assistant and ranking historian, published *Violence: America in the Sixties*, and opened by accepting the fact that the United States harboured 'the most frightening people on this earth.' Documentation was provided two years later in Thomas Rose's *Violence in America: A Historical and Contemporary Reader*, and then by Hofstadter and Wallace's *American Violence: A Documentary History*, whose final section, entitled 'Violence in the Name of Law, Order, and Morality,' recalls Lincoln's 1838 speech on 'the increasing disregard for law which pervades the country: the growing disposition to substitute the wild and furious passions, in lieu of the sober judgment of Courts; and the worse than savage mobs, for the executive ministers of justice.'[51]

At the end of the 1970s, the work of historians, lawyers, civil rights demonstrators and artists constituted a serious body of investigation that understood the law and law enforcement as the crucial site of American moral policy, domestic and imperial. The Republic began in revolt and legal proposition rather than in a continuity of what the Puritan minister Cotton Mather self-righteously considered to be life 'under the aspect of Eternity.' This brief excursion into the record has omitted crucial areas: the American comedian as social critic between 1950 and 1970 and attempts to cut him back through censorship; the extensive production of films dramatizing a wide range of criminal actions, the police, the private detective, the lawyer himself; the huge number of films concerned with wars in Korea, Vietnam, Cambodia, and Latin America; the complex issues of the Black civil rights movement; the discussion of legal change within the major law schools of the United States; and the more recent efforts of the feminist and gay liberation movements to challenge hitherto established oppressions, frequently written into law. But the issues are being tackled, at least, by activists, if only erratically by American cultural studies.

1988

Notes

Notes to Chapter One

1. Tim Findlay, 'The Revolution Was Televised,' *Rolling Stone*, 20 June 1974, pp. 6–8.

2. Caryl Rivers, 'The Vertigo of Homecoming,' *The Nation*, 17 December 1973, pp. 646–9.

3. Thomas McGuane, *The Bushwhacked Piano* (New York, 1973), p. 138. See also Larry McMurtry, *All My Friends Are Going to be Strangers* (1972; New York, 1973), pp. 8–9.

4. E.L. Doctorow, *The Book of Daniel* (New York, 1972), p. 84.

5. Louise Thorensen, with E.M. Nathanson, *It Gave Everybody Something To Do* (New York, 1974).

6. Eric Norden, 'The Paramilitary Right,' *Playboy* (June, 1969).

7. 'Alcoholism: New Victims, New Treatment,' *Time*, 4 April 1974.

8. 'Domestic Disarmament,' *The Nation*, 23 February, 1974; 'Gun Crazy,' *The Nation*, 1 March 1975; 'The Baltimore Gun Bounty,' *The Nation*, 5 October 1974.

9. Richard Hofstadter and Michael Wallace (eds), *American Violence: A Documentary History* (New York, 1970), pp. 24–5.

10. Michael Harrington, 'The Politics of Gun Conrol,' *The Nation*, 12 January 1974.

11. Perry Miller, *The Life of the Mind in America. From the Revolution to the Civil War* (New York, 1965), pp. 240, 248, 264.

12. Dixon Wecter, *The Hero in America* (Ann Arbor, 1941), pp. 352–3.

13. Odie B. Faulk, *Tombstone: Myth and Reality* (New York, 1972).

14. Hofstadter and Wallace (eds), pp. 401–3.

15. Robert Sherrill, *The Saturday Night Special* (New York, 1973), p. 3.

16. Karl Marx, *The Grundrisse*, ed. and trans. David McLellan (New York, 1972), p. 45.

17. T.K. Derry and T.I. Williams, *A Short History of Technology* (Oxford, 1960), pp. 48ff.

18. Friedrich Engels, *Anti-Dühring* (1877–8), II, iii, 'Theory of Violence.'

19. Sherrill, p. 4.

20. Sherrill, p. 17.

21. S. Lilley, *Men, Machines and History*, rev. ed. (London, 1965), p. 66.

22. Melvin Kranzberg and Carroll W. Pursell, *Technology in Western Civilization, Volume 1* (New York, 1967), p. 493.

23. Siegfried Giedion, *Mechanization Takes Command* (New York, 1948), pp. 49–50.

24. W.H.G. Armytage, *A Social History of Engineering*, 3rd ed. (London, 1961), pp. 49–59, 128, 156, 160, 183.

25. Armytage, p. 160.

26. Roger Burlinghame, *Machines That Built America* (New York, 1965), pp. 83ff.

27. Kranzberg and Pursell, p. 494.

28. P. Wahl and D.R. Toppell, *The Gatling Gun* (London, 1966); Carl P. Russell, *Firearms, Traps and Tools of the Mountain Men* (New York, 1968).

29. Tom Hayden, 'Vietnam, One Year After,' *Rolling Stone*, 28 February 1974, p. 6.

30. Lewis Mumford, *Technics and Civilization* (New York, 1934), p. 165.

31. Kranzberg and Pursell, p. 498.

32. Giedion, p. 21.

33. Walter Prescott Webb, *The Great Plains* (New York, 1931), p. 244.

34. Charles Olson, *A Bibliography on America for Ed Dorn* (San Francisco, 1965), p. 5; Webb, pp. 244–9.

35. John A. Hawgood, *The American West* (London, 1967), pp. 284–95.

36. Raymond Lee, *Fit for the Chase: Cars and the Movies* (New York, 1969), p. 14.

37. Hawgood, p. 295.

38. Orrin E. Klapp, *Heroes, Villains and Fools* (New Jersey, 1962), pp. 27ff.

39. David Riesman et. al., *The Lonely Crowd* (New York, 1950).

40. H.B. Sell and V. Weybright, *Buffalo Bill and the Wild West* (Oxford, 1955; New York, 1959).

41. Wecter, pp. 341–63; Henry Nash Smith, *Virgin Land* (New York, 1950), pp. 113–25.

42. Ron Chernow, 'John Ford: The Last Frontiersman,' *Ramparts*, April 1974, p. 48.

43. B.A. Botkin (ed), *A Treasury of American Folklore* (New York, 1944), p. 108.

44. Eugene Cunningham, *Triggernometry* (New York, 1941; London, 1967), p. 357.

45. Peter Gidal, *Andy Warhol: Films and Paintings* (London, 1971), p. 130.

46. Wilfred Mellers, *Music in a New Found Land* (London, 1964), p. 88.

47. K.L. Steckmesser, *The Western Hero in History and Legend* (Oklahoma, 1965), p. 5, n. 3.

48. Jim Kitses, *Horizons West* (London, 1969), p. 8.

49. David Lavender, *The Penguin Book of the American West* (London, 1969), p. 406; Wecter, p. 349.

50. Lavender, p. 359; Wecter, p. 349.

51. J.D. Horan and P. Sann, *Pictorial History of the Wild West* (New York, 1954), pp. 57ff; Wecter, *passim*.

52. cf. Charles A. Siringo, *A Texas Cowboy* (Chicago, 1886).

53. Steckmesser, p. 60.

54. Horan and Sann, p. 59.

55. Steckmesser, p. 68.

56. Cunningham, p. 17.

57. B.A. Botkin's *A Treasury of American Folklore* prints parts of Walter Noble Burns' *Saga, The Cowboy's Career* (St. Louis, 1881), by 'One of the Kids,' Siringo's *History of Billy the Kid*, (n.p., 1920), and 'Song of Billy the Kid' – 'Way out in New Mexico long, long ago, / When a man's only chance was his own forty four . . .').

58. Horan and Sann, p. 58.

59. Steckmesser, p. 84.

60. Michael McClure, *The Mammals* (San Francisco, 1972); *The Beard* (New York, 1965); *Star* (New York, 1970).

61. Charles Olson, *Human Universe and Other Essays* (San Francisco, 1965), pp. 139–40.

62. Louis Zukovsky, *All – The Collected Short Poems, 1956–64* (London, 1967), pp. 49–51.

63. Edward Dorn, *Gunslinger, Book I* (Los Angeles, 1968), *Book II* (Los Angeles, 1969), *Book III* (Massachusetts, 1972); *Gunslinger 1 and 2* (London, 1973); Michael Ondaatje, *The Collected Works of Billy the Kid* (Toronto, 1970; London, 1981), pp. 28, 43. Poe was president of the National Bank of Roswell, New Mexico.

64. Robert Warshow, *The Immediate Experience* (New York, 1962), pp. 89–105.

65. Eric Mottram, *William Burroughs: The Algebra of Need* (Buffalo, N.Y., 1971), p. 26.

66. Quotations in the following section are taken from Samuel R. Delany, *The Einstein Intersection* (1968; London, 1970), pp. 63ff., 87ff., 96, 101, 120, 122, 131, 136, 159.

67. Haniel Long, *If He Can Make Her So* (Pittsburg, 1968), pp. 45–49.

68. John Paul Scott, 'The Science of Nonviolence,' *The Nation*, 26 February 1973.

69. Jean Davison, 'The Triggered, the Obsessed and the Schemers,' *TV Guide* [New York], 2 February 1974.

70. Herbert Marcuse, *An Essay on Liberation* (London, 1969), p. 22.

Journal of American Studies, 10, 1 (1976), 53–84.

Notes to Chapter Two

1. W.A. Swanberg, *Luce and his Empire* (New York, 1972), pp. 390–1.

2. Stéphane Mallarmé, 'L'Action resteinte,' in *Selected Poetry and Prose*, ed. Mary Ann Caws (New York, 1982), p. 77.

3. David Mamet, *American Buffalo* (New York, 1977), p. 5.

4. Gertrude Stein, *The Autobiography of Alice B. Toklas* (1933; London, 1960), p. 194.

5. See Brian Easlea, *Fathering the Unthinkable; Masculinity, Scientists and the Nuclear Arms Race* (London, 1983).

6. Bruce Springsteen, *The River*, CBS 88510, 1980.

7. An allusion to the very fast sports car in *Smokey and the Bandit* (Hal Needham, 1977); ' "Black really burst into popularity as soon as Burt

Reynolds drove that Black Trans Am across the screen" says George Moon, the GM executive designer in charge of color.' See Kurt Andersen, 'The Allure of Darth Vaderism,' *Time*, August 19, 1985, p. 50.

8. cf. Roland Barthes, 'The New Citroen,' *in his Mythologies*, trans. Annette Lavers (1957; St. Albans, 1973), pp. 88–91 on why Citroen called their new 1957 model *Déesse*, or *Goddess*.

9. C.B. Macpherson, *The Political Theory of Possessive Individualism* (Oxford, 1962); Paul Hoch, *White Hero, Black Beast: Racism, Sexism and the Mask of Masculinity* (London, 1979).

10. Mark Williams, *Road Movies* (London, 1982), pp. 35–6.

11. Car films have been largely omitted from this paper, since the author considered them in 'Blood on the Nash Ambassador: Cars in American films,' *Cinema, Politics and Society in America*, eds. Philip Davies and Brian Neve (Manchester, 1981), pp. 221–249, reprinted in this volume. See also Gerald Silk, 'The Automobile in Art,' in *Automobile and Culture*, ed. Gerald Silk (New York, 1984).

12. Robert W. Marks, *The Dymaxion World of Buckminster Fuller* (Carbondale, Ill., 1960), pp. 96–107.

13. George Oppen, *Collected Poems* (New York, 1975) p. 4; L.S. Dembo, 'The Objectivist Poet: Four Interviews,' *Contemporary Literature*, 10, 2 (1969), p. 168.

14. David Riesman and Eric Larrabee, 'Autos in America' (1956, postscript 1957), in David Riesman, *Abundance for What? and Other Essays* (London, 1964), pp. 281–3.

15. Harry Crews, *Car* (1972; New York, 1983); David Riesman, 'The Search for Challenge,' in Riesman, pp. 345, 356.

16. Easlea, pp. 7, 27.

17. Easlea, pp. 43–44.

18. Alfred P. Sloan, Jr., *My Years With General Motors*, ed. John McDonald and Catherine Stevens (1964; New York, 1965), p. 277.

19. Thomas Pynchon, *V.* (London, 1963), pp. 28–9.

20. Stephen King, *Christine* (1983; Sevenoaks, Kent, 1984), pp. 20, 36, 244.

21. Timothy Leary, *Flashbacks* (London, 1984), pp. 51, 53.

22. Felix Guattari, *Molecular Revolution: Psychiatry and Politics* (London, 1984), p. 98.

23. Alan Harrington, *Psychopaths* (New York, 1972), pp. 241, 254. Harrington, who appears with Cassady and other Beat Generation figures under other

NOTES

names in John Clellon Holmes' novel *Go* (1952), was a witness at a Cassady wedding.

24. Harrington, pp. 243, 254.

25. Jacques Ellul, *The Technological Society*, trans. Konrad Keller and Jean Lerner (London, 1965), pp. 339, 390.

26. Quoted in V.G. Kiernan, *America: The New Imperialism* (1978; London, 1980), p. 227.

27. Williams, pp. 84–5.

28. Ellul, p. 398.

29. Jacques Derrida, 'Structure, Sign and Play in the Discourse of the Human Sciences' (1966), in *Writing and Difference* (London, 1978), p. 278.

30. cf. Gary K. Wolfe: 'Instrumentalities of the Body: The Mechanization of Human Form in Science Fiction,' in T.P. Dunn and R.D. Erlich (eds), *The Mechanical God: Machines in Science Fiction* (Connecticut and London, 1982), pp. 211–224.

31. Frederick Taylor, *Shop Management* (1903) and *The Principles of Scientific Management* (1911), rpt. in *Scientific Management* (New York, 1947); Nathan Rosenberg, *Perspectives on Technology* (Cambridge, Mass., 1976), p. 29; John A. Kouwenhoven, *The Arts in Modern American Civilization* (1948; New York, 1967), p. 183; ed. Quintin Hoare and Geoffrey Nowell-Smith, *Selections from the Prison Notebook of Antonio Gramsci* (London, 1971), pp. 277–318.

32. Ellul, p. 399. For the development of these materials, see H.T. Wilson, *The American Ideology: Science, Technology and Organization as Modes of Rationality in Advanced Industrial Societies* (London, 1977).

33. Reisman and Larrabee, pp. 279, 281, 287–8.

34. William Endicott, 'California's Fender-Benders Can Lead to Murder,' *International Herald Tribune*, Paris, 31 January 1978.

35. David Dalton, *James Dean: The Mutant King* (New York, 1975), p. 251.

36. Harrington, pp. 155–6.

37. Ellul, pp. 85–94; Riesman and Larrabee, p. 268.

38. Tom Wolfe, *The Kandy-Kolored Tangerine-Flake Streamline Baby* (New York, 1965), p. xiv.

39. Frank Trippett, "There's no Madness Like Nomadness," *Time*, 5 September 1977, pp. 41–44.

40. Riesman and Larrabee, pp. 268–71.

41. M. McClure, L. Ferlinghetti and D. Meltzer (eds), *Journal for the Protection of All Beings* (San Francisco, 1961).

42. 'Autos That Make the Statusphere,' *Time*, 15 May 1978, p. 45.

43. John Keats, *The Insolent Chariots* (1958; New York, 1959), p. 10.

44. Keats, pp. 11, 15.

45. Russell Lynes, *The Tastemakers* (New York, 1954), p. 300.

46. Hans Selye, *Stress Without Distress: How to Survive in a Stressful Society* (1974; London, 1978), p. 18. In *The Life of Poetry* (New York, 1949), p. 10, Muriel Rukeyser translates the term as 'the *in*vironment where live the inner relationships.'

47. Michael McClure, *The Mad Cub* (New York, 1970), p. 140.

48. On private armies, see Eric Mottram, 'The Persuasive Lips: Men and Guns in America, the West,' *Journal of American Studies*, 10, 1 (1976), p. 5. (Reprinted in this volume). On Manson, see Ed Sanders, *The Family: The Story of Charles Manson's Dune Buggy Attack Battalion* (New York, 1971; St. Albans, 1972), p. 13.

49. Sanders, pp. 45, 49, 102, 116–8, 122, 265–6.

50. Anderson, pp. 40–41.

51. Robert S. Lynd and Helen M. Lynd, *Middletown: A Study in Modern American Culture* (1929; New York, 1959), pp. 253ff. See also P. Olson (ed), *America as a Mass Society* (New York, 1963).

52. James J. Flink, *America Adopts the Automobile, 1895–1910* (Cambridge, Mass., 1970), p. 2. The same author's *The Car Culture* (Cambridge, Mass., 1975) adapts, develops and augments the earlier book.

53. 'The Mess in Mass Transit,' *Time*, 16 July 1979, pp. 46–48.

54. Tracy Freedman, 'Back to *Caveat Emptor* at the F.T.C.,' *The Nation*, 10 March 1984, pp. 283–6.

55. Lee Iacocca, with William Novak, *Iacocca: An Autobiography* (New York, 1984). See also Robert Reich and John D. Donahue, *New Deals: The Chrysler Revival and the American System* (New York, 1985).

56. Counter-Information Service [London], *Ford: Anti-Report* (London, 1978), pp. 43–47.

57. *Time*, 5 September 1977.

58. Recently reproduced by Digest Books, Northfield, Illinois, nd.

59. Henry Ford, with Samuel Crowther, *My Life and Work* (London, 1924), pp. 43, 73, 98.

60. Gilles Deleuze and Félix Guattari, *Anti-Oedipus: Capitalism and Schizo-phrenia* (1972; New York, 1977), p. 17.

61. Félix Guattari, 'Psychoanalysis and Schizo-Analysis, '*Semiotext(e)* [New York], 11, 3, p. 79.

62. Guattari, 'Everybody Wants to be a Fascist,' *Semiotext(e)* [New York], 11, 3, pp. 87–98.

63. Jean Baudrillard, *Simulations* (New York, 1983), p. 112.

Notes to Chapter Three

1. Marshall McLuhan, *Understanding Media* (London, 1964), p. 18; Victor Turner, 'Themes in the Symbolism of Ndembu Hunting Ritual,' in John Middleton (ed), *Myth and Cosmos* (New York, 1967), p. 269; Hans Selye, *Stress Without Distress* (London, 1977), p. 18.

2. Stanley Milgram, *Obedience to Authority* (New York, 1974).

3. William Gaddis, *The Recognitions* (New York, 1955), p. 844.

4. Lawrence Alloway, *Violent America: the Movies, 1946–1964* (New York, 1971), p. 7.

5. Michel Carrouges, *Les Machines célibataires* (Paris, 1954).

6. Stan Brakhage, *Film Biographies* (Berkeley, Calif., 1977), p. 175.

7. Brakhage, pp. 155–6.

8. François Truffaut, *Hitchcock* (London, 1969), p. 324.

9. Pier Paolo Pasolini, 'The Cinema of Poetry,' in *Movies and Methods*, ed. Bill Nichols (Berkeley, Calif., 1976), pp. 544–5.

10. Peter Gidal, 'Theory and Definition of Structural/Materialist Film,' in Peter Gidal (ed), *Structural Film Anthology* (London, 1976), p. 3.

11. Christian Metz, *Film Language* (New York, 1974).

12. Charles Olson, 'An Ode on Nativity,' in *Archeologist of Morning* (London, 1970), np.

13. Cahiers du Cinéma, 'John Ford's *Young Mr Lincoln*,' in Nichols (ed), pp. 493–529; Pasolini in Nichols (ed), p. 545; Umberto Eco, 'Articulations of the Cinematic Code,' in Nichols (ed), pp. 593–4. See also Umberto Eco, *A Theory of Semiotics* (London, 1977), pp. 191ff.

14. Raymond Lee, *Fit for the Chase* (New York and London, 1969). For the

car industry see, for example, James J. Flink, *America Adopts the Automobile, 1895–1910* (Cambridge, Mass., 1970); Joseph J. Schroeder, *The Wonderful World of Automobiles, 1895–1930* (Northfield, Ill., 1971).

15. Nicholas Ray, 'Story into Script,' in *Hollywood Directors, 1941–1976*, ed. Richard Koszarski (Oxford and New York, 1977), pp. 244–56 (quotation from p. 253).

16. cf. Michael Balint, *Thrills and Regressions* (New York, 1959).

17. David Dalton, *James Dean: the Mutant King* (New York, 1975), pp. 290, 301, 358.

18. Donald Allen (ed.), *The Collected Poems of Frank O'Hara* (New York, 1972), pp. 228–31; Kenneth Anger, *Hollywood Babylon* (Phoenix, Ariz., 1965), p. 181; John Dos Passos, *Mid Century* (New York, 1961), pp. 468–75.

19. Malachy McCoy, *Steve McQueen* (London, 1974), from which the following information and quotations are derived.

20. James Goode, *The Story of the Misfits* (New York, 1963).

21. William Friedkin, 'Anatomy of a Chase,' in Koszarski, pp. 392–403.

22. McLuhan, pp. 42, 220.

23. Gilles Deleuze and Felix Guattari, *Anti-Oedipus*, trans. Robert Hurley, Mark Seem, and Helen Lane (New York, 1977), p. 18.

24. Leonard Berkowitz, 'The Effects of Observing Violence,' *Scientific American* (February, 1964), p. 35.

25. Arthur Penn, '*Bonnie and Clyde*: Private Morality and Public Violence,' in Koszarski, pp. 360–4 (quotation from p. 360).

26. Cited in Michael Pye and Linda Myles, *The Movie Brats* (London, 1979), p. 120.

27. Truffaut, p. 331; Alloway, p. 25.

28. Jay Berman, *The Fifties Book* (New York, 1974), pp. 76–7.

29. Colin McArthur, *Underworld USA* (London, 1972), pp. 23–24.

30. Metz, p. 47; James Monaco, *How to Read a Film* (New York, 1977), pp. 150–1.

31. McArthur, pp. 30, 32.

32. Deleuze and Guattari, p. 235.

33. Alloway, p. 15.

34. Antonio Gramsci, 'Americanism and Fordism,' in *Selections from the Prison*

Notebooks, ed. Quentin Hoare and Geoffrey Nowell-Smith (London, 1971), pp. 279–322.

35. Ivan Illich, *Tools for Conviviality* (London, 1973), p. 2.

Philip Davies and Brian Neve (eds), *Cinema, Politics and Society in America* (Manchester, 1981), pp. 221–249.

Notes to Chapter Four

1. Charles Olson, *Letters for Origin, 1950–1956*, ed. Albert Glover (London, 1969), pp. 103–6.

2. At this point Olson's argument resembles that of Paul Feyerabend, *Against Method* (London, 1975).

3. Feyerabend, p. 35.

4. Charles Olson, *The Maximus Poems* (New York, 1960), pp. 9–12, 72–3.

5. Ralph Waldo Emerson, 'Napoleon, or the Man of the World' (1845), from *Representative Men* (1850), in *The Portable Emerson*, ed. Carl Bode and Malcolm Cowley (1946; New York, 1981), pp. 325–6.

6. Herman Melville, *Moby Dick; or, The Whale*, ed. Luther Mansfield and Howard Vincent (New York, 1962), pp. 165–6.

7. Henry Nash Smith (ed), *Popular Culture and Industrialism, 1865–1890* (New York, 1967), pp. 23–41.

8. Max Lerner, 'Big Technology and Neutral Machines,' in Hennig Cohen (ed), *The American Culture* (Boston, 1968), p. 187.

9. Henry David Thoreau, *Walden* (1854): 'Economy' – 'the first news that will leak through into the broad, flapping American ear.'

10. Perry Miller, *The Life of the Mind in America* (New York, 1965), p. 312.

11. Alfred Kazin and Daniel Aaron (eds), *Emerson: A Modern Anthology* (New York, 1958), p. 340.

12. Nathaniel Hawthorne, "Selections from the *American Notebooks*," in *The Portable Hawthorne*, ed. Malcolm Cowley (New York, 1948), p. 558.

13. Henry Nash Smith, *Virgin Land* (New York, 1950), p. 138.

14. Lynn White, Jr., *Dynamo and Virgin Reconsidered* (Cambridge, Mass., 1968), pp. 89–90.

15. Norbert Wiener, *The Human Use of Human Beings*, 2nd rev. ed. (New York, 1954; London, 1968), p. 141.

16. The future of Emerson's attitudes lies with John Dewey's instrumentalism and Marshall McLuhan's concept of technology as the extensions of man.

17. Siegfried Giedion, *Mechanization Takes Command* (New York, 1948), p. v.

18. Marvin Fisher, *Workshops in the Wilderness* (New York, 1967).

19. Smith, *Popular Culture*, pp. 51–56.

20. Smith, *Popular Culture*, pp. 57–70.

21. Arthur O. Lewis (ed), *Of Men and Machines* (New York, 1963), pp. 194, 233–6.

22. Nathan Rosenberg, *Perspectives on Technology* (Cambridge, 1976), p. 29.

23. John A. Kouwenhoven, *The Arts in Modern American Civilization* (1948; New York, 1967), p. 183.

24. Quintin Hoare and Geoffrey Nowell-Smith (eds), *Selections from the Prison Notebooks of Antonio Gramsci* (London, 1971), pp. 277ff.

25. James Burnham, *The Machiavellians* (London, 1943), p. 185: 'The democratic totalitarians . . . are consistent in being uniformly directed against the foundations of freedom. Not unity but difference, not the modern state but whatever is able to maintain itself against the state . . .'

26. Lewis Mumford, *Technics and Civilization* (London, 1934), pp. 12–18.

27. See Bruce Mazlish (ed), *The Railroad and the Space Program* (Cambridge, Mass., 1965).

28. Quoted in Bruce Mazlish, 'Historical Analogy: The Railroad and the Space Program and Their Impact on Society,' in Mazlish (ed), p. 37.

29. Henry George, 'What the Railroads Will Bring Us,' in Dennis Hale and Jonathan Eisen (eds), *The California Dream* (New York, 1968), p. 19.

30. Thomas Parke Hughes, 'A Technological Frontier: The Railway,' in Mazlish (ed), p. 53.

31. Hughes in Mazlish (ed), p. 71.

32. Constance Rourke, *Trumpets of Jubilee* (New York, 1927), p. 173.

33. Smith, *Popular Culture*, pp. x–xi.

34. Richard Hofsadter and Michael Wallace (eds), *American Violence: A Documentary History* (New York, 1970), pp. 133–84.

35. Harvey Wish, *Society and Thought in Modern America* (London, 1952), p. 78.

36. F.O. Matthiessen, *From the Heart of Europe* (New York, 1948), p. 88.

37. Charles Noider (ed), *The Complete Humorous Sketches and Tales of Mark Twain* (New York, 1961), p. 286.

38. Lee Kennett and James La Verne Anderson, *The Gun in America* (London and Connecticut, 1975), p. 89.

39. Rosenberg, pp. 9–31.

40. Kennett and Anderson, p. 120.

41. John F. Kasson, *Civilizing the Machine: Technology and Republican Values in America, 1776–1900* (1976; New York, 1977), p. 183.

42. Rosenberg, p. 21.

43. See Eric Mottram, 'The Persuasive Lips: Men and Guns in America, the West,' *Journal of American Studies*, 10 (1976), 53–84; rpt. in this volume.

44. Walter Prescott Webb, *The Great Plains* (New York: 1931), pp. 244–9.

45. Rosenberg, p. 24.

46. Henry Adams, *The Education of Henry Adams* (1906; New York, 1928), p. 340.

47. In Chapter 18 of his *Brighter Than a Thousand Suns* (1958; Harmondsworth, 1960), p. 272, Robert Jungk has a note on the Eniwetok atomic explosion in 1952: the American author and painter, Gilbert Wilson, noted that 'only a century after Herman Melville wrote his great book our own American atomic engineers unwittingly selected almost the very spot in the broad Pacific, some few thousand miles south-east off the coast of Japan, where the fictional *Pequod* . . . was rammed and sunk by the white whale. . . . Melville had Ahab describe the Whale with an image remarkably similar to the conventional symbol of the atom used by artists, "O trebly hooped and welded hip of power." '

48. Justin Kaplan, *Mr. Clemens and Mark Twain* (New York, 1966), Chapter 14.

49. W.H.G. Armytage, *The Rise of the Technocrats* (London, 1965), p. 243.

50. Rosenberg, p. 43.

51. Armytage, pp. 167–8.

52. His short story 'Entropy' (1960, rpt. in Richard Kostelanetz (ed), *Twelve From the Sixties* (New York, 1967), pp. 22–35 and Thomas Pynchon, *Slow Learner. Early Stories* (London, 1985), pp. 80–98), describes the results of social-natural equilibrium in Washington; *Gravity's Rainbow* (New York, 1973) concerns world society entirely given over to the politics of engineering.

53. Henry James, *The American Scene* (London, 1907), p. 463: His response to 'the general conquest of nature and space' apparently affirmed by the Pullman – 'If I were one of the painted savages you have dispossessed, or even some tough reactionary trying to emulate him, what you are making would doubtless impress me more than what you are leaving unmade . . . your pretended message of civilization is but a colossal recipe for the *creation* of arrears and of such as can but remain forever out of hand.'

54. Giedion, pp. 449, 694.

55. The enquiring hero of H.P. Lovecraft's 'The Picture in the House' explores the Miskatonic Valley in 1896 by bicycle, 'despite the lateness of the season.' (H.P. Lovecraft, *The Shadow Out of Time* (London, 1968), p. 20).

56. Neville Williams, *Chronology of the Modern World, 1763 to the Present Time* (London, 1966), pp. 325–403; Isaac Asimov, *Biographical Encyclopedia of Science and Technology*, rev. ed (London, 1975), passim.

57. D.B. Steinman, *The Builders of the Bridge* (1945), quoted in Oliver W. Larkin, *Art and Life in America*, rev. ed. (New York, 1960), p. 283.

58. Brom Weber (ed), *Complete Poems and Selected Letters and Prose of Hart Crane* (London, 1968), pp. 43–117.

59. R.J. Forbes and F.J. Dijksterhius, *A History of Science and Technology*, Vol. 2 (London, 1963), pp. 453–4.

60. Larkin, p. 230.

61. Larkin, p. 242.

62. Smith, *Popular Culture*, p. 74.

63. Christopher Davis, *A Peep Into the Twentieth Century* (New York, 1971).

64. In 1852 Hawthorne had made his utopianist social engineer of *The Blithedale Romance* a reformer of criminals and the inventor of a Benthamite panopticon.

65. At the beginning of George Roy Hill's film *Butch Cassidy and the Sundance Kid* (1969), also based on this robbery, while the town marshall fails to recruit a posse to hunt down the Hole in the Wall gang, a safety bicycle salesman easily attracts a crowd.

66. Brooks Adams, *The New Empire* (1902; Cleveland, 1967), p. 135.

67. Charles Olson, 'Brooks Adams' *The New Empire*,' in his *Human Universe* (San Francisco, 1965; New York, 1967), p. 135.

68. Henry Adams, *Education*, p. 501.

Notes to Chapter Five

1. Hugo Gellert, 'Us Fellas Gotta Stick Together,' *American Dialog* (Autumn, 1967).

2. Louis Adamic, *Dynamite: The Story of Class Violence in America*, rev. ed. (New York, 1934), pp. 407–8.

3. Daniel Aaron, *Writers on the Left* (New York, 1961), p. 403.

4. Lionel Trilling, *Partisan Review* VI, (Fall, 1939), p. 109, quoted in Aaron, p. 403.

5. Stan Brakhage, 'Sergei Eisenstein,' *Caterpillar*, 15/16 (1971), p. 124.

6. David Meltzer (ed), *The San Francisco Poets* (New York, 1971), p. 18.

7. Robert Warshow, 'The Legacy of the 30s,' in his *The Immediate Experience* (1962; New York, 1964), pp. 3–5.

8. cf. Eric Mottram, 'Mississippi Faulkner's Glorious Mosaic of Impotence and Madness,' *Journal of American Studies*, 2 (1968), pp. 121–9.

9. Margaret F. Thorp, *America at the Movies* (London, 1946), pp. 30, 65, 133.

10. Joseph North (ed), *New Masses: An Anthology of the Rebel Thirties* (New York, 1969), p. 47.

11. John Tipple, *Crisis of the American Dream. A History of American Social Thought, 1920–1940* (New York, 1968), p. 165.

12. James B. Gilbert, *Writers and Partisans: A History of Literary Radicalism in America* (New York, 1968), p. 125.

13. Gilbert, p. 204.

14. Gilbert, p. 220.

15. George Orwell, *England Your England* (London, 1953), pp. 131–4.

16. North, p. 51.

17. Marshall Stearns, *The Story of Jazz* (London, 1967), p. 187.

18. Earl Hines and his Orchestra, *Swinging in Chicago*, Decca Coral CP 63, 1970.

19. Stearns, p. 197

20. Langston Hughes, *The Big Sea* (New York, 1945), p. 258.

21. Norman Kagan, 'Reviving "The Emperor Jones,"' *Village Voice*, 24 June, 1 July 1971. (The term 'Negro' in this and subsequent paragraphs is retained from its common usage in the period under discussion.)

22. cf. LeRoi Jones, 'City of Harlem' and 'The Myth of Negro Literature,' in his *Home: Social Essays* (New York, 1966), pp. 87–93, 105–115; Harold Cruse, *The Crisis of the Negro Intellectual* (New York, 1968).

23. Roi Ottley and W.J. Weatherby (eds), *The Negro in New York* (New York, 1967), vii.

24. Marshall McLuhan, *The Mechanical Bride* (New York, 1951), pp. 102–3; see also p. 123, 'The Law of the Jungle,' on business mythology.

25. D.M. White and R.H. Abel, *The Funnies: An American Idiom* (New York, 1963), p. 3.

26. White and Abel, p. 4.

27. Alan Dutscher, 'The Book Business in America,' in B. Rosenberg and D.M. White (eds), *Mass Culture: The Popular Arts in America* (Glencoe, Ill., 1957), p. 133.

28. Warshow, p. 147.

29. Rosenberg and White, p. 147.

30. Bernard Berelson and Patricia Salter, 'Majority and Minority Americans: An Analysis of Magazine Fiction,' in Rosenberg and White (eds), pp. 235–250.

31. Paul Rotha and Richard Griffith, *The Film Till Now* (London, 1949), p. 435.

32. Arthur Knight, *The Liveliest Art* (New York, 1957), p. 115.

33. 'Crime and Racketeering,' in Fred J. Ringel (ed), *America as Americans See It* (New York, 1932).

34. James Thurber, *The Thurber Carnival* (London, 1945), p. 148.

35. Edward Dahlberg, "From *Those Who Perish*," in Louis Filler (ed), *The Anxious Years* (1962; New York, 1964), pp. 197–8.

36. Meltzer, pp. 10–12.

37. Marius Bewley, *The Eccentric Design* (London, 1959), p. 10.

38. Peter Viereck, *Dream and Responsibility* (Washington, 1953), p. 61.

39. Malcolm Cowley, *Exile's Return*, rev. ed. (New York, 1951), p. 223.

40. Harry Slowchower, *No Voice is Wholly Lost* (London, 1946), p. 71.

41. Christopher Lasch, *The New Radicalism in America* (New York, 1965), pp. 110–111.

42. Harvey Swados (ed), *The American Writer and the Great Depression* (New York, 1968), p. xxxiv.

43. Thorp, pp. 44, 84.

44. See Frederick R. Benson, *Writers in Arms: The Literary Impact of the Spanish Civil War* (New York, 1968).

45. Seymour Krim, *Shake It For the World, Smart Ass* (New York, 1967), pp. 3–25.

46. Aaron, pp. 406–7.

47. Tipple, pp. 273–4.

48. Stuart Hughes, *Consciousness and Society: The Reorientation of European Social Thought, 1890–1930* (London, 1959), pp. 414ff.

49. *Times* [London], 2 November 1971, p. 8.

50. Eric Mottram, *William Burroughs: The Algebra of Need* (Buffalo, N.Y., 1971), p. 26.

51. Joel Oppenheimer, 'Poem for Bonnie or Clyde,' *In Time: Poems 1962– 1968* (New York, 1969), p. 162.

Journal of American Studies, 6 (1972), 267–287.

Notes to Chapter Six

1. *The Deming Graphic* [Luna County, N.M.], Vol. XIV, No. xxviii, 10 March, 1916, p. 1.

2. Eric Mottram, 'Norman Mailer: Frontline Reporter of the Divine Economy,' in *American Autobiography*, ed. A. Robert Lee (London, 1988), pp. 217–43.

3. *Rolling Stone*, 15 August 1974.

4. Leonard C. Lewin, *Report From Iron Mountain on the Possibility and Desirability of Peace* (Harmondsworth, 1968).

5. Alan Lovell, *Don Siegel* (London, 1975), p. 15.

6. William Johnson (ed), *Focus on the Science Fiction Film* (New Jersey, 1972), pp. 72, 75.

7. Alfred McCoy, *et. al.*, *The Politics of Heroin in Southeast Asia* (New York, 1972), pp. 14, 352–4.

8. Dave Pirie, 'Friendly Invasion,' *Time Out*, 23–29 March 1979, p. 14.

9. See Colin McArthur, *Underworld USA* (London, 1972), pp. 11–21.

10. Jeff Rovin, *A Pictorial History of Science Fiction Films* (New Jersey, 1975); Franz Rottensteiner, *The Science Fiction Book* (London, 1975).

11. McArthur, p. 23.

12. Brian Ash (ed), *The Visual Encyclopedia of Science Fiction* (London, 1975).

13. Stan Brakhage, *The Brakhage Lectures* (Chicago, 1972), pp. 12–14.

14. Parker Tyler, *Underground Film: A Critical History* (New York, 1970); Sheldon Ronan, *The Underground Film* (London, 1968); Gregory Batcock (ed), *The New American Cinema* (New York, 1967).

15. D.A. Levy, *Collected Poems* (Ephraim, Wisconsin, 1976), p. 25.

16. Charles Perry, 'From Eternity to Here,' *Rolling Stone*, 26 February 1976.

17. Daniel Ben-Horin, 'The Alternative Press: Journalism as a Way of Life,' *The Nation*, 19 February 1973.

18. Ben-Horin, *passim*.

19. Andrew Kopkind, 'Are We in the Middle of a Revolution?' *New York Times Magazine*, 11 November 1968.

20. H. Bruce Franklin, *From the Movement Towards Revolution* (New York, 1971); Peter Stansill and David Zane Mairowitz (eds), *Bamn* (London, 1971). See also Lawrence Leamer, *The Paper Revolutionaries: The Rise of the Underground Press* (New York, 1972); Robert J. Glessing, *Outlaws of America: The Underground Press and its Context* (London, 1972); Jesse Kornbluth (ed), *Notes From the New Underground* (New York, 1968); and Mel Howard (ed), *Countdown: A Subterranean Magazine*, nos. 1–3 (New York, 1970).

21. Peter Clecak, *Radical Paradoxes: Dilemmas of the American Left, 1945–1970* (New York, 1973), p. 1.

22. John R. Stilgoe, *Common Landscape of America, 1580 to 1845* (New Haven and London, 1982), p. 341.

23. Douglas T. Miller, *The Birth of Modern America, 1820–1850* (New York, 1971), p. 44.

24. Cheng-tsu Wu, *Chink! A Documentary History of Anti-Chinese Prejudice in America* (New York, 1972), pp. 37–8.

25. Mary Roberts Coolidge, *Chinese Immigration* (New York, 1909), p. 120.

26. Gustavus Meyers, *A History of Bigotry in the United States* (New York, 1960).

27. Richard Hofstadter, 'The Paranoid Style in American Politics,' in David Brion Davis (ed), *The Fear of Conspiracy* (Ithaca, N.Y., 1971), pp. 2–9. A fuller version of Hofstadter's essay is in his *The Paranoid Style in American Politics and Other Essays* (London, 1966), pp. 3–40.

28. Davis, p. xiv; Quentin Anderson, *The Imperial Self* (New York, 1971).

29. cf. Robert Greenfield, *The Spiritual Supermarket* (New York, 1975).

30. Davis, p. xix.

31. Roger Daniels, *Concentration Camp USA: Japanese Americans and World War II* (New York, 1971). See also Roger Daniels, 'Pearl Harbor and the Yellow Peril,' in *The Underside of American History, Vol. 2: Since 1915* ed. Thomas R. Frazier (New York, 1974).

32. Davis, pp. 55–57.

33. Hofstadter, pp. ix, xii, 4, 5, 31–32.

34. Eric Bentley, *A Century of Hero-Worship*, 2nd edition (London, 1957).

35. Vernon Stauffer, *New England and the Bavarian Illuminati* (New York, 1918).

36. J.G. Frazer, *The Scope of Social Anthropology* (London, 1908), pp. 15–16; reprinted in Frazer, *Psyche's Task*, 2nd ed. (London, 1913), p. 170. Lévi-Strauss commemorates Frazer's lecture in his own inaugural lecture as professor at the Collége de France in 1960, 'The Scope of Anthropology,' first published in English in *Current Anthropology*, 7, 2 (1960), pp. 112–23, and reprinted in *The Scope of Anthropology* (London, 1968).

37. Bertolt Brecht, *Poems, 1913–1956*, ed. J. Willet and R. Mannheim (London, 1976), p. 252.

38. David Boadella, *Wilhelm Reich* (New York, 1975), pp. 88–89.

39. Chung Tsu-wu, pp. 37–38, 40, 41.

40, Alexander Saxon, *The Indespensible Enemy: Labor and the Anti-Chinese Movement in California* (Berkeley, Calif., 1971), pp. 139–40.

41. Coolidge, p. 120.

42. Coolidge, p. 96. The information on San Francisco and the Chinese is indebted to Patty Limerick, 'Corralling the Chinese,' *Rolling Stock* [Boulder, Colorado], 11 (1986).

43. A. Derleth and D. Wandrai (eds), *Selected Letters of H.P. Lovecraft, Vol. 1, 1911–1924* (Sauk City, Wisconsin, 1965), pp. 333–34. See also L. Sprague de Camp, 'H.P. Lovecraft: Master of Fantasy,' *Dialog*, 5, Nos. 3–4 (1975).

44. L. Sprague de Camp, *Lovecraft: A Biography* (New York, 1976), pp. 233–6, 249.

45. Derleth and Wandrai (eds), *Selected Letters of H.P. Lovecraft, Vol. 1*, p. 90; Derleth and Wandrai (eds), *Selected Letters, Vol. 2, 1925–1929* (Sauk City, Wisconsin, 1968), p. 308.

46. Jack London, 'The Yellow Peril' (1904), in his *Revolution and Other Essays* (New York, 1910), p. 281.

47. cf. Elmer C. Sandmeyer, 'Anti-Chinese Sentiment in California,' in *The Underside of American History, Vol. 1: Before 1915*, ed. Thomas R. Frazier (New York, 1974), and Daniels in ed. Frazier.

48. H.P. Lovecraft, 'The Shadow Out of Time,' in H.P. Lovecraft and August Derleth, *The Shadow Out of Time and Other Tales* (London, 1968), pp. 42–113.

49. Lovecraft, pp. 60, 68–9, 77, 112; Kurt Vonnegut, Jr., *Slaughterhouse Five* (1969; London, 1972), p. 80; Charles Platt, *Who Writes Science Fiction?* (London, 1980), p. 209.

50. Robert Shea and Robert Anton Wilson, *Illuminatus!* Parts 1 to 3 (New York, 1975); Robert Anton Wilson, *Cosmic Trigger: The Final Secret of the Illuminati* (New York, 1977).

51. Harry R. Warfel, *Charles Brockden Brown* (Gainseville, Florida, 1949), p. 98.

52. David Lee Clarke, *Charles Brockden Brown* (1952; North Carolina, 1969), pp. 169, 174.

53. Warfel, pp. 195, 206–211, 216.

54. Eric Mottram, '"The Infected Air" and "The Guilt of Interference": Henry James's Short Stories,' in *The Nineteenth-Century American Short Story*, ed. A. Robert Lee (London, 1985), pp. 164–90.

55. F.W. Dupee (ed), *Henry James: Autobiography* (London, 1966), pp. 479–81, taken from Chapter 12 of James's *Notes of a Son and Brother* (1914), rpt. in M.D. Zabel (ed), *The Portable Henry James* (New York, 1951), pp. 675–6.

56. Dupee, pp. 196–8, taken from Chapter 25 of James's *A Small Boy and Others* (1913), rpt. in Zabel, pp. 676–8.

57. E.C. Benson (ed), *Henry James: Letters to A.C. Benson and Auguste Monod* (London, 1935), p. 35.

58. Henry James, *The Art of the Novel: Critical Prefaces* (New York, 1934), pp. 72, 76–78.

59. A.L. Lowe (ed), *Henry James: English Hours* (London, 1963), pp. 13, 16, 86.

60. Oscar Cargill, *The Novels of Henry James* (New York, 1961), pp. 146–73.

61. Igantius Donnelly, *Caesar's Column* (London, 1891), pp. 4, 11.

62. Herman Melville, *Billy Budd, Sailor*, ed. Harrison Hayford and Merton

M. Sealts (Chicago, 1962), pp. 2, 75. See also Eric Mottram, 'Orpheus and Measured Forms: Law, Madness and Reticence in Melville,' in *New Perspectives on Melville*, ed. Faith Pullin (Edinburgh, 1978), pp. 229–54.

63. Donnelly, p. 222.

64. Donnelly, p. 285.

65. Donnelly, pp. 342, 344.

66. Norman Mailer, *The Short Fiction* (New York, 1967), pp. 188–207.

67. Donnelly, p. 367.

68. Tom Robbins, *Another Roadside Attraction* (New York, 1971), p. 250.

69. Shea and Wilson, *Illuminatus!* Part 3, pp. 15–17.

70. Jack London, *The Assassination Bureau, Ltd.*, completed by Robert L. Fish (New York, 1963); Eric Norden, 'The Paramilitary Right,' *Playboy*, June 1969; 'Neo-Nazi Groups: Artifacts of Hate,' *Time*, 28 February 1977, p. 32; Michael T. Klare, 'Rent-a-Cop: The Boom in Private Police,' *The Nation*, 15 November 1975.

71. London, *Assassination Bureau*, pp. 9, 31–4, 40, 43, 53, 67, 87, 92, 94, 104, 112, 116, 139, 141, 178; William Burroughs, 'The Four Horsemen of the Apocalypse,' in *Man, Earth and the Challenges* (New Mexico, 1981).

72. William Gaddis, *The Recognitions* (New York, 1955), p. 388.

73. Ed Sanders, *The Family* (New York, 1971), pp. 127–8.

74. Harriet Beecher Stowe, *Uncle Tom's Cabin* (New York, 1966), pp. 84, 91.

75. Damon Knight, *Charles Fort: Prophet of the Unexplained* (London, 1971), p. 61.

76. This and the following quotations are taken from Charles Fort, *The Book of the Damned*, introd. Tiffany Thayer (New York, 1969), pp. 11–13, 20–21.

77. Quoted in Knight, p. 206.

78. Paul Feyerabend, *Against Method. Outline of an Anarchistic Theory of Knowledge* (London, 1975), p. 21.

79. Eric Mottram, 'Ross Macdonald and the Past of a Formula,' in *Essays on Detective Fiction*, ed. Bernard Benstock (London, 1983), pp. 97–118.

80. Alfred Korzybski, *Science and Sanity* (Chicago, 1933); Marshall McLuhan, *The Gutenberg Galaxy* (London, 1962); M. Alterton and H. Craig (eds), *Edgar Allen Poe: Representative Selections* (New York, 1962), pp. 123–4, 129.

81. Ross Macdonald, *The Underground Man* (London, 1971), p. 208.

82. C.G. Jung, 'Flying Saucers: A Modern Myth of Things Seen in the Sky' (1958), in *Collected Works*, Vol. 10 (London, 1964); John Mitchell, *The Flying Saucer Vision: The Holy Grail Restored* (London, 1967); Ivan T. Sanderson, *Invisible Residents* (New York, 1970).

83. *The Nation*, 11 December 1967. See also R. Harris Smith, *OSS: The Secret History of America's First Central Intelligence Agency* (Berkeley, Calif., 1972); Frank Donner, 'Hoover's Legacy,' *The Nation*, 1 June 1974.

84. Gaddis, pp. 362, 377, 472; Harold Bloom, *The Anxiety of Influence. A Theory of Poetry* (New York, 1973).

85. Thomas Pynchon, *The Crying of Lot 49* (Philadelphia and New York, 1966), pp. 25, 170, 181–2.

86. Georges Bataille, quoted in Michele Richman, *Reading Georges Bataille: Beyond the Gift* (Baltimore, 1982), p. 65; Bataille, 'Extinct America,' *October 36* [Cambridge, Mass.], Spring 1986.

87. Richman, p. 67.

88. Quoted in Edwin Schlossberg, *Einstein and Beckett* (New York, 1973), p. 74.

89. Thomas Pynchon, *Gravity's Rainbow* (New York, 1973), pp. 209, 303, 410–11, 509, 647ff, 703, 720, 722; Thomas Pynchon, *V.* (London, 1963), pp. 226ff.

90. Thomas Pynchon, 'A Journey Into the Mind of Watts,' in *The California Dream*, ed. Denis Hale and Jonathan Eisen (New York, 1968), p. 260; Robert Anton Wilson, *Right Where You Are Sitting Now* (New York, 1982).

91. John Mackay, 'Illuminatus! . . .' *The Guardian* [London], 19 April 1977.

92. Wayne Morse, 'Supremacy and Secrecy: The Deeper Meaning of Watergate,' *The Nation*, 18 June 1973.

93. H. Hertzberg and D.C.K. McClelland, 'Paranoia,' *Harper's Magazine*, June 1974.

94. Geoffrey Ripps, *The Campaign Against the Underground Press* (San Francisco, Calif., 1981).

95. William Levy (ed), *Certain Radio Speeches of Ezra Pound* (Rotterdam, 1975), n.p. [address of 4 May 1942].

96. Jeremy Leggett, 'Conspiracy to Commit Murder is a Crime,' *New Statesman*, 21 November 1986.

Notes to Chapter Seven

1. Poe quoted in Richard Schickel, 'Entertainment Arts: Theater, Music and Film,' in Daniel Boorstin (ed), *American Civilization* (London, 1972), p. 251.

2. Norman O. Brown, *Love's Body* (New York, 1966), p. 161.

3. Norman O. Brown, *Life Against Death. The Psychoanalytical Meaning of History* (Middletown, Conn., 1959).

4. Robert Jay Lifton, *Boundaries. Psychological Man in Revolution* (New York, 1970), pp. xi–xii; Thomas Kuhn, *The Structure of Scientific Revolutions* (Chicago, 1962).

5. Lifton, pp. 37–63.

6. Pierre Boulez, 'Musical Technique,' *Boulez on Music Today*, trans. Susan Bradshaw and Richard Rodney Bennett (London, 1971), pp. 59–60.

7. Richard Meltzer, *The Aesthetics of Rock* (New York, 1970), pp. 225–29.

8. Meltzer, p. 235.

9. Samuel Delany, 'Corona,' (1966) in *Driftglass* (New York, 1971).

10. Charlie Gillett, *The Sound of the City* (New York, 1970; London, 1971), p. i.

11. Alfred Willener, *The Action-Image of Society*, trans. A.M. Sheridan-Smith (London, 1970), p. 230.

12. Allen Ginsberg, *Planet News, 1961–1967* (San Francisco, 1968), pp. 83–4, 102–3, 110–32.

13. David Morse, *Motown and the Arrival of Black Music* (London, 1971), p. 18.

14. Walter J. Ong, *In the Human Grain – Further Explorations in Contemporary Culture* (New York and London, 1967), p. 28.

15. Albert Goldman, 'The Emergence of Rock,' *New American Review*, 3 (1968), pp. 118–39.

16. Perry Miller, *The Life of the Mind in America. From the Revolution to the Civil War* (London, 1966), p. 33.

17. Richard Schechner, *Public Domain: Essays on the Theater* (New York, 1969), pp. 215, 228.

18. Schechner, *Public Domain*, p. 228.

19. Goldman, p. 127.

20. *The Rolling Stone Interviews*, compiled by the editors of *Rolling Stone* (New York, 1971), pp. 208–9, 212, 214.

21. *Rolling Stone Interviews*, p. 214.

22. Mike Jahn, *Jim Morrison and the Doors* (New York, 1969), p. 64.

23. *Rolling Stone Interviews*, pp. 229–30.

24. Schechner, *Public Domain*, p. 228.

25. Richard Schechner (ed), *Dionysus in 69* (New York, 1970).

26. Robin Blaser, 'The Fire,' *Caterpillar*, 12 (July 1970), p. 20.

27. Norman Mailer, *Advertisements for Myself* (New York, 1960), p. 319.

28. Georges Bataille, *Death and Sensuality. A Study of Eroticism and the Taboo* (New York, 1962), pp. 86–88.

29. Lawrence Lipton, *The Holy Barbarians* (New York, 1959), p. 244. The same terms describing the same essential phenomena are used in Norman Mailer's essays in *Advertisements for Myself*: 'The Man Who Studied Yoga' [1951], 'The White Negro' [1957], and the notes on *hip, hipster, beatnik*, and *square* [1957–58].

30. E.R. Dodds, *The Greeks and the Irrational* (Boston, 1951), quoted in Lipton, p. 245.

31. Walter J. Ong, *The Barbarian Within* (New York, 1962), p. 283.

32. Ong, *Barbarian*, p. 284.

33. Jerry Hopkins, et al., *Festival!* (New York, 1970), pp. 11–16.

34. The social history is given in two of Leary's volumes: *High Priest* (New York, 1968), and *The Politics of Ecstasy* (New York, 1968).

35. Sanders is a distinguished poet, organizer of the Peace Eye Bookshop in New York, and author of *The Family*, in 1972, an account of Charles Manson's degenerate commune. Kupferberg was a major Beat figure in the 1950s and 1960s, a poet, publisher of Birth Press editions, political clown, and a star of Dusan Makavejev's film *WR: Mysteries of the Organism* in 1971 – subtitled 'a cinematic testament to the life and writings of Wilhelm Reich.'

36. The festival is described in Tom Wolfe, *The Electric Kool-Aid Acid Test* (1968; New York, 1969), pp. 222–234.

37. Franz Kafka, *America*, trans. Edwin and Willa Muir (1949; Harmondsworth, 1967), p. 246.

38. Michael McClure, 'Wolf Net,' *Io*, 20 (1974), pp. 166–72.

39. David Horowitz, Michael P. Lerner, and Craig Pyes (eds), *Counterculture and Revolution* (New York: 1972), p. 98.

40. Craig Pyes, 'Rolling Stone Gathers no Politix,' in Horowitz, et. al., p. 107.

41. Sol Stern, 'Altamont: Pearl Harbor to Woodstock Nation,' in Horowitz, et. al., pp. 113–4.

42. Brown, *Life Against Death*, pp. 302–5. The passage quoted by Brown comes from Henry Miller, *Sunday After the War* (1944).

43. Stern in Horowitz, et. al., pp. 113–131.

44. Timothy Leary, *Jail Notes* (New York, 1970), p. 147.

45. Ben Fong-Torress (ed), *The Rolling Stone Rock'n'Roll Reader* (New York, 1974), p. 541.

46. Fong-Torres (ed), p. 547.

47. Stern in Horowitz, et. al., p. 124.

48. 'Beat Godfather Meets Glitter Mainman,' *Rolling Stone*, 28 February 1974.

49. William Burroughs and Daniel Odier, *The Job* (London, 1970), p. 183.

50. Hunter Thompson, *Hell's Angels* (New York, 1967), pp. 346–9.

51. Michael McClure and Frank Reynolds, *Freewheelin' Frank. Secretary of the Angels* (1967; New York, 1974); Michael McClure, *The Beard* (New York, 1967); *The Blossom, or Billy the Kid* (New York, 1967); *The Sermons of Jean Harlow and the Curses of Billy the Kid* (San Francisco, 1968), reprinted in *Star* (New York, 1970).

52. McClure and Reynolds, pp. 8, 23.

53. Allen Ginsberg, 'How to Make a March/Spectacle,' *Liberation* (Jan, 1966).

54. Allen Ginsberg, 'First Party at Ken Kesey's With Hell's Angels,' in *Planet News*, p. 104.

55. Wolfe, p. 153.

56. Wolfe, p. 159.

57. Don McNeil, *Moving Through Here* (New York, 1970), pp. 33–4.

58. George Leonard, *The Ultimate Athlete* (New York, 1975); Johan Huizinga, *Homo Ludens: A Study of the Play Element in Culture* (1944; Boston, 1955). Leonard's previous book was *Education and Ecstasy* (New York, 1968).

59. Mick Brown, 'Hollywood Anger,' *Crawdaddy* (September, 1976).

60. Richard Grossinger, *Book of the Earth and Sky, Book Two* (Los Angeles, 1971), pp. 60, 65.

61. Grossinger, pp. 65–66.

62. Grossinger, p. 67.

63. Norman O. Brown, *Closing Time* (New York, 1973), pp. 62, 74.

64. Robert Duncan, *Caesar's Gate* (San Francisco, 1972), p. iv.

65. Robert Duncan, 'Passages 30/Stage Directions,' in *Bending the Bow* (New York, 1968; London, 1971), pp. 130–1.

66. Allen Ginsberg, 'Interview with Allen Young, in *Gay Sunshine Interview 5, Vol. 1*, ed. Winston Leland: San Francisco, (Calif., 1978), p. 120.

67. Mircia Eliade, *The Two and the One*, trans. J.M. Cohen (London, 1965), pp. 79–80.

Reprinted with revisions for the Open University from *Other Times* [London], No. 1 (November 1975–January 1976), pp. 38–48.

Notes to Chapter Eight

1. Denis Diderot, *Ramean's Nephew* (New York, 1956), p. 58.

2. Carl Sauer, *Land and Life: A Selection From the Writings of Carl Ortwin Sauer*, ed. John Leighly (Berkeley, 1967), p. 359.

3. James Fenimore Cooper, *The Prarie*, ed. James Elliott (Albany, N.Y., 1985), p. 27.

4. Bob Dylan, *Writings and Drawings* (London, 1973), p. 87. 'Them' are 'weapons of the chemical dust.' See also Anthony Scaduto, *Bob Dylan*, rev. ed. (London, 1977).

5. Gerald Stanley Lee, *Crowds*, (New York, 1913), p. 362.

6. Gregory Ratoff, dir., *The Heat's On*, (Columbia, 1943).

7. Terence Butler, *Crucified Heroes: The Films of Sam Pekinpah* (London, 1979), p. 119.

8. Walt Whitman, *Leaves of Grass: Comprehensive Reader's Edition*, ed. Harold Blodgett and Sculley Bradley (New York, 1965), p. 587.

9. Whitman, pp. 119, 597, 608–9.

10. William Kapp, *The Social Costs of Private Enterprise* (New York, 1971), p. 245.

11. Edward T. Hall, *The Silent Language* (Middletown, Connecticut, 1966), p. 117.

12. Herbert Marcuse, *Counter-Revolution and Revolt* (London, 1972), p. 36.

13. Scaduto, p. 117.

14. Herbert Marcuse, *One Dimensional Man* (Boston, 1964), p. 2.

15. Norman Mailer, *The Presidential Papers* (London, 1964), [preface].

16. William Eastlake, *Dancers in the Scalp House* (New York, 1975), p. 170.

17. Brion Gysin and Terry Wilson, *Here to Go/Planet R-101* (San Francisco, 1982), p. 75.

18. Alexis de Toqueville, *Democracy in America, Vol. 1*, ed. Phillips Bradley (New York, 1961), pp. 283, 288–9.

19. Victor H. Li, *Law Without Lawyers: A Comparative View of Law in China and the United States* (Boulder, Colo., 1978), pp. 9, 36–38.

20. Ross Macdonald, *Find a Victim* (1954; London, 1971), p. 132.

21. Eldridge Cleaver, *Soul on Ice* (New York, 1968), p. 14.

22. Calvin Hernton, *Sex and Racism in America* (London, 1969), p. 11.

23. William S. Burroughs, *The Naked Lunch* (Paris, 1959), p. 72.

24. Alec Barbrook and Christine Bolt, *Power and Protest in American Life* (Oxford, 1980), p. 40.

25. Victor Navasky, *Naming Names* (New York, 1980), pp. 22–23.

26. Charles Brockden Brown, *Wieland*, ed. F.L. Pattee (New York, 1960), p. 99.

27. Nathaniel Hawthorne, 'Earth's Holocaust,' in *Works, Vol. 10, Mosses From an Old Manse*, Centenary Edition (Ohio, 1974), pp. 381–404.

28. Ezra Pound, *Selected Poems*, ed. T.S. Eliot (London, 1928), p. 174.

29. John Steinbeck, *The Log From the Sea of Cortez* (London, 1964), pp. 111, 120, 223–9.

30. John Steinbeck, *In Dubious Battle* (1936), in Pascal Covici (ed), *The Portable Steinbeck* (New York, 1971), p. 204 (See also John Steinbeck, 'Dubious Battle in California,' in J. Salzman and B. Wallenstein (eds), *Years of Protest* (New York, 1967), pp. 66–72); John Steinbeck, *The Grapes of Wrath* (1939; New York, 1959), p. 204; *Cannery Row* (1945; Harmondsworth, 1961), p. 187.

31. R.G.H. Siu, *The Portable Dragon* (Cambridge, Mass., 1971), p. 71.

32. Michel Foucault, *The Order of Things* (London, 1970), pp. 374–5.

33. Garry Wills, 'Robertson and the Reagan Gap,' *Time*, 22 February 1988, pp. 28–9.

34. The following materials are drawn from Perry Miller, *The Life of the Mind in America* (New York, 1965), pp. 105–6, 143–4, 148, 160–1, 176, 184, 187, 243.

35. Murray Bookchin, *The Ecology of Freedom* (Palo Alto, Calif., 1982), pp. 165–6.

36. Wendell Gluck (ed), *Henry D. Thoreau: Reform Papers* (Princeton, N.J., 1973), pp. 65, 70, 73–4; Richard Slotkin, *Regeneration Through Violence* (Middletown, Conn., 1973), pp. 517–65.

37. Slotkin, p. 536.

38. Walter E. Bezanson (ed), *Herman Melville: Clarel* (New York, 1960), p. 233. [Part II, Canto xxvi].

39. Robert Nozick, *Anarchy, State and Utopia* (Oxford, 1974), pp. ix, 238.

40. Sterling P. Lamprecht (ed), *John Locke: Selections* (New York, 1928), p. 69.

41. Robert Dworkin, *Taking Rights Seriously* (London, 1977), p. xi.

42. Dworkin, pp. 184–5, 188, 200–201; *The Walker Report to the National Commission on the Causes and Prevention of Violence* (New York, 1968); *Report of the National Advisory Committee on Civil Disorder* (New York, 1968); Allen Ginsberg, *Chicago Trial Testimony* (San Francisco, 1975); Judy Clavir and John Spitzer (eds), *The Conspiracy Trial* (London, 1971).

43. John Rawls, *A Theory of Justice* (London, 1972), p. 225.

44. Robert Duncan, *Bending the Bow* (New York, 1968), pp. 70–73.

45. Robert Duncan, "The Lasting Contribution of Ezra Pound." *Agenda* [London], 4, 2 (Oct.–Nov. 1965), p. 23.

46. Richard Harris, *Justice: The Crisis of Law, Order and Freedom in America* (New York, 1970), p. 240.

47. Michael Lewis, *The Culture of Inequality* (New York, 1979), pp. 190, 199–201.

48. Carl Resak (ed), *War and the Intellectuals: Essays by Randolph S. Bourne, 1915–1919* (New York, 1964), pp. 65–104.

49. Norman O. Brown, *Closing Time* (New York, 1973), p. 56.

50. *New York Times*, 1 October 1968, p. 50.

51. Richard Hofstadter and Michael Wallace (eds), *American Violence: A Documentary History* (New York, 1971), p. 476.

Acknowledgements

Acknowledgements and thanks to the following for permission to reprint essays and to reproduce lyrics, and for providing occasions for lectures and courses:

The *Journal of American Studies* for 'Living Mythically: The Thirties' (*Journal of American Studies*, 6 (1972)) and 'The Persuasive Lips: Men and Guns in America, the West' (*Journal American Studies*, 10 (1976)).

Valencia University Press for the first version of 'That Dark Instrument: The American Automobile', from Enrique Garcia Diáz (ed), *American Studies in Spain* (Valencia, 1988); and to the British Association for American Studies, and the International Conference on American Studies, Valencia 1985.

Manchester University Press for 'Blood on the Nash Ambassador: Cars in American Films', from Philip Davies and Brian Neve (eds), *Cinema, Politics and Society in America* (Manchester, 1981).

Christopher Brookeman and the American Studies Resources Centre, Polytechnic of Central London, for 'The Metallic Necessity and the New American: Culture and Technology in America, 1850–1900', from *Essays by Eric Mottram and Philip Davies* (London, 1978); and to the Institute of United States Studies, University of London.

Hanne Bramness and Shamoon Zamir, the editors of *Talus*, for 'Out of Sight But Never Out of Mind: Fears of Invasion in American Culture', from *Talus* No. 1 (Spring, 1987), and the revised version of 'That Dark Instrument: The American

Automobile', from *Talus* No. 3 (Spring, 1988); and to the editors of *The New Hungarian Quarterly* No. 80 (1980) for an initial version of 'Out of Sight', drawn from the proceedings of the conference on *The Origins and Originality of American Culture* at Eötvös University, Budapest, 1979; and to the British Association for American Studies.

Paul Brown, the editor of *Other Times*, for 'Dionysus in America,' from *Other Times* No. 1 (November 1975–January 1976).

King's College University of London, where the first version of 'Laws Scribbled by Law-Breakers: Law, Confidence and Disobedience in American Culture' was delivered as Eric Mottram's inaugural lecture as Professor of English and American Literature, November 29, 1983; and to the British Association for American Studies conference in April 1988.

Westminster Music Ltd. and Mirage Music Ltd. for lines from 'Street Fighting Man' and 'Sympathy for the Devil' by Mick Jagger and Keith Richards from The Rolling Stones, *Beggar's Banquet*, copyright © 1968.

Doors Music Ltd., Nipper Music, and the American Society of Composers, Authors, and Publishers for lines from 'Break on Through (to the Other Side),' 'Twentieth Century Fox,' and 'The End' from *The Doors*, copyright © 1967; 'When the Music's Over' from *Strange Days*, copyright © 1967; and 'Not to Touch the Earth' and 'Five to One' from *Waiting For the Sun*, copyright © 1968, all written and recorded by The Doors.

Bruce Springsteen for lines from 'Cadillac Ranch' by Bruce Springsteen from Bruce Springsteen, *The River*, copyright © 1980.

Index

INDEX

INDEX

275

INDEX

INDEX